W9-AQN-707

ADVANCE PRAISE FOR *MONEY AND LOVE*

"There is a huge difference between spending and investing. That's true with money. It's true with time. And it's true with love. And it's beautifully illustrated by Strober and Davisson in their book, *Money and Love*. With all the trade-offs we face in life, let this book be your operating handbook for making your most important decisions."

—Greg McKeown, podcaster and author of two *New York Times* bestsellers, *Effortless* and *Essentialism*

"Having been CEO of three brands while raising four children, I believe it's possible to have *both* money *and* love—but only if you're intentional. In a real and relatable way, Strober and Davisson guide us through the big decisions we make, empowering us to build a full, joyful, and purposeful life."

—Nancy Green, former CEO of Old Navy and Athleta

"Reframing big problems into manageable ones and adopting a doable decision-making process are power tools for navigating the complexities of modern adult life. And nothing is more complex than money and love."

—Dave Evans, coauthor of *Designing Your Life: How to Build a Well-Lived, Joyful Life*

"According to the Beatles, 'money can't buy me love,' but Strober and Davisson show how to think about your choices so that careers and relationships can jointly flourish. Great reading on life's most difficult and important decisions."

—Andrew Scott, economics professor at London Business School and author of *The 100-Year Life*

"Strober and Davisson have written a book that delivers on provocative ideas and information—and, far more importantly, a truly useful framework—for tackling life's most important decisions."

—Seth Stephens-Davidowitz, author of *Don't Trust Your Gut* and *Everybody Lies*

MONEY AND LOVE

**MYRA STROBER &
ABBY DAVISSON**

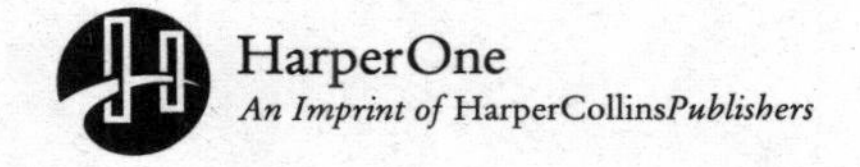

MONEY AND LOVE

AN INTELLIGENT ROADMAP FOR LIFE'S BIGGEST DECISIONS

MONEY AND LOVE. Copyright © 2023 by Myra Strober and Abby Davisson. All rights reserved. Printed in the United States of America. No part of this book may be used or reproduced in any manner whatsoever without written permission except in the case of brief quotations embodied in critical articles and reviews. For information, address HarperCollins Publishers, 195 Broadway, New York, NY 10007.

HarperCollins books may be purchased for educational, business, or sales promotional use. For information, please email the Special Markets Department at SPsales@harpercollins.com.

FIRST EDITION

Designed by Bonni Leon-Berman

Library of Congress Control Number: 2022944181

ISBN 978-0-06-311751-8

23 24 25 26 27 LBC 5 4 3 2 1

To our husbands
Jay Jackman, in loving memory
and Ross Davisson

CONTENTS

INTRODUCTION

Lauren blinked back tears, wondering how the day's happy events had made her feel so unhappy. Soon after she'd been accepted to a top graduate school in New York—with a full scholarship, no less—her boyfriend of three years, Greg, had announced that he couldn't leave California because of his recent promotion. To her surprise, he had then gotten down on one knee and proposed.

Both her acceptance to graduate school and Greg's proposal were moments Lauren had long hoped for, but now, neither piece of exciting news felt the way she'd imagined. Would she really have to choose between her relationship and her career? In a single day, Lauren had come face-to-face with the intricate, often challenging connections between love and money. Which would she choose? Perhaps more important, how would she make such an agonizing decision?

Throughout our lives, we inevitably encounter similarly fraught decisions around money and love. In addition to choosing a life partner and a career, we may have to decide whether to marry (or not) or become a parent (or not); how to care for a sick or disabled family member or cope with our own illness or disability; select where to live; determine how to divide household tasks; decide whether to go for that promotion or big job; reconcile different spending, saving, and investing habits; and figure out whether or how to combine parenthood with a career, as well as how and when to change careers. We may also need to figure out how to strengthen a relationship or end it. As our parents age, helping with eldercare and end-of-life planning may be necessary. As we ourselves age, we must manage postretirement life, which may include caring for a life partner.

These kinds of money and love decisions were never simple, and we are now confronting them during a time of rapid and profound change. The coronavirus pandemic forced millions to set up workstations in their kitchen, living room, or bedroom, all while caring for loved ones of all ages. Suddenly, the illusion of work/life separation was exposed, and we could no longer ignore just how intimately these parts of our lives are linked. That forced millions to reassess how and where they live and work. As our reality continues to evolve, our love and money decisions will likely involve a laundry list of additional complexities:

- Dual-career household norms will continue to change. Before the pandemic, the number of stay-at-home dads was rising; will this trend continue, even accelerate? How many women who opted out of the workforce at the height of the pandemic will reenter, and what will that look like?
- In an increasingly tech-based economy, some jobs will be phased out while others are created.
- We will encounter a noticeably larger remote workforce. Zoom fatigue, anyone? How about home office envy?

Even the effects of climate change—water shortages, wildfires, devastating storms and other extreme weather—may increasingly inform how, where, and with whom we conduct our lives. While navigating all these massive shifts, we're immersed in an online world that can skew perspectives, presenting idealized alter-realities of what our lives should look and feel like. In short? Money and love decisions are becoming more complex as our world becomes more complex.

Rest assured, however, that this book is *not* an exercise in doom-scrolling. It's quite the opposite, in fact. This book is a guide to help you navigate love and money decisions. We never tell you *what* to decide; only you can do that. Instead, we give you a framework, relevant research, and exercises to help you identify your priorities and make decisions that are aligned with what *you* want. The result? You will experience more ease and feel more confident, knowing that even when external factors beyond your control impact your life, you have a solid, proven framework you can use to course correct. Little by little, leap by leap, you'll move your life toward your bigger goals and dreams, feeling a greater sense of control—not over just one part of your life but over the most essential parts of your life and how they work together to shape your larger life journey.

Challenging times can force us to reassess our lives in ways that ultimately lead to better outcomes. In 1970, Myra, a labor economist, was told by her then-employer, the University of California, Berkeley, that she would never be hired for a tenure-track position because she was a mother of two young children. Determined to overcome this bias, she proposed a seminar on work and family. That seminar was given the green light, and it soon turned into a full-fledged course. Two years later, UC Berkeley offered her a tenure-track position, but she turned it down to become the first-ever woman faculty member at Stanford Graduate School of Business (Stanford GSB). In the decades that followed, she led thousands of students through the hugely popular Work and Family course that eventually inspired this book. Myra retired in 2018 as a tenured professor at Stanford Graduate School of Education (Stanford GSE) and Stanford GSB.

While teaching the Work and Family course, first at UC Berkeley and then at Stanford University, Myra was herself navigating many of the topics it covered: arranging childcare, in an era when group childcare was scarce; getting divorced and later remarrying; and caring for her elderly mother and then her husband after he was diagnosed with Parkinson's disease. As her life evolved, more women entered the workforce and our overall culture changed in various ways. During her forty years of teaching the course, Myra continually updated it to reflect her and others' life experiences, as well as new research and expertise from guest contributors.

The enduring popularity of the Work and Family course was due in part to Myra's consistent yet flexible approach. Throughout, she adhered to her core philosophy: be direct and matter-of-fact about the way things are; rely on accredited data, but carefully examine their limitations; make use of personal perspectives and experience to inform the discussion; and empower students to embrace their role in changing their families, their workplaces, and our society.

While staying faithful to this core approach, the course itself evolved over time to reflect changing cultural beliefs and norms. Stanford GSB is an elite private institution that does not reflect the larger population or all groups within it, but as the school did more to prioritize diversity, the focus of the Work and Family course shifted, too. Increased numbers of international students led European pupils to voice their surprise about American students' "fixation" on marriage. "Why get married at all?" they asked. Meanwhile, some men from Pakistan and India shared their relief regarding the arranged marriage system in their home countries, which would spare them from having to choose a life partner. (Interestingly, no woman or nonbinary person from these countries voiced the same support of arranged marriage.) Having more diversity in race, ethnicity, gender, and sexual orientation also prompted the class to consider issues particular to historically marginalized groups. How does being Black affect marriage prospects? How does being gay affect decisions about having children? How does being a member of an underrepresented group affect career goals or decisions about where to live?

From the course's inception, thousands of students—from different races and ethnic backgrounds; female, male, and nonbinary; single, in a relationship, or married; and of all sexual orientations—enrolled in it, and many told Myra that it was one of the most useful courses they had ever taken. Years after graduation, they write to say that the course prepared them for life better than any other undergraduate or graduate class and that they are still using the information and approach they learned.

One such student was Abby, who took Myra's course in 2008 while in business school with her then-boyfriend, Ross, whom she'd been dating for only a year. With graduation looming, Abby and Ross needed to decide whether to accept jobs in the same city and, if so, whether to move in together. Initially too intimidated to broach the topic in any meaningful way, they learned in Myra's class how to engage in thoughtful, effective decision-making.

Myra's teaching proved so helpful that Abby and Ross made the topic of living together before marriage the focus of their final paper. That assignment turned out to be the first of many joint productions: more than a dozen years of marriage and two kids later, Abby and Ross agree that the class changed their lives by giving them a blueprint to successfully navigate the high-wire act of dual-career parenthood.

After graduating, Abby and Ross stayed in touch with Myra, and soon Myra began inviting them to her class as guest speakers. They returned as speakers annually for nearly a decade, using the forty-five-minute drive from San Francisco to Palo Alto to take stock of their relationship satisfaction, sometimes noting with humor that their car conversations had resulted in a redistribution of household tasks. As Abby climbed the career ladder in a Fortune 200 company, she observed how often family matters impacted colleagues' career decisions—a fact that wasn't widely discussed or acknowledged, despite a family-friendly culture and a majority-female workforce. Abby realized the power of the lessons she'd learned in Myra's class and imagined the legions of people who would benefit if they had access to the course's framework and insights.

One day, after Myra retired, she told Abby over lunch that she was thinking of writing a book about the course to bring it to a broad audience beyond the Stanford classroom. She looked at Abby across the table, and it struck her that she had found her coauthor. Who better to help tackle the subject than a former student who was in the trenches of combining family and work—caring for aging parents and raising two children while successfully navigating her career? From that very first lunch, we have been committed to writing this book together.

The stories we tell in the book come from multiple sources and perspectives. Many come from Myra's students, as well as her colleagues and friends. Abby, too, has contributed stories from her peers, family, and friends. To expand our reach, we also completed a survey that included graduates of Stanford GSB and others and conducted follow-up interviews with dozens of respondents who offered unique perspectives. We are grateful to those who let us include their unvarnished stories in these pages. While names and identifying details have been changed to protect privacy, we have tried to uphold the spirit of each person's story. In addition to stories, we've included research from academic journals and popular literature. We drew on research included in Myra's Work and Family course, updating it and adding new sources where relevant.

The injustices in our society regarding race, gender, sexual orientation, age, ability, and class do, in our view, create undeniable disparities in choice. For example, several Black interviewees noted that they had opted for entrepreneurial career paths because of the racism they encountered in corporate America. As one person put it, "The main impact of being Black on my career is that it never made sense to strive for the top of a large organization. [Advancing to a top leadership role] requires too many promotion steps that are subject to bias—either in the assessment of skills or in access to sponsorship." A Black single parent who had risen to a vice presidency in a Fortune 100 company was even more blunt: "Corporate America was not designed for people like me." When talented Black professionals see striking out on their own as less risky than staying in large companies, it's clear that disparities in choice exist even for those with credentials from top schools and employers. While we acknowledge the disparities and discuss some ways to address them, the full extent of systemic change needed for true equity is beyond the scope of this book.

HOW TO USE THIS BOOK

This book is designed to provide a uniquely integrated approach to decision-making that flexes alongside your goals and priorities. As different parts of your life naturally ebb and flow over time, you may find that certain sections resonate more than others. Once you've read chapter one, where we lay out our 5Cs decision-making framework, feel free to either read the chapters sequentially or flip to the ones that feel most relevant at a particular moment in time.

The book begins by outlining the framework that so many have used to make fulfilling decisions that are authentic to their lives, goals, and circumstances. While this framework is structured, it informs your decision-making *process*, not its results, giving you the flexibility to determine how to proceed, with your eyes wide open. From there, we explore highly charged money and love topics, arranged roughly in the order that people tend to encounter them.

That exploration begins in chapter two, where we look at key decisions related to choosing mates. These decisions can set the tone for the many life-cycle decisions that follow. Subsequent chapters delve into deciding whether to marry; choosing to have children (or not); dividing household work; deciding where to live and when to move; combining a family with a career; traversing rough spots in a relationship and possibly divorcing; and providing eldercare. Finally, we step back and look at the big picture: how societal norms change and how you can become a change agent at your workplace and in your community.

However you use this book, we hope you will return to it often, allowing its 5Cs framework to add ease to your decision-making and improve your confidence. We also hope its stories will reassure you that you are in good company, especially during trying times in life.

Life is full of twists and turns, and tough decisions are inevitable. Yet there are no courses in high school devoted to decision-making, and there is no curriculum that teaches us how to organize alternatives and consider likely consequences. Instead, decision-making is too often presented as an overly limiting and linear exercise, dictating that career decisions be weighed against career goals and love decisions against personal desires. By insulating our priorities from each other, however, we turn love and money into an either/or option, forcing us, for example, to choose the big career *or* the happy marriage. Instead of accepting that premise, we ask, why not find a way to accommodate both?

To be clear, we're not talking about "having it all," or even having it all (but just not at the same time). We're talking about getting very clear about what you want and then making informed trade-offs to pursue your personal and professional goals. As women born nearly four decades apart, our experiences have proven that we can all ultimately realize more of what we desire—whatever our gender or life stage—if our approach to decision-making is sufficiently integrative and thoughtful. This book, and the 5Cs framework presented within its pages, provides that flexible yet sturdy framework, which factors in the many important priorities *and* people in your life. As a result, you will become able to uncover more options, create better results—and experience more ease and enjoyment along the way.

Money and love, love and money. Popular culture got it wrong; love is not a fairy tale, and money is not a limitation. Both money and love are at their most powerful when they're working together, to help you and your loved ones build and grow the life you most desire.

We wrote this book to offer something that has been missing from existing decision-making content: a career and life guide that takes relationships into account; a decision-making framework that applies to the most personal of choices; and a roadmap for making the biggest decisions of your life—those about love and money—that will resonate with everyone.

We consider ourselves optimistic realists. We tackle a host of thorny issues in this book, yet many of our early readers said they found the book comforting, and we hope you will, too—but we also hope it will spur you to action at both a personal and a societal level. And we hope you will share it with family, friends, and connections of all ages, including younger ones. The earlier in life people start making well-considered decisions, the happier and wiser they will be.

Few aspects of our lives are as fundamental to health and happiness as love and money, yet historically they have been pitted against each other. Which matters more? Which one do you choose? This book is titled *Money and Love* because in our experience, money and love are an invitation to live a life that's more closely aligned with our values and desires. We hope you'll accept that invitation and use these pages to access the untapped potential in yourself and your life.

ONE

INTRODUCING THE 5Cs FRAMEWORK

They say hindsight is 20/20, but what if our decision-making "vision" is merely clouded rather than impaired? When Lauren suddenly and unexpectedly had to choose between marrying Greg (and staying in California) or accepting a full scholarship to a top graduate school (and moving to New York), she was understandably overwhelmed. Should Lauren marry a man she loved and had been dating for three years? Or should she attend a selective school that would pave the way for the career she wanted? How could she possibly choose? If her choice was "wrong," would she sabotage her entire future?

Philosopher Ruth Chang argues that *big* decisions are life-altering, but only when they have desirable alternatives are they also *hard* decisions.[1] In other words, when more than one choice has positive attributes, a big decision also becomes a hard one.

As a society, we've been programmed to believe that it's practical to make tough decisions in a compartmentalized way. Conventional career wisdom doesn't take account of choices about relationships, and typical relationship guidance doesn't tell us how to make career decisions in light of those relationships. Instead, we're counseled that if we have a professional decision to make, we should think about the job and career we want. If we have a romantic decision to make, we should think about the love life we desire. Realistically speaking, as in Lauren's case, emotional decisions (love) inevitably affect financial well-being (money), and vice versa. We can't make good decisions about our lives without looking at the whole picture.

OVERRIDING THE QUICK-DECISION IMPULSE

Making holistic decisions that optimize for the long run isn't easy. Social science research (and experience) underscores our innate tendency to narrowly focus on the short term, on a limited subset of factors, or both. In his landmark book *Thinking, Fast and Slow*, Nobel laureate Daniel Kahneman describes two systems the brain uses to form thoughts.[2] System 1 is intuitive and emotional, and it is the system we typically default to when we're tired, rushed, or in an especially optimistic mood. This is the part of our brain that convinces us to mutter "Sure, whatever," when we're too overwhelmed to consider consequences or "Let's go for it!" when we're feeling so upbeat that we can hardly imagine a negative outcome. System 2 is something else altogether. As the more thoughtful and logical approach, System 2 requires deliberate effort. This is the part of our brain that hears our "Sure, whatever," or "Let's go for it!" and asks, "Wait, is this really a good idea?" or says, "Hang on; let's take a step back and consider all the factors."

System 2 thinking can provide a crucial check on our impulsivity and biases. Much of this book is dedicated to helping you engage System 2 when making decisions about love and money—to slow down your process, creating the space for you to examine your decisions from more than one angle. By doing this, you'll be likely to make decisions that are more informed and intentional. This isn't always as simple as it seems. At times, people *believe* they are making considered decisions, but they are still relying on knee-jerk responses that may not serve them in the long run.

THE VALUE OF PLANNING . . . IN AN IMPERFECT, UNCERTAIN WORLD

Even the best-laid plans can go sideways when we least expect. As the old Yiddish saying goes, "Man plans, and God laughs." It's a catchy maxim that's sometimes quoted as the reason to forgo planning altogether. After all, the thinking goes, what's the point of planning when outcomes are inherently unknown? There's another saying that, however cliché, may better capture the realities of planning: "When you fail to plan, you plan to fail." No one can guarantee that planning will net you your intended outcome. Case in point—how many of us sat down in 2019 to plan how we'd adapt to pandemic life in 2020? (Hearing crickets? We are, too.) However, even in our imperfect, uncertain world, planning remains a valuable and important exercise. By skipping planning, you significantly increase your chances of *not* getting what you want.

When you make decisions about love and money, much of the information you may assume you need will be unattainable because it requires predicting an undefined future. For example, planning to have a second child means accepting that you don't yet know about that child's health or temperament. Even with this uncertainty, making intentional decisions using a thorough process will improve the quality of your thinking and your decisions. If the outcomes aren't what you expected, your "mental muscle" will be better equipped to adjust your decisions to your new circumstances.

A LOGICAL APPROACH TO LOVE AND MONEY

How, when, and how often we plan is, to some extent, a reflection of personality. Some of us start planning at a young age and never stop. Abby, at just nine years of age, kept a journal at summer camp that she used to preselect what she'd wear each day (a story she still can't tell without chuckling with mild embarrassment). We also know a woman who creates a spreadsheet listing everything she needs to pack for each vacation she takes. Whether by nature, habit, or some combination of both, people like these undeniably qualify as "planners." Planning is just what they do. Others, however, abhor planning and everything it entails. For some, it feels too tedious; for others, it seems like a fun-killer. People have different styles, and it's important to honor that fact. However, even the most spontaneous soul can benefit from advance consideration of major decisions involving love and money, if only to minimize regret.

Popular culture has long drummed the idea into our heads that true love "sweeps you away." Given that planning is a deliberate, cerebral exercise, some initially view love and planning as inherently incompatible. In reality, however, taking a deliberate approach toward love doesn't diminish it. Rather, by entering into a relationship with a clear-eyed view, you're more likely to enjoy more love for a longer period precisely because you're able to avoid some of the pitfalls associated with relationships. The same is true of money. By considering how to use it well, you ultimately gain more freedom to enjoy the possessions and experiences you do invest in.

If it's not in your nature to do so, you don't ever have to crack open a journal or create a spreadsheet, but by using the decision-making framework we lay out in this chapter, you can expand and elevate the thinking behind your money and love decisions. This will help to clear the mental and emotional fog we all inevitably experience when we face decisions that are both big and hard. In other words, this approach will bring your decision-making vision closer to the 20/20 level we once assumed was achievable only through hindsight.

THE 5Cs FRAMEWORK

"When we seek advice, we rarely want to be told which option to choose. We're usually seeking guidance on how to approach the decision," observed organizational psychologist Adam Grant. "The best advice doesn't specify what to do. It highlights blind spots in our thinking and helps us clarify our priorities."[3]

Our five-step framework, which we call the 5Cs, can improve the quality of your decision-making about both love and money and your confidence in the outcomes it produces. The 5Cs will also give you the courage to face tough choices you might otherwise avoid.

Step One: *Clarify* What's Important to You

To make an effective decision, you first need to consider what you really want. This means thinking carefully about what you care about and what you don't. Making that distinction often sounds easier than it is. When Lauren took time to think about whether she'd marry Greg or attend graduate school, she realized just how much she wanted a loving marriage *and* a fulfilling career. What she didn't want was to have to choose between two parts of her life that felt intrinsic to her well-being. Coming to this realization was more complicated than it seemed. She had been dating Greg for three years, and her friends and family expected her to marry him. Rejecting the need to choose between her relationship and her career might mean losing Greg and then disappointing all the people who cared about them as a couple.

Being willing to consider our own desires takes courage because often, we're unconsciously jumping through hoops other people have set up for us. High achievers in particular may relish checking off accomplishments on a list. We could all be more diligent about making sure the only items we allow on our "life lists" are the ones we truly want, not the ones our parents or society expects.

Defining our wants apart from those of others is made more difficult by something we all experience called "mimetic desire," a term coined by French anthropologist René Girard that describes desires shaped by those around us. For example, if your friends all start buying houses, you may start feeling that you should, too, even if you're happy renting. Often, we don't realize how influenced we are by the behavior of people we admire. Of course, brands and advertisers have been aware of this phenomenon since at least the 1700s, when Wedgewood made a tea set for King George III's wife and marketed its products as having "Royal" approval.[4]

By taking the time and space to engage in thorough self-reflection, you can determine what *you* do and don't want. During this process, it's important to let your deep-down preferences rise to the surface and to separate those preferences from emotions such as jealousy, anger, sadness, and fear. As you acknowledge your emotions, you can generate self-compassion and gently put your emotions aside to pinpoint your true desires. This can require some digging because big emotions tend to be front and center and may mask, or even hide, your true preferences. Taking time to yourself, away from the thrum of daily life, can help you focus. The time-out doesn't need to be elaborate—sometimes a simple solo walk in a natural setting will do the trick. At other times, it may take a longer period of time, not only for you but also for your partner, if you have one.

Marion and Anika had both been married to men before they came out as gay. Now both divorced with adult children, they had been in a loving relationship for five years. When same-sex marriage was legalized in their state, Marion wanted them to get married. However, Anika was unsure, and after months of discussion, she still felt unwilling to make that commitment. She had felt rushed when her husband proposed marriage many years earlier but had married him after her parents encouraged her to accept. She didn't want to repeat the same mistake. Marion suggested they pause their relationship while Anika figured out what she wanted. Anika agreed to reach out to Marion once she had clarity. Much to Marion's surprise, she didn't hear from Anika for almost a year. During that time, Marion dated other women, but her experiences only reminded her how much she missed Anika.

When Anika finally appeared at Marion's front door saying she was ready, she'd been in therapy for a year and felt she'd learned a lot about herself and what she wanted. Marion was ecstatic to see her and delighted to hear that Anika wanted to renew their relationship. Marion and Anika soon married, and they have been together for more than ten years. Their time apart wasn't easy, but it deepened their bond and gave Anika the opportunity to gain much-needed clarity.

When to Postpone Decision-Making

According to traditional philosophers such as Plato and Descartes, passion should never inform rigorous decision-making.[5] It just gets in the way. However, in the real world, human decisions almost always involve emotion, and this is particularly true when the decisions concern money and love because the people making the money decisions are in loving relationships—with partners, spouses, parents, or adult children—and because every decision has both financial and emotional dimensions.

Still, it's important to engage System 2 thinking—logic and thoughtful consideration—in your decision-making. As a rule of thumb, it's best to avoid making important decisions in haste, anger, or fear. Remember, too, if you have a partner, to seek out their insight and perspective, even in decisions that seem to affect only you.

Step Two: *Communicate*

As you clarify what you want, you need to communicate with the other person or people who will be most affected by your decision. Two-way dialogue is the cornerstone of every healthy relationship. John Gottman and Julie Gottman, relationship experts and bestselling authors, assert that trust and commitment are the two main pillars of a sound relationship. Both are strengthened by frequent communication.[6]

Given that communication about a relationship requires both people to be clear about what they want, self-reflection and two-way communication should occur in tandem. Each new topic raised in the relationship requires additional self-reflection, followed by more communication. You might think of it as a double helix, which is the shape of a double-stranded DNA molecule, with two spiral staircases wound around each other.

When Lauren initiated this kind of communication with Greg, she learned that he was envisioning a traditional marriage in which he would be the breadwinner and she would stay home. That gave her the opportunity to ask herself whether she was willing to let go of her dream of having a family *and* a career. The answer to that question was ultimately a hard no. Although saddened by the situation, Lauren ended her relationship with Greg and accepted her scholarship. To this day, she maintains that it was one of the best decisions she's ever made. Currently the chief curator at a major museum, she has been happily married for more than a decade. She and her husband divide household responsibilities, are equally involved parents, and are supportive of each other's careers and other dreams.

When and How to Communicate

The pattern of communication that couples establish early in their relationship is important. Patterns can certainly shift over time (especially with intentional effort), but the way you start out will likely affect your communication throughout your relationship. If you're dating or in a newer relationship, overinvest in communication during the early months and years. Share how you're feeling about things that happen to you and decisions you make, both big and small, and share why you feel that way, even if it seems obvious to you. If you're in a more established relationship, try opening the lines of communication slowly; suddenly unleashing a torrent of thoughts and feelings may be overwhelming to you both.

Good communication isn't always polite and calm. Sometimes it's incredibly awkward and uncomfortable. Sometimes it involves raised voices and, later, apologies for what was said in the heat of the moment. If you grew up in a household in which your parents didn't openly disagree, you'll need to learn how to do this productively. As one couple expressed on the eve of their ten-year anniversary, "We have figured out our cadences through practice, some tense conversations and more than a few full-out fights, and in general a ton of communication. Even if not all of it is done well, we don't shy away from trying to talk about it." The operative word here is "trying"—even if you don't always succeed, it is far better to keep trying to communicate than to withdraw or shut down, a practice known as stonewalling. The Gottmans have called stonewalling one of the "Four Horsemen of the Apocalypse." Along with criticism, contempt, and defensiveness, it is one of the negative communication styles that they believe can predict the end of a relationship.[7] Investing in communication is a signal that you value the other person and their feelings and viewpoints.

Step Three: Consider a Broad Range of *Choices*

Before making a decision, it's important to generate a broad range of possible choices. Few decisions are strictly either/or, and one key to better decision-making is widening your alternatives. Have you inadvertently taken possibilities off the table that deserve consideration? Have you framed a decision too narrowly and created a false choice between two options? Are there any solutions that would allow you to have your cake and eat it, too?

Min and Yong, both originally from Shanghai, met when they were working for a large investment bank in San Francisco. After they married, they attended the same business school, both focusing on finance. When Min gave birth to their first child, she took a year off from school to care for their daughter full-time, with some help from Yong, who continued his studies. When Yong graduated and began a full-time job based in San Francisco, Min returned to school. By then, however, Yong was traveling frequently and could help care for their daughter only on weekends. On the recommendation of a classmate, Min joined a childcare cooperative with two other student families. For a while, the arrangement worked. But soon Min found that the number of hours that she needed to provide care for her own daughter plus the other young children made it difficult to keep up with her studies. When a slot opened at the university day-care center, she placed her daughter in day care with great relief.

By the time of her graduation, Min had received a job offer from the same prestigious company that employed her husband. Accepting the job meant they would both be based in San Francisco, but it also meant they would both have to travel a lot. Min very much wanted to accept the job, but what would they do about childcare? Daytime childcare alone wouldn't work because they would need evening and some weekend care also.

They soon began interviewing for a live-in nanny but couldn't find an applicant who would make a suitable "third parent." With demanding jobs that required so much time away, they had to find someone they could trust completely with the care and, to some degree, the upbringing of their child. "We need to think out of the box here," Min told her husband.

After several weeks of thinking and talking with each other, as well as with friends in dual-career couples, Yong had an idea. They needed to be near their families! That seemed to be how many dual-career couples with travel-heavy jobs made parenthood work.

His employer (soon to be hers as well) had offices in Shanghai, where both sets of parents still lived. Would the company agree to transfer them to Shanghai? And would their parents be willing to play a major role in raising their daughter? Thinking broadly paid off. Their employer agreed to base them at the Shanghai office, and their parents were equally enthusiastic about helping to raise their granddaughter. Min and Yong were fortunate to have such support, but they also put time and energy into brainstorming options that initially seemed "out there."

Step Four: *Check In* with Friends, Family, and Other Resources

At different points in the decision-making process, it can be helpful to check in with others. These check-ins can serve different purposes. For Lauren, talking with trusted confidants helped her gain clarity about what she wanted. (Vocalizing thoughts and feelings can be especially helpful if you do your best thinking when talking aloud.) For Min and Yong, reaching out to friends in similar situations opened their eyes to a broader set of options they could consider.

Before Abby took Myra's class in graduate school, she was planning to work part-time after becoming a parent. To explore that option in more depth, she did some check-ins, but instead of consulting only friends and colleagues, she also sought out published research. During that process, she learned about the wage penalty of at least 20 percent for part-time work. In Myra's class, she then discovered that part-time workers also typically receive fewer employee benefits (more on this topic in chapter seven).[8]

Since equity has always been one of Abby's core values, the idea of making less per hour for the same work done by someone who worked full-time did not sit well. Scrapping her plan to work part-time, she resolved to figure out a way to work full-time after having kids and to try to effect much-needed change in this area (we explore that in chapter ten.)

Sometimes the best check-ins come from unlikely sources. A neighbor, an acquaintance, or even a stranger may offer just the inspiration you need. For Ava, her most beneficial check-in was an indirect one. After she had spent twenty years out of the workforce, her youngest was graduating from high school, and she was ready to return to work. The idea of getting a job, however, felt overwhelming. "Who would want someone with a two-decade gap in her resume?" she asked her husband, Mike, adding that she didn't even know what kind of job or which industry she would pursue.

Mike was supportive of Ava's desire to return to work, and he casually mentioned her predicament to someone on his adult league baseball team. "Ah," Mike's teammate said, "my sister just went through the same thing. I'll give you her email in case Ava wants to contact her."

When Ava reached out to this woman she'd never met, a new world opened before her. To Ava's surprise, there were now companies that specialized in helping women return to the workplace after pausing their careers. Suddenly, she had access to a wealth of online information—blogs, coaches, webinars, and fellow job seekers. While her job-hunting journey proved circuitous, she eventually began a new career that she loves, working as a paramedic. It all started with Mike casually mentioning Ava's situation to his teammate.

There are some money and love decisions, such as how to return to the workplace after a career pause, where it's helpful to have as many conversations as possible; however, for other decisions, seeking input from only a few people can be the best course of action. One woman noted that when she was deciding whether to have a child, she limited her check-ins to just a few people whose opinions she really trusted. She felt that getting too much input too early on could be overwhelming, even discouraging.

It can also be helpful to get creative. Nadia's husband has a physical disability that emerged years into their relationship (the Centers for Disease Control and Prevention estimates that one in four adults in the United States lives with a disability that impacts major life activities).[9] Since the onset of his disability, her husband has been unable to complete most household tasks, and the bulk of that work now falls on her. When they began to contemplate having children, she found that traditional advice for dual-career households wasn't relevant to their situation. However, when she checked in with friends and colleagues who are single parents, she found their insight both pertinent and useful.

When you're doing check-ins, stay open. You may be surprised by which perspectives and sources lead you toward the most optimal solutions.

Step Five: Explore Likely *Consequences*

Arguably one of the most difficult aspects of decision-making is trying to predict the likely consequences of each major alternative. We all lack the crystal ball we would like for this work, but even amid massive uncertainty, you'll make better choices after considering the possible consequences of alternative paths. You may already do some version of this when you make a decision, and if so, remember that love and work are intricately intertwined, so a work decision will likely have repercussions for those you love, and vice versa.

Anticipating likely consequences begins with categorizing possible outcomes. For example, suppose you are thinking of accepting a job in another city. First, look at the job itself. What might go wrong? This is similar to conducting a "premortem," which has become popular in the business world. In a premortem, you proactively predict what could cause a project to fail so you can construct appropriate safeguards in advance.[10] Asking what might go wrong is an excellent way of beginning to unearth a decision's possible consequences, but you should also be sure to ask yourself what might go *right*. What consequences might prove advantageous?

Using that same example of considering a new job in a new city, here are some specific questions you might ask to anticipate consequences of a new job: How do you feel about the person who will be your boss? How would you describe the company culture, based on what you've seen, heard, and experienced? Is the amount of travel you have negotiated likely to change? If the new company is a start-up, what is your backup plan if it fails? What are some potential advantages of the new job? Then, considering the move to a new city, you might ask questions like these: How might living in the new city affect your partner and their career? How about your kids, parents, and friends? Do you know anyone in the new city who can serve as your "anchor friend" (someone who will introduce you to their friends in the area), or will you have to develop a new network on your own? What are some likely benefits of the new city?

Once you've considered potential consequences, assign probabilities to each. No one can do this perfectly. As with communication, the goal here is simply to try; do your best based on whatever information and experience you can access. Doing check-ins can help you get a more realistic picture of probabilities. For example, connecting with parents of kids of similar ages as yours could prove helpful. You also might spend a week in a rental in the city or neighborhood you are considering to get a more realistic picture of what living there might be like—to prototype the experience, in the parlance of design thinking.

You might also consider how your decision might play out over different time horizons. We like to frame the consequences this way: the immediate (the next few months); the short term (the next six months to two years); and the long term (beyond the next two years). Often, what may seem like negative consequences in the immediate or short term end up becoming neutral or even positive over the long term. Returning to our moving example, it might be challenging to make new friends in a new city immediately, but you'll likely have developed some friendships in two years' time.

If seeking answers to these questions seems like a long and winding road to analysis paralysis, rest assured, it's not. Many of these questions are likely already in the back of your mind. By consciously focusing on them, you can face your fears and get the information you need. In other words, bringing all the likely consequences into the open helps you tame the bogeymen and prepares you to make an intentional decision.

Matt and Claire discovered how to get through a bottleneck in their decision-making during the coronavirus pandemic. For years, Claire had been turning down job offers in other cities because Matt was reluctant to move away from his professional and social network. Once the pandemic hit, however, he changed his tune. Sheltering in place without in-person contact with friends and colleagues for months on end made Matt realize that what he needs most in life is Claire and their children. Once he had that clarity, he became much more open to the idea of moving.

As we move forward and explore some of the dynamics behind commonplace, sometimes hot-button, love and money decisions, we'll continually refer back to the 5Cs framework—clarify, communicate, consider a broad ranges of choices, check in with trusted sources and confidants, and explore likely consequences.

CHAPTER ONE EXERCISE:

Framework for Making Decisions About Money and Love

This exercise is designed to help you apply our 5Cs framework to a money/love question that is top of mind for you right now. Jot down your initial thoughts here, and then refine your answers as you continue reading subsequent chapters.

CLARIFY

What money/love question is top of mind for you right now?

___

What matters most to you about this decision?

___

I WANT:	I DON'T WANT:
1.	1.
2.	2.
3.	3.

COMMUNICATE

Who will be most affected by this decision (besides you)?

___

What would you like to tell them?

___

What would you like to ask them?

___

CHOICES

What are some potential solutions? (Try to generate at least four or five.) Have you framed the options broadly enough? Revisit these after the next step, adding to your list if possible.

CHECK IN

How will you learn more?
People who may be helpful:
Other resources to explore (books, articles, etc.):

CONSEQUENCES

Using your best guess, how do you think your decision might play out in the following time frames?

Immediate (next few months):

Short term (next six months to two years):

Long term (beyond two years):

What are some ways you might prevent potential negative consequences?

When you're ready, write down your decision, along with a few notes on why you landed there. Continue to refine your thoughts as you read. Keep the paper where you can find it if you have misgivings later, and then move on with your life.

TWO

FINDING YOUR PERSON

Dating and Mating

From Hollywood and the music industry to Bumble, Tinder, and social media, it's clear that we're still madly in love with love, weddings, and honeymoons. Yet even as growing numbers of people swipe right or click on their ideal match, marriage rates—which were at a historic low by 2018—have continued to decline.[1]

Meanwhile, popular culture perpetuates the ideas that "real" love leads to marriage, that marriage is only about love, and that if it's *true* love, money doesn't matter. But is love really all it takes for a long-term relationship, married or not, to succeed? As gender roles shift, and our lifestyles and priorities are continually rocked by everything from technology to a pandemic, decisions about dating, mating, and deciding whether or not to marry feel more loaded than ever. Increasingly, the way we approach these decisions is paramount.

IS MARRIAGE STILL THE GOAL?

The institution of marriage has been a fundamental building block of society for millennia. Not surprisingly, it has also had an enormous impact on how we define committed relationships. As a result, most discussions about long-term relationships still lead to a discussion of marriage. However, that may be changing as more couples delay marriage or even opt out of it altogether.[2]

Our collective focus on marriage as the end point of any good relationship, particularly in the United States, isn't always positive. In fact, focusing on marriage too early in the dating and mating process sometimes lessens the chances of creating a mutually supportive, loving relationship. Given this, as well as the fact that more people are delaying or opting out of marriage—only time will tell which of these is actually occurring—the discussion in this chapter integrates marriage but doesn't assume that wedlock is the de facto goal. The topic of marriage is covered in more depth in chapter three.

A NEW LTR MINDSET

In January 2022, the *New York Times* published an essay by Kaitlyn Greenidge in which she reflected on the loneliness and joy of her pandemic life as a newly single mother living in her own mother's house with other relatives. Framing her experience in the context of the overall decline in marriage rates, she wrote: "We are living through a time when all the stories the larger culture tells us about ourselves are being rewritten: the story of what the United States is; what it means to be a man or a woman; what it means to be a child; what it means to love oneself or other people. We are imagining all of this again so that these stories can guide and comfort us rather than control us."[3]

This enlightened, hopeful approach is an important starting point for our discussion of dating, long-term relationships (LTRs), and marriage. According to the 2020 Census, there are approximately thirty-six million solo dwellers in the United States.[4] This isn't new news; the number of single people has been increasing steadily for decades.[5] While research has indicated that married people live longer and are likely to have better health outcomes in some circumstances, those health benefits vary by gender, socio-economic status, and the marriage itself.[6] Separate research also indicates that single people are discriminated against at work, by being expected to work longer hours without extra pay, and medically, by being viewed as of lower priority when they need certain kinds of urgent procedures.[7] This bias against single people may explain some of the health "benefits" of marriage.

There are advantages to being single, too. Single women in particular may have improved career opportunities.[8] Furthermore, as the number of single people has increased, the stigma associated with having children outside of wedlock has been steadily fading, which may help to reverse the bias against unmarried adults.[9] Our point? Progress is never perfect, but the historical norms dictating that real love leads to marriage seem to be changing. Even if marriage rates do eventually rebound, our collective approach to lifelong commitment will likely look noticeably different for you than it did for your parents. With increased flexibility about what a successful long-term relationship is, we may discover new options. Ironically, with less pressure to get married, we may also be better able to create the authentic outcomes that we desire, whether these are loving relationships, fulfilling careers, and perhaps parenthood, as well as our desired lifestyle.

FINDING A MATE

Looking for someone to build a life with is an extremely emotional process. It produces the highest of highs when it's going well and the lowest of lows when it isn't. There's also still a lot of societal pressure to find someone "soon" (before the biological clock runs down) and to find the "right" someone. Even though using our framework and recommendations can smooth the process and help you make more satisfying decisions, you may feel as if lady luck has abandoned you for significant chunks of time. This doesn't mean you will be alone forever.

Time spent alone can be valuable, helping you to define what you want and need in a life partner. As much as you can, try to relax and enjoy the ride. Being single doesn't have to equal loneliness. In fact, people in couples (and even parents with multiple children) can and do experience loneliness. Single people also tend to be more social, and have larger social networks, than married individuals.[10] Remember also that these and other societal norms are changing. Instead of succumbing to the idea that being single is a burden, embrace it and the opportunities it provides. Changing jobs or careers, moving to a new city or country, pursuing additional education, overhauling your entire lifestyle—these options and others are often more accessible for singles. Your freedom is at a peak. You may use it in whatever ways you most desire.

SHELVING THE STORYBOOK

As popular legend has long told it, we're each destined to meet "the one." But with nearly eight billion people on the planet, the myth that we each have a "one and only" seems unlikely. Chasing this mythical individual you're "destined" to end up with can be counterproductive and add unnecessary stress, especially for those feeling the pull of the biological clock.[11] Instead of searching for your one and only, focus on finding someone who's as well suited to you and your needs as you are to theirs. The quality of the connection between two people is the heart and soul of any successful, lasting relationship.

As you shed the burden of needing to find your "destined" mate, you can also cast off the love at first sight—or lust at first sight—fantasy. If your pheromones don't go wild at first glance, if your heart doesn't pound out of your chest but instead just keeps beating regularly, that doesn't mean intense mutual attraction is off the table. Starting as "just friends" can give people time to build an important foundation for a long-term relationship. Myra and her second husband, Jay, were "just friends" for almost thirty years. In fact, Jay was her first husband's friend and an usher at their wedding. Many years later, after they'd each been divorced for almost ten years, at one lunch everything changed for Jay, and not long after, it did for Myra also.[12]

Abby and Ross also started off as "just friends" in business school, enjoying hikes, dinners, and other adventures together. It wasn't until time apart over spring break that Abby felt ready to admit her feelings for Ross. They soon began dating, surprising no one when their relationship quickly grew serious. Relationships can and often do change over time. While you don't want to try to force attraction, it's important not to undervalue a mate because a relationship hasn't developed in a traditional storybook way.

ERASING "THE LIST"

Just as we've been taught to expect our relationships to develop in a specific way, many of us begin the search for love with a list of the qualities we want in a potential mate. Sometimes we write down those characteristics, but mostly we keep them in our heads (and our daydreams). That exercise can help you to understand what you think you want in a partner, yet "the list" is not always helpful. In the survey we sent out while writing this book, one respondent described how her list proved to be misleading:

When I first met my husband through mutual friends, it was NOT love at first sight. Even when we started dating, I wasn't "all in" because he didn't meet the made-up requirements I had conjured up as a teenager: he wasn't tall, dark, or even handsome in the way I had pictured. He didn't sweep me off my feet with his charisma or seduce me with his moves. He didn't impress me with his title or promise me a lavish life with his paycheck. Quite the opposite! It took me years to overcome my own misguided perceptions of what love and the perfect guy look like. I think a lot of people, including myself, were surprised with "the one" I chose, but thirteen years, two kids, and a global pandemic have confirmed my choice.

Physical good looks and career or financial success may seem like what you want in a partner at first, but over the long haul, what you may value most is the person's dedication to parenthood or willingness to prioritize your career alongside their own. Stay open to people you connect with, regardless of how well they fit your "list."

LIKE ATTRACTS LIKE

Another reason to ditch the list is that it may be inherently unnecessary, since people tend to couple with others who share similar traits, which social scientists call "positive assortative mating."[13] Research confirms that beautiful people marry other beautiful people, tall people marry each other, and members of a couple often have similar levels of education, wealth, and body mass index (BMI).[14]

This tendency to partner with someone like ourselves may come from a natural human penchant for comfort; someone who resembles us may feel inherently familiar, at least to some degree. However, this phenomenon may also reflect a societal structure that makes it more challenging to know many people who are inherently *unlike* ourselves. One recent study found that social structures are key to assortative mating and that couples in both the United States and Germany who met online tended to be more unalike in their education, race, religion, and ethnicity than the control group of couples who met without the help of online platforms.[15] However, economist Paul Oyer points out that with respect to attractiveness and wealth, positive assortative mating is quite alive and well on dating sites.[16]

Although many believe that assortative mating has increased since the 1950s (remember how the executives in *Mad Men* married their secretaries?), in fact assortative mating has declined among those with a college education and increased for those with a low level of education.[17]

Does assortative mating affect marital happiness? The findings are thin and unclear. There is no definitive evidence that marrying someone with a similar education or, say, from a comparable socioeconomic background is a recipe for a lasting partnership. Your happiness will likely depend more on the particular person you choose and the kind of relationship you create as a couple.

WHAT DO YOU WANT?

One of the most important steps you can take before—and during—your search for a long-term partner is getting clear about what *you* want in life and what *you* want from a relationship. This can be more challenging than it seems, since our mates and relationships will inevitably be scrutinized by friends, family, and society as a whole. Without our conscious awareness, their expectations can take on outsize importance, as one of our survey respondents experienced in her first marriage:

I married the "ideal" husband at twenty-five. High earning potential, smart, attentive, from a politically influential company, White (my family is Asian) . . . everything to make my mother happy. I realize now that at that time, I was more concerned with being ahead of my cohort, having a nice fancy wedding (while a lot of my friends were still waiting to get proposed to) than listening to my own feelings. We got divorced ten years later, and although we remain good co-parents, I am sorry that I hurt my ex-husband through this marriage. That decision to marry came from a place of fear of being alone and unwanted and from a deep desire to make my mother proud. None of them great reasons to marry.

What values and principles are most important to you, and which of these do you need your mate to have as well? Political and social views, religion and spirituality, life goals, and priorities can all fall under these categories. Keep in mind, values and principles, unlike characteristics and attributes such as having a good job, are about core beliefs. They highlight how we view ourselves, one another, our lives, and the world at large.

The idea of sharing core values and principles was echoed by many survey respondents who have enjoyed long, happy relationships. This woman shared how she knew her husband was the one she wanted to build a life with:

Mostly because of the way I felt when I was with him. I felt happy, respected, engaged, full of life. We shared a view of the world, even though we came from very different backgrounds. He made me laugh . . . and challenged my thinking. He respected me and my work. Life felt like more of an adventure, and I had the right level of "spiritual safety" with him by my side. And I thought he was good-looking.

While "the list" approach to mate finding is often counterproductive, studies show that two characteristics are especially important in predicting successful unions—*self-control* and *conscientiousness*.[18] These traits lead to follow-through on promises, which is helpful for significant priorities, such as not cheating, and others, like completing household chores. Sometimes noticing seemingly small clues, like your date's attention span and whether they stick with plans, can give you useful insights.

Another important question to consider is how you want your potential life companion to treat you and interact with you. While passion may be at a high point early in the relationship, couples who remain the happiest over a longer period attribute their satisfaction to more than chemistry. Deep and abiding friendship and mutual trust as well as affection and attraction are critical to building connections that endure life's inevitable twists and turns. If you're already dating or in a relationship, ask yourself how comfortable you feel sharing your most private thoughts, feelings, and dreams with this person. Does this person treat you with respect and regularly take your preferences into consideration? Answering questions such as these honestly before making a significant commitment is essential.

It may also be important to consider other characteristics. Do you feel strongly about partnering with someone of the same race or ethnicity? Is age, family culture, or birthplace important to you? You may find that being more open about some of these characteristics is helpful because it can lead to a larger pool of potential mates. As this survey respondent expressed:

> *My husband and I have a big age difference (almost eighteen years). When I met him, I was very suspicious because I knew that in his culture, educated men from a good family would already have been married years ago. We started dating, and I looked out for red flags that indicated he had commitment issues—but to my (happy) surprise, I realized he simply had never met the right one. When we [had been to-*

gether for] around three months, I knew he was the one for me. It felt like the perfect fit, and I just had no words but all feeling to know why. Despite the differences in age, culture, and religion, we bonded deeply on a completely different level. We shared the same core values and principles.

WHEN TO COMMIT AND WHEN TO QUIT

Deciding when to take a relationship to the "next level," whatever that may mean, can be challenging. It's a personal, emotional decision but also a practical one. According to economists, it's important to weigh the costs of continuing your search against the costs of stopping it. When search costs exceed the likely benefits of that search, it may be time to stop looking. With online dating, the financial search costs are low, but the time and energy costs can be high. If you are a woman who wants to have a child, declining fertility can be a reason to stay in a relationship, since waiting for a better partner—whatever that means to you—can have significant consequences. On the other hand, continuing to search may provide an opportunity to get clear about what you're looking for in a relationship and find someone more compatible. The choice is yours and depends entirely on which priorities rank highest.

Research completed by professor Baba Shiv suggests that *simultaneous choice*—examining all the options at once—leads to greater satisfaction and commitment than sequential choice, which is examining each option separately, one after another.[19] Shiv's study, in fact, was inspired by his own arranged marriage. Shiv grew up in India. When he felt ready to settle down, he told his mother, and per common custom, she then presented him with three or four potential partners (simultaneous choice), and he chose one. Fortunately, his future wife also chose him from her own pool of potential mates. They married and recently celebrated their thirtieth wedding anniversary.

While arranged marriage is not common in the United States, the rising demand for matchmaking services suggests that Americans are starting to see the value of seeking professional help in finding a potential mate, compared with endlessly swiping left and swiping right.[20] Professional matchmaking and arranged marriage are certainly not universal solutions, but Shiv's research is helpful in highlighting our bias toward "the eternal quest for the best." Believing that there's always a better option out there, as many dating apps lead users to believe,[21] may encourage people to forgo relationships that would otherwise hold promise.

Lori Gottlieb, a vocal proponent of stopping the search sooner rather than later, also thinks that people looking for a mate are often unrealistic about the need to endlessly search for perfection. In a much-quoted *Atlantic* magazine article titled "Marry Him! The Case for Settling for Mr. Good Enough," she argued that women should "settle" much earlier than they do. "What makes for a good marriage isn't necessarily what makes for a good romantic relationship," Gottlieb wrote.[22] This argument holds for people of all genders and successful long-term relationships in or out of wedlock.

CHOOSING A MATE IS ALSO CHOOSING A RELATIONSHIP

What kind of relationship do you want? Do you want a partnership in which you raise children together? Do you want both careers to be equally advantaged? Do you want to prioritize one partner's career while the other partner focuses more time and energy on home life?

Again, it's important to try to cast aside any conditioning about what kind of relationship you've been taught or told you should want. Focus instead on what *you* desire in a relationship. To get you thinking, the sections that follow describe two distinctly different relationships—one that aims to give both partners' careers equal priority and another that prioritizes one partner's career. These, of course, are just two of many possible scenarios, so allow these to inspire your thinking rather than limit you to a choice of either/or.

Scenario A

When we decided to marry (two MBAs six years apart), we actively decided that our two careers would have equal priority, even though I was already an executive and she was just starting out. We agreed we'd make decisions about where to live and how to invest in childcare with the core belief that we wanted her to be on a path to being an executive as well. We talk about her career weekly, especially since it's been difficult to navigate it during the pandemic.

Scenario B

This wasn't the reason I married him, but deciding to marry my husband, whose priority is more on family versus work, has had a very positive impact on my career and life. He's not as career focused as I am and has been happy to take on much of the running of the household and finances and more of the child-related duties. We have a one-year-old and a three-year-old.

We're not the first to assert that the most important career decision you'll make is about whom to marry and what kind of relationship you will have. If you're pursuing a high-powered, time-intensive career, finding a potential mate who supports that is important. If you think you want to pause your career when you have children, find out whether your potential mate is on board with that plan. The point here is to communicate your hopes and dreams early in the relationship. Everything doesn't need to be decided in advance, especially since people often change their minds as a relationship moves forward or they become parents. However, if you know you want a high-powered career and your potential mate prefers that you focus on homelife, that may create substantial challenges in the future.

The only changes you can count on are the ones under your own control. During the dating stage, take your potential mate at their word and don't assume that time or other forces will someday lead to a change of heart.

FINDING A PARTNER

As you move along in your search for a mate and reflect on your experiences, your preferences may shift. Gary Becker's economic theory of marriage conceptualized the dating process as a marriage market where people seeking a mate come together with diverse attributes and disparate values and eventually find a match. Noneconomists may not call the process a marriage market, but in talking with students over the years, Myra has found that most of them agree that, consciously or not, they are participating in a kind of market.

One advantage of looking at dating as a marketplace is that it allows you to value the experience you gain over time and how that can help you make more informed decisions. Just as the more you shop for fruit, the better you get at choosing the right bananas, people who date increase their knowledge and understanding of themselves and what they are looking for. (To be clear, we're not suggesting you or your mate is a banana or equivalent to one. We're just saying that finding a banana that's to your specific liking is no easy task!) One survey respondent put it this way:

> *I dated a tech entrepreneur and then a tech manager whose goal was to be CEO of a media company, and from both I learned what it was like to be with someone whose time was scarce. I then dated and married a bartender turned farmer who has lots of time flexibility. I decided that for me, an abundance of time and flexibility with time were the most important assets I was looking for in a spouse.*

Through experience, this woman learned that her previous emphasis on finding a mate with a high-powered career didn't reflect what she wanted. Instead, she valued availability and time flexibility.

BIG CONVERSATIONS TO HAVE EARLY ON (BEFORE YOU FEEL ENTIRELY COMFORTABLE)

By the time Lauren and Greg, whom we met in the introduction, realized that they had different priorities—she wanted a career while he wanted a wife whose primary focus was on home and family—they were already living together. By that point in their relationship, their friends and family expected them to marry, thereby further complicating Lauren's decision to break off their union. For a lot of couples, taking this all-too-familiar path of least resistance can feel easier than breaking up. If there's love and commitment, the thinking goes, the rest can be ironed out. However, as we also discussed in chapter one, the communication pattern that's established early in a relationship is important. Going with the flow, so to speak, can feel good by allowing you to avoid important conversations early in a relationship, but by doing this you are likely to create bigger challenges later. Instead, when you feel a relationship has promise, initiate conversations about big topics early. By airing your viewpoints sooner rather than later, you will not only understand your partner's priorities better but also gain practice in talking through emotionally charged issues.

People sometimes forgo or delay these conversations out of an unacknowledged fear that unearthing differences will lead to a breakup. While that fear is entirely understandable, in the long run you're better off discovering these differences early in a relationship. If you and your partner do discover incompatible goals and preferences, you may surprise yourselves by finding a compromise, as Abby and Ross did when they discussed religion early in their relationship. Abby knew she wanted to raise her children in the Jewish faith, as she'd been raised, but Ross didn't feel strongly about any one faith. He told Abby he was comfortable raising their children in the Jewish tradition, provided he didn't have to take the lead in incorporating faith into their lives. To Abby that felt like a major milestone, even though being married with children still felt far off.

If you discover a topic where you and your mate can't come to any kind of agreement, conversations like this may lead to the end of a relationship. However painful that may be in the moment, keep in mind that your perspective may change over time. Several of Myra's students have thanked her years afterward for encouraging them to have difficult conversations that led to a breakup. As a result of ending that relationship, they were able to find someone better suited to them and their goals and dreams. In other words, if a disagreement about a high-priority issue is unresolvable, it's better to know now, before your lives are even further intertwined.

The following are topics that are important to discuss sooner rather than later in a relationship. When you decide to broach them, you may feel quite anxious. You may also worry that it's too early or that your relationship isn't yet ready for such weighty discussions. Remember, discussing emotionally charged issues is a large part of what strengthens a relationship. Deep down you know that if the topic is important to you, you will *have to* talk about it. You can wait, but that diving board will probably not get any lower. Knowing that, take the plunge. If it doesn't work, chalk it up as experience you'll benefit from later. We've included an exercise at the end of this chapter that can serve as a guide.

Question 1: Where Will You Live? How Will You Decide Whether and When to Move?

The decision about where to live often involves trading off matters of love and money. It's a major decision because it can be life-altering. It's a tough decision because there are so many alternatives, especially in today's global economy and distributed work environment. One student from Spain was already married to another Spanish student when the couple took Myra's class. They had numerous choices about where to live following graduation. The summer after they graduated, they went on a road trip through all the countries and cities they were considering for their next move, starting in Amsterdam, going south through Belgium, Luxembourg, and Switzerland, and then returning through Paris to London. All along the way, they talked with friends and alumni to get their perspectives. They told Myra that the trip really helped narrow down their choices, and they ultimately decided to settle in Luxembourg, where they have lived happily for several decades.

The Spanish couple were lucky in that they agreed on their preferences. That wasn't the case for Tandice, who assumed that she and her girlfriend, who were both from California, would live there after graduation. However, her girlfriend wanted to go wherever she could find the best career opportunities, which ended up being New York City. They lived there for a few years, but Tandice was miserable. One winter, she took a trip to visit friends in Los Angeles and never boarded her flight back. Eventually, her girlfriend was advised by a mentor to settle where she wanted to live and then *make* the career opportunities happen wherever she was. About a year later, she joined Tandice in Los Angeles. They got engaged and have lived there ever since. Looking back, they regret not discussing their living preferences earlier, as it might have saved them a good deal of heartache.

Never assume you know your potential partner's preferences. Ask early in the game, making sure to tell them about your preferences also.

Even when you agree on where to live, there is merit in agreeing on broad parameters for possible future moves. For instance, some couples agree in advance that they won't move to a new place if the move seems likely to make either partner worse off. This strategy provides stability and allows family members to develop strong local friendships and community ties while still permitting an advantageous move if all the stars align. In a way, this approach is like a Hippocratic oath for moving: first, do no harm to your partner.

The calculus may be different for LGBTQ couples or multiracial couples because in addition to considering where their family is or where their best career prospects are, they need to prioritize where they feel safe, comfortable, and supported. One woman in a same-sex marriage shared, "The longer I stay in the [San Francisco] Bay Area, the more I realize how nice it is to be out. When I was younger, I thought I could live anywhere in the world. Now I'm not sure if it's worth the 'covering'; there are big chunks of the world where I would not feel comfortable even traveling anymore."

One multiracial couple shared a similar hesitation. When they created a spreadsheet of cities where they could live, given their chosen industries, one midwestern city ranked high on the list. Ultimately, they omitted it as an option because "our children's last name would stick out, and we wondered whether they would be more comfortable in a blended community. . . . We wanted to be where there was diversity."

Another important factor if you have children and both partners are employed, or if you are raising a child as a single parent, is the availability and affordability of high-quality childcare. We discuss this in greater depth in chapter seven.

If you and your partner decide to live separately so that each of you can take a dream job in a different city, that decision might benefit each of you individually, but it will likely test the limits of your relationship. In that case, prioritize nourishing the relationship while you are apart so that your bond continues to grow rather than dissipate. If you allow your relationship to become stagnant, you predispose it to wilting. Myra's husband, Jay, a psychiatrist, introduced her to the idea that a loving partnership consists of three entities: each of the partners and the relationship they create. Jay's work with couples taught him that the care and feeding of the relationship is as central to its success as the care and feeding of each partner. Couples should frequently ask: Does this decision (or practice) serve our relationship in addition to serving each of us individually? This is an important perspective to keep in mind when broaching the question of where to live, among other tough questions.

Question 2: How Will You Handle Finances?

Gulp. Sigh. Eyeroll. Talking about money often ranks high on the list of least favorite conversations. Some of us were taught that discussing money is too personal (or downright impolite), or we may fear being judged for limited means, good fortune, or how we spend the money we have. Whatever the case, finances tend to be an emotionally fraught topic. However, being able to discuss money openly and honestly is critical to the long-term health of any relationship. This means disclosing debt and addressing long-term financial goals.

We also recommend constructing a shared approach to handling finances, especially if your future is likely to include living together, getting married, or having children.

Experts agree that the way couples approach their finances often represents more than just their method for managing money—it symbolizes their priorities and their attitudes about their relationship. That means it's worth taking the time to determine an approach that you both feel good about.[23]

Before diving into the tactics, have a candid conversation (or several) about spending habits, saving habits, and your financial "stories." Did a childhood that involved moving multiple times because the rent was overdue leave you with an inclination to save every penny? Are you used to giving and receiving generous gifts because that's how your family showed affection? Have your parents lived in the same two-bedroom apartment forever, choosing to invest in their retirement accounts instead of renovating or moving? Do you like to upgrade your phone, computer, and car every time the next model comes out? Share that with your partner! Money-related issues frequently lead to discord—and even divorce—so it's important to address them *before* they become a source of conflict. Once you've discussed your financial philosophies and have your eyes wide open about any differences, you'll be better positioned to tackle the specifics about how to combine your finances.

There are a few options for handling finances as a couple:

- *Pooling:* merging all assets into a joint account. This is often a process as you figure out different priorities for spending and lifestyle, short-term desires and long-term goals, and so on.
- *Partial pooling:* merging some assets, whether the minimum required to cover household expenses (rent or mortgage, groceries, and utilities) or combining most assets but keeping individual accounts. In this case, you'll need to define guidelines

for how much to contribute to the joint account (a fixed amount versus a percentage of salary, especially if you and your partner earn different amounts) and which expenses will be paid out of the joint account rather than individual accounts.

- *Independent management:* keeping entirely separate individual accounts. Keep in mind, this option still requires that you discuss in detail how shared expenses will be paid, as well as optional ones such as eating out and travel.

Financial experts agree that for married couples or domestic partners, having at least one joint account is best practice.[24] Beyond that, expert opinions diverge. Some believe it's important to keep at least some independent money—either to pay for gifts for the other person or to be able to make "no questions asked" expenditures; others think separate accounts create too much potential for deception.

Ultimately, all agree that regardless of the selected approach, what's key is communicating about finances with transparency and being willing to revisit and adjust your approach over time as circumstances change. For example, if one person leaves the workforce and is no longer earning an income, or if someone inherits a significant sum, it may be necessary to reassess how finances are handled.

Often, the process of having these conversations and discussing each of your preferences is in some ways more important than the outcome of those discussions. One survey respondent shared this:

> *Ultimately, we decided I would manage finances (since I work in finance), but we would each have an individual account in addition to our joint account. We went through the process of [determining] how much to allocate to our joint account versus individual accounts and decided on the thresholds where we would run financial decisions and purchases by each other.*

Another pointed out how his and his partner's approach to finances changed as the trust between them deepened:

When we were engaged, we decided on a formula for how to pool and divide our income. The idea was to allocate the same amount to each of us per paycheck for personal expenses (we didn't come up with a strict definition, instead defining it as expenses that are clearly benefiting one person and are discretionary and nonessential) and pool the rest toward a shared family cash pool. The logic of choosing this approach (over a percentage of salary approach) was that regardless of who earns more, we would both feel we have an equal and meaningful "fun fund" that each of us could spend guilt-free. Over the years, however, we both realized we fully trust each other, and this mechanism was only creating overhead (accounting, keeping track of things). At this point, we just pool everything into a single account, and each of us is welcome to spend as we see fit.

Question 3: Do You Want Children? How Many, and When?

We discuss this subject at much greater length in chapter four, but we want to put in a placeholder for the topic because it deserves time and attention early in your relationship. For some couples this is an easy discussion; for others it's as challenging as discussing money or more so. Regardless, it's a fundamental issue that should be addressed sooner rather than later.

Some are surprised by how aligned they are with their potential mate about having children, as this couple found:

Early in our dating, I shared with my husband that I was interested in growing our family through adoption. It turns out he shared the same interest. . . . I'm happy to report we have two beautiful adopted children now!

The next story illustrates the importance of taking your potential mate's preferences at their word.

When I first met my ex-wife, I fell hard, and when she told me she didn't want children, I figured I could eventually change her mind. We were married for seven years, but I never succeeded in convincing her that we should have children. I have always wanted children, and so ultimately I asked her for a divorce. I'm remarried now and I have two children, but I wish I had believed what my ex-wife told me in the first place.

As with the questions before this one, it's helpful to know your own views on the subject before broaching it with your potential partner, so take some time to self-reflect prior to the conversation. It's okay if the answer is "I'm not sure," provided you can articulate the reasons for your uncertainty.

USING THE 5Cs FRAMEWORK: CHOOSING A MATE

Rather than rushing into love decisions or basing them on emotions and inherited social norms, take time to consider what you truly want, whom you're with (or may want to be with), and how you envision your shared life unfolding. By grounding your love choices in the practical realities of daily life, you can not only feel more certainty about your decisions but also likely experience deeper connection, commitment, and joy in your relationship.

Step One: *Clarify*

If you're trying to decide whether the one you're with might be your life partner, it can be tempting to get swept up in the excitement and skip this step. Please don't. Knowing that no one person is likely to meet every criterion on any long list, identity your high-priority must-haves and be honest about whether the person you're dating feels like a true fit.

Some people find online exercises designed to help clarify core personal values helpful.[25] Reflecting on formative experiences that have shaped you and times when you have felt happiest or most fulfilled may also prove worthwhile. What about those situations and people made you feel so good? The clearer you are about what matters most to you, the better able you'll be to assess your long-term compatibility with a potential partner. Finally, once you're clear about your core values, think about couples whose relationships you admire. What do you find so noteworthy about their partnerships? Identifying those characteristics may help you to define what kind of long-term relationship you'd like for yourself.

Step Two: *Communicate*

It's no secret that good communication is at the heart of any successful, enduring relationship. How effectively and honestly do you and your partner communicate? Have you told each other what you want from your relationship? Can you discuss the strengths *and* weaknesses of your relationship? Are you comfortable being vulnerable with each other?

When thinking about communication, people tend to focus on how well they express their feelings. While that's certainly important, equally important is being a good listener. Attentive listening means fully concentrating on what your partner is saying and letting them know that you are absorbing what they're saying. "I hear you" is a response that can signal attentive listening.

What psychologists call "mirroring" is also a powerful way to connect when your partner is voicing their thoughts and feelings.

Repeating what they've said indicates to your partner that they have been heard. Since most people rarely feel that their words are carefully listened to, the experience may stand out.

When you're practicing attentive listening, it's important not to judge the other person. It's also important to give the other person the floor, so to speak. If, for example, you interject a story of your own, you may be disrupting an opportunity to develop greater intimacy. Listening means paying attention to what your partner is saying and letting them determine when *they* feel ready to stop sharing.

Over time, it's equally critical to learn how to become attentive to the other person's entire being—their history, their hopes, and, most of all, their fears, traumas, and triggers. Each of us walks around with some amount of baggage, and accepting that you and your partner each have some can help you to understand their negative or somehow undesirable actions and reactions. Viewing these moments and behavioral patterns in the context of who your partner is and what they've lived through can help you see that they're responding to their own history as much as they are to the moment at hand. By not taking these interactions or reactions so personally, you may be able to create additional opportunities to communicate on ever-deeper levels.

Finally, keep in mind that communication is a skill that you and your partner will ideally continue to work on, and improve upon, as your relationship moves forward. A shared commitment to improving the way you communicate with each other can go a long way. However, before making a long-term commitment, make sure the basic foundation for constructive communication is alive and well.

Step Three: Consider a Broad Range of *Choices*

When it comes to choosing a life partner, as Shiv's research indicates, it may make sense to limit your choice instead of broadening it. If you feel ready to settle down with someone but aren't sure if you want to do that with your current partner, you can reap the benefits of Shiv's research without introducing new partners. To do this, compare your present option—the potential mate you're considering—with past options you thought highly of or that you may even regret not choosing. How does this person compare with "the one that got away" (as in the Katy Perry song), as well as the other one or two partners you dated for the longest or loved the most? Essentially, by comparing your present option with past options, you can trick your brain into reframing a sequential choice as a quasi-simultaneous one.[26]

This may seem risky, but if the present option doesn't at least equal the one that got away, you may be better off continuing your search.

Step Four: *Check In*

Remember our recommendation to think about long-term relationships you admire? Take that one step further and find out how those couples decided to stay together. You might also want to introduce your potential partner to some of these couples and then call them afterward to ask them what they think of the two of you together. If they have reservations, are there any you feel are worth taking into consideration? (It's better to end an ill-suited relationship than realize later, when your lives are even more intertwined, how many red flags you overlooked early on.)

Notice also how your family and friends feel about your potential mate. This can be tricky for a variety of reasons, but if their opinions about your partner matter to you, take note. If friends and family are hesitant to tell you their true feelings, read between the lines. Actions speak louder than words. You know how your family and friends react when they really like someone. Do they react in those ways to your potential mate? If not, you may want to ask them directly about their reservations. Keep in mind also that if your parents dislike your potential mate, that might have substantial implications for the future. Even if their opinions don't matter to you now, you may feel differently if you have children.

Step Five: Explore Likely *Consequences*

Try to anticipate the consequences of your relationship decision by pressure-testing it. While time is its own kind of pressure test, undergoing stressful situations as a couple can give you new insights. Some people live together before marriage to see how their relationship stands up to the mundane but real pressures of everyday life. Traveling can also provide valuable information about how you and your partner behave and relate to each other in unpredictable situations. The peak points of the coronavirus pandemic also pressure-tested relationships in unique and enduring ways. If you were together, how did you and your mate fare during those periods? Do you and your partner tend to emerge from stressful periods stronger and closer? Have your tough times as a couple ultimately reinforced your bond or weakened it? Noticing how well you can weather life's storms as a cohesive unit is critical to predicting how your union will develop over time.

In addition to a career in business and teaching, Joel Peterson has raised seven children with his wife. He has spoken about the importance of having a "no off-ramps" mentality once you commit to someone.[27] If your partnership feels worthwhile, instead of heading to the exit when the going gets tough, think about ways to turn the rough patches in your relationship into opportunities to communicate better and grow closer.

CHAPTER TWO EXERCISE:

How Do You Feel About the Big Questions? (Part I)

This exercise focuses on the CLARIFY and COMMUNICATE steps of our 5Cs framework. Take some time to consider your own answers to the questions that follow.[28] *Then discuss them with your partner, if you have one. We suggest you spend at least thirty minutes talking about each category (some of them might take longer—you don't have to discuss them all in one sitting!). Note that there is a part II of this exercise at the end of chapter three. Consider how you might make this a loving discussion—we like the idea of going on a picnic or a hike.*

HOME

What place feels like home to you? Why?

____

Where do you want to live in the near term? Is that different from the long term?

____

What's important to you in a place to live (both geographically and a physical dwelling)?

____

How important is it to you to have a clean house and an organized living space?

____

How will you decide whether and when to move?

____

MONEY

What is your earliest money memory?

____

How do you want to handle finances (pool everything, pool some, keep everything separate)?

____

Do you have any debt (educational, credit card, other), and if so, how much?

____

What budget item, if any, do you spend "reckless amounts of money" on?

____

FAMILY

Do you want kids? If so, how many and when?

____

What if you can't conceive easily?

____

How do you imagine your role as a parent?

____

What type of spirituality, faith, or belief system were you exposed to while growing up? Is it important for you to raise your children within this same belief system?

____

What is your relationship like with your family (parents, siblings), and how often do you expect to see them?

____

THREE

POP THE QUESTION (OR SKIP IT ALTOGETHER?)

Getting Married

"Why get married at all?" some of Myra's students have asked over the years. It's an interesting question and one that still feels surprisingly radical in some cultures, including the United States. By their early twenties, young people may still hear about how all the "good ones" will be taken if they don't find a mate who's "marriage material." What does this even mean now that gender roles are changing so quickly? And who wants to be weighed down by the "old ball and chain" now anyway? Can a real feminist even be a wife? Should marriage still be considered the end goal of a committed, long-term relationship?

These questions are important, especially now, when our collective views about marriage are so different from what they were even a generation ago. In 2019 in the United States, only 16 percent of men and 17 percent of women said that marriage was essential for living a fulfilling life (versus 57 percent of men and 46 percent of women who said that a job or career they enjoy was essential for living a fulfilling life).[1] With marriage rates continuing to slide downward, it's clear that more people are on the fence about how, when, and even whether marriage fits into their lives. What does this mean for us collectively and individually? Are we moving away from marriage for good, or are we merely pausing to redefine it to better meet our current needs? And how does all of this impact you if or when you're deciding when, or whether, to take the proverbial walk down the aisle?

THE TRUE HISTORY OF MARRIAGE

The notion that by a certain age, young adults need to aggressively pursue victory in a collective race toward coupledom, and then marriage, dates back millennia. For most of human history, marriage was first and foremost an economic arrangement. Once married, a couple was more likely to have children, which was essential to the well-being of the community. By marrying off their younger members, families increased their labor force. Practically overnight, there were more farmhands available and, in some cases, increased landholdings, too. As a result, couples who married were more likely to be able to support themselves and their families, and by extension, entire communities could survive or even thrive.

Interestingly, while marriage became intrinsic to the structure of society, throughout history the institution of marriage has been more fluid than most of us realize. For the majority of human history, two people were considered married once they agreed to be. Prior to the sixteenth century, no ceremony, priest, official, or license was required.[2] For centuries, the church simply trusted couples who self-identified as married. Also, as recently as the nineteenth century, marrying for love was considered absurd, even irresponsible. The thinking was that a love-based marriage would be too unstable. In her book *Marriage, a History: How Love Con-*

quered Marriage, Stephanie Coontz elaborated on the tenuous relationship between love and marriage:

> *People have always fallen in love, and throughout the ages many couples have loved each other deeply. But only rarely in history has love been seen as the main reason for getting married. When someone did advocate such a strange belief, it was no laughing matter. Instead, it was considered a serious threat to the social order. . . . In some cultures and times, true love was actually thought to be incompatible with marriage. . . . Even when past societies did welcome or encourage married love, they kept it on a short leash. Couples were not to put their feelings for each other above more important commitments, such as their ties to parents, siblings, cousins, neighbors, or God.*[3]

The love marriage began to take hold only during the Enlightenment, and it gained traction slowly, over several generations, eventually morphing into what we now call a traditional marriage. That begs the question, is it traditional or merely the way a handful of recent generations have been taught to define marriage?

THE MYTH OF THE TRADITIONAL MARRIAGE

The traditional marriage, as we define it currently, is based largely on the 1950s ideal—two young people (clearly heterosexual, since we're talking about a 1950s ideal) fall for each other and marry. The wife then stays at home, tending to the house and kids, and the husband goes to work, doing his duty by supporting his family financially. In fact, as Coontz explains, this so-called ideal evolved over the approximately 150 years prior to the 1950s. In other words, what we've been taught to view as a traditional marriage is a relatively new invention.

Throughout most of human history, in heterosexual couples the husband and wife both performed paid work. While women were deprived of critical rights, including property ownership, it was entirely normal, even expected, for a wife to grow crops and slaughter pigs and then sell them in the market. Not only was she working for money (or necessary goods, when trading occurred); she was doing so outside of the home. This isn't to suggest that marriage was an egalitarian arrangement. On the contrary, though women did historically earn money, they were also tasked with household upkeep and child-rearing, among other family and community responsibilities.

This sounds a lot like the "second shift" that employed women typically still take on.[4] Before and after completing a full day of paid work, many women still face hours of cooking, cleaning, and childcare. This all-too-familiar history may not be comforting, especially to younger women who hesitate to shoulder this double load, but it does underscore the fact that marriage hasn't always looked like the 1950s ideal that we somewhat misguidedly call a traditional marriage.

Perhaps, at this time in our history, we're now pausing to define marriage on new and more equal terms, rather than slowly doing away with it altogether, as some media outlets have suggested. What if, instead of forcing us to "take the plunge" or "get hitched," marriage wasn't about sinking or getting stuck? What if it could be a way to build a life that's authentic to who you are, how you live, and what dreams you aspire to realize individually and as a couple?

OUR EVOLVING IDEAS ABOUT MARRIAGE

As coauthors with a nearly forty-year age difference, we were fascinated to discover how different our own expectations and ideas about marriage were. Thinking back on what she expected marriage to be for her, Myra reflected:

My view of marriage as a young woman in the 1950s and early 1960s was conflicted. On the one hand, my mother, who was an undeclared feminist and worked the whole time my sister and I were growing up, frequently told us that "marriage is not the be-all and end-all of life." Repeatedly, she told us that we would have to be able to support ourselves in case of a "rainy day," which, to her, meant being widowed. At the same time, she would reinforce the culturally dominant message: "Marriage is critical to a woman's well-being, and while you are in college you need to figure out who you are going to marry."

My friends and the culture surrounding us put the icing on the marriage cake: "If you're not married by the time you're twenty-five, everybody good will be taken and you'll be an old maid." Dinner conversations at my sorority house during my senior year were frequently about choosing wedding gowns, china and silver patterns, and honeymoon venues. There were no conversations that I can remember about what marriage would be like or what it would take to have a successful marriage.

Nobody talked about whether their marriage was successful or not. I knew plenty of my aunts and uncles and friends of my parents who were in unhappy marriages, but I knew only one man who had been divorced. If you were in an unhappy marriage, you simply made the best of it (and often joked about it). Divorce was difficult to achieve in New York State, and only people with means could afford to try to prove that their spouse had been unfaithful. It wasn't until the early 1970s, when the divorce laws were eased, that people began thinking about how to make their marriage "successful."

Nobody really talked about sex, either, except to tell you to stay away from it, lest you become pregnant, or to talk about a "fallen" sister who needed an abortion or got married earlier than expected and had a child soon after. Condoms were iffy, diaphragms required a doctor's prescription (which generally required you to tell the doctor of your intention to be married soon), the pill was not available until 1962, and IUDs were not widely used until even later. Abortions were illegal and often dangerously botched. So, all in all, it took considerable courage to have sex without some assurance that the child's father would make you "an honest woman" should you become pregnant.

When I told my parents that the dean of my college suggested I consider getting a PhD, the first question they asked was what my boyfriend (who later became my husband) thought of the idea. "Will he still marry you? Won't he mind if you have a PhD?" (He was in medical school and, to my good fortune, said he didn't mind at all.) "Well," my parents finally concluded, "if he will still marry you, then it's okay with us." The parents of a friend of mine, who was also considering getting a PhD and didn't yet have a boyfriend, told her that it was a bad idea. "If you get a PhD, you'll have to find a husband who has two PhDs," they advised.

My fantasies about marriage were that I would fall in love and get married. My husband and I would work hard to achieve our work goals and eventually have children, who would bring us enormous pleasure. We married when I was twenty-two and my husband was twenty-three. Neither of us had the foggiest notion of what it would be like to try to succeed at two demanding careers while raising children, and it turned out that while he supported the idea of my getting a PhD, once we had children, he was unwilling to do any of the housework or child-rearing (in part because he didn't enjoy them and in part because these activities interfered with his career). The only part of my original fantasy that turned out to be realistic was that I have always gotten enormous pleasure from my children.

When I talk to my twenty-something grandchildren today, I am astonished that when I was their age I was already married. One of the best things about our current society is that the average age of marriage has been pushed up and that women are not spending their early twenties frantically looking for a mate. The second-best thing is that they have access to effective birth control and talk openly about sex and its importance in relationships.

Less than four decades later, Abby was herself a young woman. By then, her expectations about marriage were measurably different:

Like many in my generation, my marriage fantasy was influenced by 1980s movies like The Princess Bride *and* When Harry Met Sally. *The former taught me that marrying someone you didn't want to marry was worthy of suicide, whereas true love was worth risking your life in a fire swamp. From the latter I learned that when someone's the right person for you, you'll just know "the way you know about a good melon."*

Of course, both movies, and many others I watched, are about the lead-up to marriage—the quest to find the right person—but not about the state of being married. I had absolutely no idea about what being married was like, aside from observing my own parents' marriage. And while their marriage was a happy one, I couldn't help but notice that my mother had given up an awful lot. She had moved nine hundred miles away from her hometown (and friends) for my father's job; she had given up her career—albeit temporarily—to raise children; and she did pretty much everything around the house except for a few specific chores my father took on (e.g., post-dinner cleanup and lawn mowing). And because my father had a long commute and traveled upward of one-third of the time for his job, she was often on her own, having to deal with everything from the daily schlepping to school and afterschool activities to trips to the emergency room (my father was away for every. single. one.), and so much more. Meanwhile, my dad got to travel all over the world for his work, which often involved schmoozing with colleagues over good meals. I didn't have a model for what an egalitarian marriage looked like, but I certainly didn't want the deal my mom got. While she only ever complained about the emergency room visits, I knew I wanted something altogether different.

I never doubted that I would get married, but I wasn't in any rush. Over time, I developed a dating philosophy of "better alone than poorly accompanied." I had a few boyfriends here and there in high school and college, and even though some felt serious at the time, I never fantasized about being married to them. Birth control was relatively easy to get, so there was never a sense of needing to wait until marriage to have sex or worry about getting pregnant (though being a worrier, of course I worried). I had a beloved cousin who remained single through her thirties, unlike my parents, who married at age twenty-four, and I admired her greatly.

When I graduated from college, moved to San Francisco, and began to navigate the world of postcollege dating, I developed a test for whether I wanted to go on a second date with someone: would I rather spend time with this person, or would I rather read a book? Many times I decided I would rather read a book. The thing is, I never wanted to give up things that were important to me—my independence, or my ambition, for example—just to be married. My marriage fantasy was finding "a good melon" who would support me in keeping those things.

What a difference a few decades can make!

THE MODERN MARRIAGE

While Hollywood and social media still inundate us with idyllic notions of eternal love, we're simultaneously told that marriage is hard work. What's the actual truth, in the context of our lives today?

In his book *A Treatise on the Family*, economist Gary Becker argues that the notion of falling in love is far too simplistic an explanation for marriage. In his view, people marry to make themselves better off economically and emotionally. Lori Gottlieb takes a similarly balanced view. "Once you're married," she wrote, "it's not about whom you want to go on vacation with; it's about whom you want to run a household with. Marriage isn't a passion-fest; it's more like a partnership formed to run a very small, mundane, and often boring nonprofit business. And I mean this in a good way."[5]

This idea that marriage is about love *and* money seems to bear out. According to research, while love is cited as a primary reason for moving in together as well as getting engaged and married, economics are hardly irrelevant. In fact, financial unreadiness is commonly cited as a reason to delay marriage. Also, while most still view moving in together as a step toward marriage, convenience and finances are often cited as reasons for cohabitating.[6] Looking beneath the surface, then, it seems that even while we adore the idea of "true" love, in our real lives many of us remain unwilling to be swept away by love alone. In the light of day, we recognize that marriage isn't an *either* love *or* money proposition.

The Economics of Marriage Today

The current economics of marriage vary enormously. In the United States today, in 30 percent of married couples with children under the age of eighteen, one partner is out of the labor force and earns no income.[7] On the other hand, in a 2019 survey by TD Ameritrade, 21 percent of women reported earning more than their male partners (and 26 percent reported earning the same as their male partners).[8]

Whether you're in a relationship now or looking ahead to envision the future you intend to create with the partner you choose, here are some questions to discuss before making your decision, and ideally early in your relationship.

Question 1: Will You Get Married?

It turns out that the answer to this question is partly based on demographics. Being aware of these trends may be helpful as you consider whether to marry.

People with higher incomes are more likely to get married. In 2018, 80 percent of those in the top quintile were married, compared with only 38 percent in the lowest quintile. Over the past four decades, the marriage rate for the upper quintile remained much the same (declining by only 2 percentage points), but the rates in the lower quintiles dropped substantially.[9]

At the same time that the marriage rate has decreased, the average age at which people marry has markedly increased. In 2019, the average age was thirty for men and twenty-eight for women.[10] Declining wages for men and increases in women's earnings relative to men's have led to a situation in which more women look to their own earnings for financial security rather than to the earnings of a potential marriage partner. The decline in men's wages has been steepest in the middle of the wage distribution, which is where the marriage rate has declined the most.

The decline in wages has been particularly steep for Black and Hispanic men, and this has been reflected in their marriage rates.[11] In 2015, in the United States as a whole, 48 percent of those fifteen years of age and older were married, but among Black men, the rate was only 32 percent, and among Black women, it was only 26 percent.[12] Marriage rates among Black people are low not only because of a decrease in Black men's earnings but also because the ratio of women's to men's earnings is higher in the Black community. As a result, the economic advantage of marriage tends to be lower for Black women than it is for White women.[13] Black women earn 96 percent of what Black men earn (as compared with White women, who earn only 82 percent of what White men earn).[14] Also, for Black heterosexual women who wish to marry a Black partner, two additional factors reduce the available pool: (1) social, political, and economic circumstances that lead to high incarceration rates for Black men; and (2) the fact that Black men are twice as likely as Black women to marry a partner who is not Black.[15] Within the Hispanic/Latinx population, there has also been a decline in the rate of marriage, mirroring the decline in the earnings of Hispanic and Latino men. Only Asians have continued to marry at the same rate. At 61 percent, Asians are marrying more commonly than all other races.[16]

As more states have legalized same-sex marriage, the number of same-sex married couples has increased considerably, from 142,000 in 2008 to 592,000 in 2018.[17] However, some same-sex couples have opted to remain domestic partners, citing the "marriage tax" that can penalize couples in which both individuals earn incomes on the higher or lower ends of the spectrum.[18] One survey respondent in a fourteen-year relationship noted that she will likely marry at some point, largely because of benefits such as Social Security inheritance. "If being domestic partners afforded the same benefits as marriage," she explained, "I probably wouldn't consider [getting married]. I don't equate marriage with depth of commitment—that comes from how we treat each other daily."

Another woman shared how she agonized over whether to marry her partner:

> *I put a lot of pressure on myself when I decided to marry my husband. I am very happy with the decision, eight years and three kids later, but at the time, I had enormous anxiety about it. I had always been in high-pressure environments (e.g., Harvard, Stanford) and never had any anxiety or trouble sleeping at night. However, when it came to deciding on a life partner, I felt (I think correctly) that it was the biggest decision I would ever make, and I was petrified of making the wrong decision. I developed severe anxiety (something totally new to me) and couldn't*

sleep. I went to see a therapist for the first time ever, and I cried and cried about it. I loved my then-boyfriend, but he wasn't perfect, and he wasn't what I had envisioned. His family was different from mine, and he wasn't like the guys I had dated previously. I was worried that if I married him, I would wake up one day and regret the decision, which seemed like the end of the world. Ultimately, I think it was a comment from my mom that helped me feel comfortable with the decision. She said something along the lines of "I can't make this decision for you, and I don't know what I can tell you, but if it were me, I'd marry him!" She made me see that I would never have perfect information (i.e., I couldn't date every potential partner to see whether other relationships would be better than the one I had in hand), but I had dated enough men to know that my boyfriend was special. He had all of the most important qualities (kindness, honesty, integrity) in spades, and I realized that he had the qualities that I needed (even if he didn't have every quality that I had dreamed of).

Question 2: Will You Live Together Before Marrying?

Some of the decline in marriage rates may result from the increase in cohabitation, or living together before or without marrying. Between 2013 and 2017, almost 60 percent of adults aged eighteen to forty-four reported that they had lived with an unmarried partner at some point, and among cohabitators, slightly over half cited financial unreadiness as their reason for not marrying.[19] Since the 1990s, several studies have looked at the effects of cohabitation on marital stability. Their findings are inconsistent. Some older studies from a period when cohabitation was less common found that couples who lived together before marrying were more likely to divorce, a phenomenon called the "cohabitation effect."[20] It may be that in the past, those who were willing to flaunt social norms about cohabitation were also more willing to get divorced. But currently, researchers suspect that the cohabitation effect is more likely for couples who treat the initial decision to cohabitate relatively casually, choosing to move in together because it is more convenient or because they want to save money on rent, and then "slide into marriage" rather than consciously decide to marry. Unfortunately, most studies on the effects of cohabitation don't take into account couples' intentions when they move in together; those that do show that the cohabitation effect largely disappears for couples who intend to marry or get engaged when they move in together.[21]

Given that laws in the United States have not kept up with the ways families are formed, there are other reasons to live together before marrying, as this survey respondent shared:

> *My partner is transgender, and our kids were conceived with the help of a known sperm donor. Because of this, my partner needs to adopt our children, even though we are living and parenting and making major life decisions together. That adoption takes time and money, even in our progressive state, so we decided to delay marriage until we believe our family is complete so we can do a single adoptive process. Fortunately, my progressive employer provides benefits to domestic partners, which enabled us to carry out this plan even once my partner was staying home with the kids.*

Regardless of the reason for cohabitation, once a shared living arrangement is made, it is almost as hard to leave as a marriage. In general, the research agrees that the cohabitation effect can be mitigated by clear communication, including about the expectations of what the living arrangement means for the longer-term relationship. We encourage all couples who are considering moving in together to have a frank conversation about each of the topics discussed in this chapter and in chapter two. As in chapter two, we've included a worksheet at the end of this chapter with prompts designed to assist you.

Some states permit couples to register as domestic partners, and others allow them to create a civil union. Each of these categories has important tax implications that couples will want to examine. For example, if a cohabitating couple splits up, in some states there continue to be unresolved tax issues concerning support and property division.

Whether you decide to cohabitate, marry, or register as domestic partners, when you decide to live together, you should consider writing a will. Many of Myra's students have resisted this, mistaking youth for immortality. But sometimes a student relates an experience of surviving a serious accident or illness, and afterward other students show an understanding of vulnerability and mortality that was absent earlier. Your property may not be worth a great deal, but most young adults nonetheless have possessions they care about—maybe a special bike, a photo collection, or a musical instrument—and once you are living with someone, if you die, the possessions may not go to the people you wish to have inherit them. Raising these topics in an intentional way before you start living together is worthwhile.

If you have children, a will is even more essential, specifically one that designates guardians should their parents die or become incapacitated. Unfortunately, this advice is too seldom heeded; approximately half of parents with children under eighteen have a will, and 37 percent are without life insurance, which would otherwise provide for the children's needs if the parents are deceased.[22]

Question 3: Will You Have a Prenup?

Prenuptial agreements are on the rise: a recent survey of the American Academy of Matrimonial Lawyers found that a majority of attorneys have seen an increase in the number of millennials requesting them. Reasons for the rise include the fact that millennials are marrying later in life (and therefore have more time to accumulate assets and debts) and the fact that one-third of millennials grew up with single or divorced parents (so they understand from personal experience that not all marriages succeed).[23]

Prenups tend to be a highly charged topic. For some it's considered unacceptable, even coldhearted, to acknowledge that economics factor into marriage decisions. Additionally, some don't like the idea of openly discussing the prospect of a marriage's failure at its hopeful beginning. Myra had a student who shared how she had broken off an engagement over a prenup. She told Myra and the class, "My fiancé was quite wealthy, and as our wedding got closer, he wanted me to sign a prenup saying that if we got divorced, I wouldn't get any of his money. So even though I loved him a lot, I broke off our engagement. If he wouldn't share his money with me, I didn't want to share my life with him."

In other circumstances, creating a prenup can lead to marriage, as it did for one couple in their early forties. Each owned a successful small business, and neither was interested in having children. One day, the man asked the woman if she would ever consider marriage. "Only if we had a prenup so there'd be no chance that when I die, you'd inherit my business. I've promised my company to my niece," she replied. The man was delighted. He also wanted a prenup but hadn't dared to ask for it. They each engaged a lawyer and signed a mutually agreeable document, and they were married soon after.

Even in the absence of significant financial wealth, it can be important to have open discussions about the potential division of assets. One survey respondent explained how he and his partner broached the topic: "We decided to be fully transparent with each other about our financial situations and went through the questions a couple would go through if they were to do a prenup, without actually creating one." This approach provides most of the value of deliberation but without lawyer bills. Some prefer to create a nonbinding agreement to articulate how they will set up their relationship to succeed (as opposed to articulating what will happen to their assets if it doesn't).

If you do decide to go through the prenup process fully and sign a document, be sure that the lawyers you hire don't make the procedure unduly argumentative. Myra and Jay signed a prenup using a single lawyer. Since sharing legal representation is unusual, they also signed a document stating that they understood that neither of them was being "represented." In some sense, the lawyer was representing their relationship rather than them as individuals.

USING THE 5Cs FRAMEWORK: TO TIE THE KNOT OR NOT?

Once you've considered some of these foundational topics, use our framework to decide whether to get married.

Step One: *Clarify*

The majority of Americans see commitment as a prerequisite to cohabitation as well as marriage.[24] If you're already in a commitment-based relationship, why get married? Given that same scenario, others might ask, why *not* get married? Both questions offer valid and important perspectives.

Overall, married couples report feeling that their relationship is going well more often than unmarried cohabitators. Also, married couples are more likely to say they trust their partner to be faithful, act in their best interest, tell them the truth, and handle money responsibly. Married couples also report higher satisfaction than cohabitating couples around the division of household chores, how well their spouse balances work and life, and how effectively they communicate. The one area where cohabitating couples and married couples report similar levels of satisfaction is in their sex lives; for both groups, about one-third of couples say they are very satisfied.[25] Perhaps the relative bonuses of being married lie in the simple willingness to "make it official," which itself may inspire couples to put more time and energy into their relationship. Whatever the reasons, the advantages of marriage will likely apply to your partnership only if you and your mate feel good about your decision.

Before deciding to marry (or not), get clear on why you want (or don't want) to marry in the first place. What does marriage mean to you? Also ask yourself what you expect to change in your relationship once you marry. When you answer these questions, try to push aside your feelings about the wedding and honeymoon. As wonderful as both can be, neither is ultimately likely to shape your life and relationship as a married couple in any significant way.

Step Two: *Communicate*

Talk to your mate about your feelings about getting married. Even if you both agree that you want to get married, you may approach the decision differently. One person may think of marriage as the first step in building a life together, for instance, while the other may feel that certain milestones—career, financial, or other—need to be met first. Discuss these different ideas and try to stay open-minded if your partner has views that don't mesh with yours. If one person wants to wait while the other would rather get married sooner, that doesn't automatically mean that the first person has doubts about the relationship. It may simply indicate a different view of marriage. The goal here isn't to agree on every detail but instead to understand how each of you envisions marriage within the context of your relationship.

Step Three: Consider a Broad Range of *Choices*

Once you understand how each of you feels about getting married, consider the choices that follow that decision to get married or not. If marriage is a next step that you both agree on, when do you each want to marry? Does either of you have stipulations attached? For instance, do you imagine getting married and then moving back to your hometown? Or, if you decide to wait to marry, you may want to set a period of, say, six or twelve months, after which you'll revisit your decision. Alternatively, if you decide not to marry, consider what's next for your relationship, remembering that marriage isn't required for a committed, connected partnership.

Step Four: *Check In*

Again, you may want to discuss your decision with friends and family members whose opinions you value. Also, this could be a good opportunity to talk with couples you admire about their decision to get married (or not), if you haven't yet done that. If any of your check-ins provide valuable insights or give you reasons to reconsider your thinking or decision, think about it carefully, and discuss it with your mate, if possible.

Step Five: Explore Likely *Consequences*

Take some time to assess likely consequences of your decision about marriage. If you aren't on the same page as your partner, is that likely to lead to resentment? If so, how will you address that? Will your decision be a sticking point with your parents or other important people in your life? How might you bring that up with them and have a conversation about it? Going into the decision with your eyes wide open about the possible consequences or side effects of your choice will help address these issues proactively, which can reduce the second-guessing that can happen after major decisions.

CHAPTER THREE EXERCISE:

How Do You Feel About the Big Questions? (Part II)

This exercise focuses on the CLARIFY and COMMUNICATE steps in our 5Cs framework. Take some time to consider your answers to the questions that follow.[26] Then discuss them with your partner, if you have one. We suggest you spend at least thirty minutes talking about each of the following categories (some of them may take longer—you don't have to discuss them all in one sitting!). This exercise is intended to be paired with part I, which is at the end of chapter two. As with the previous exercise, consider how you might make this a loving discussion.

MARRIAGE

Do you want to get married? Why or why not?

____

What does marriage mean to you?

____

What do you expect to change in your relationship after marriage?

____

LIVING TOGETHER

How do you feel about living with someone before getting married?

____

If you move in together, do you have expectations about what it will lead to in the longer term? What are they?

____

How will you divide chores? (See more detail in the exercise for chapter five.)

___

How much time alone do you need? When do you most want to be alone?

___

OTHER

How would you describe your parents' relationship? How did they handle conflict?

___

How do you feel about prenups? Would you want one?

___

How satisfied are you with sex now? What could make it better? How important is sex to you?

___

FOUR

BAY TALK

Having Children

Should I (or we) have children, and if so, when is the best time? These weighty questions have no simple answers. Given that biology plays a large role, outcomes and timing are only partially under our control, so even when we decide we want children, the universe doesn't always cooperate. This experience can have a significant impact on our lives, as this woman shared:

> *[My partner and I] were on the same page [about when to start trying]; however, we had five years of infertility and finally had a child through an embryo transfer after years of IVF cycles. This one area of our lives had the greatest impact over everything: our relationship, my career, where we are choosing to live. It has also brought to light our differences in parenting philosophies as well as our general outlook, approach, educational differences, and so forth.*

Questions related to having children are hot-button issues partly because, like marriage, having children often feels like the default choice in the United States—a remarkable fact, given how little support American policies provide to working families. The vast majority of adults in the United States have at least one child. Only 15 percent of women between the ages of forty-five and fifty do not,[1] and that doesn't include adopted children or stepchildren.[2] Among men aged forty to forty-four, only 20 percent are childless.[3] The birth rate, which is now 1.7 (below the replacement rate of 2.1), has decreased only because the average number of children in families has fallen, from 2.4 in 1965 to 1.9 currently.[4]

Like marriage rates, birth rates tend to vary across races and ethnicities. In 2019 in the United States, Native Hawaiian and other Pacific Islander women had the highest birth rates (at 58 births per 1,000 women); White and Asian women had the lowest (at 50 and 48 births per 1,000 women, respectively); and Latina and Black women fell in between (at 54 and 52 births per 1,000 women, respectively).[5]

Norms and expectations for whether and when to have children differ significantly across generations. People today are having children later in life than their parents and grandparents did. The average age at first birth is now twenty-six for all women and thirty-one for women who are college graduates. On average, men become fathers at thirty-one.[6] Often, people delay having children because they want more time to enjoy travel and other leisure activities or to have more time to further their careers, particularly in "greedy professions" that require exceedingly long workdays and extreme responsiveness to clients. The time-based demands of work, in fact, seem to have increased for many workers. In 2019, full-time employees worked 8.78 hours per day,[7] which suggests that even those not in demanding careers are working longer hours. Americans work far more hours than workers in other developed countries.[8] Those in low-wage jobs face different but arguably more challenging problems, including unpredictable hours that make it difficult to arrange quality childcare, among other important priorities.

Raising children is also costly. Some people delay childbearing until they have paid off school loans, have saved for childcare, and can afford a home large enough to accommodate a family. Also, waiting until they are higher on the career ladder, some wager that they will be more successful in negotiating paid parental leave and greater flexibility in hours and assignments when they return to their jobs post-baby.

Many people defer having children because they don't yet have a partner. Thanks to advances in medical sciences, new childbearing options are available to those without partners. Over the past fifty years, the number of children born to unmarried people in the United States has increased considerably. In 2014, 40 percent of all births were considered out-of-wedlock births, with the rates varying markedly by race: 29 percent for Whites, 53 percent for Hispanics, and 71 percent for Blacks. In 1964, the national average was below 10 percent, and there was less variation across racial and ethnic groups.[9]

The main reasons why people don't have *more* children parallel their reasons for postponing children in the first place, with one additional motivation: a desire to have more time and money to spend on the child or children they already have.

REASONS TO HAVE CHILDREN (OR NOT)

People who want children may feel a deep yearning to experience the creation of a new life, a deep desire to give and receive unconditional love and help their children live meaningful, purposeful lives. Some say they want to pass on their genes, family values, and family name. Some want to fix the mistakes they think their own parents made, to have kids as a kind of do-over. Some feel they just don't have the strength to buck the tremendous social pressures and expectations they feel from family and friends. Some may want children so that their offspring can help them in old age. And, of course, some experience several of these desires simultaneously.[10]

People who don't want children have their own list of reasons. Some feel parenthood is too much work and too stressful, particularly the early months of sleep deprivation, which is as shortsighted as opting to have a child because you "love babies." Others are more interested in fostering their careers or doing good in the wider world than in raising children. Some want a career or life that involves a great deal of travel, which they assume is incompatible with parenthood. Some have strong ideological objections to bringing more people into a world that is already overpopulated, polluted, and increasingly affected by climate change.[11] Many have deep-seated fears—about passing on family physical or mental health problems, about not having the "instincts" to be a good parent, or about raising a child in an uncertain and cruel world.[12]

Some also fear that having a child may put too much stress on their relationship. For two-thirds of married couples, in fact, satisfaction with marriage takes a nose dive when a baby enters their lives.[13] However, declining satisfaction with one's marriage is not an inevitable result of having children. Psychologists John Gottman and Julie Gottman report that couples who participate in a workshop they have developed for parents *before* their baby is born are more likely to remain satisfied with their marital relationship after they become parents.[14]

Fertility is also an important factor in people's decisions not to have children. Some who have waited a long time to begin to try to have children find that they no longer can. Unwilling or unable to undergo costly, painful treatments, they discover that the alternatives—surrogacy and adoption, for example—are also challenging and expensive.

In a culture where having children is still considered the norm, people who don't want them are often expected to justify their preference. However, these choices are intensely personal and worthy of our respect—without explanation. To this day, Myra regrets her (unsuccessful) attempts to change her sister's mind about having children. At the time, she felt she was advising her sister from a place of love. Feeling over the moon about her own babies, she wanted her sister to feel the same joy. In retrospect, however, she now realizes that she put her sister under unnecessary stress every time she raised the topic.

Even if you discuss your desire to have children with your prospective partner before getting married, you can still end up with divergent views. Abby's beloved paternal aunt and uncle resolved their differences after deciding not to have their own children:

> *I did not want to have children, but my wife did. Our final decision did not come easily or without some charged discussions. I would lay out my logical concerns, and my wife's only counter was that she just wanted children. Eventually she admitted that some of her desire to be a parent was left over from childhood programming and that when she was younger, career options for women were much more limited. In the end, we each honed and pursued our own talents and goals and have had very satisfying careers. My wife got an MA in education and has had a lasting impact on many children's lives, and we have stayed in touch with quite a few of those former students and their families. We do worry at times about who will help us with late-life challenges and decisions, but we agree that this concern could not dictate how we have lived the bulk of our full and rewarding lives. We are still very much in love after fifty-one years of marriage.*

At their fiftieth anniversary celebration, Abby was struck by how their friends spoke about them and their contributions. It was yet more proof that, with or without children, two people can have a significant impact on young people and on their community as a whole.

THE COSTS OF RAISING CHILDREN

Financial Costs

Through the mid-1800s, children were an essential part of the labor force, making them into economic assets.[15] Today, of course, child labor laws, as well as an increasingly knowledge-based economy that makes schooling critically important, have turned children into economic investments rather than assets.[16]

Some are surprised at how much it costs to have a child, let alone two or more. Those who want to go in with their eyes wide open should plan to budget half a million dollars to raise a child and fund college tuition. While this is a considerable expense, it's also a profoundly galvanizing one. If necessity is indeed the mother of invention, many parents find that supporting the well-being of their children is the most powerful motivator of all. Somehow, some way, in spite of the odds, parents often "make it work." However, it's important to note that this financial burden is disproportionately heavy for low-wage workers, who are often people of color.

Here's how that expense breaks down over time: a little more than half of the cost is incurred before college. The latest data indicate that a married couple in a middle-income family ($59,200–$107,400 per year) can expect to spend $285,000 to raise a child to age eighteen.[17] Housing costs account for close to 30 percent of these expenses (a larger home or apartment, more furniture, and higher utility bills), and higher food costs contribute almost 20 percent. That number assumes that your children go to public school and does not account for the cost of extracurricular activities or summer programs.

College costs then enter the equation.[18] For a middle-income family with a child attending a four-year private college, the cost for four years is currently over $200,000 per child. Attending a public institution within your own state is considerably less expensive yet still costly.[19] However, many students receive financial aid in the form of scholarships, loans, or work-study opportunities. And sometimes grandparents are in a position to contribute to a 529 plan (a tax-advantaged educational savings plan) to help defray the costs of college.

For people who wish to have a job or career after having a child, there is also the cost of childcare. And there is an additional cost for mothers in the workforce because having a child can have a negative effect on earnings. Women who become mothers often take time out of the workforce to raise their children, and their earnings are heavily penalized when they return. Sometimes their earning potential is decreased because they seek jobs that have fewer time demands (and therefore pay less), and sometimes it happens because employers perceive them as not fully committed and pass them up for advancement opportunities. Fathers, however, do not experience an earnings penalty. On the contrary, fathers tend to gain an earnings premium compared with men of similar age and education level who are childless. In Japan, earnings premiums for fathers are built into formal wage structures.

Time Costs

Having a child is also a significant time investment, especially in recent years as parenting has become increasingly demanding.[20] A study of time spent parenting in eleven rich countries found that parents spend more than twice as much time with their children than parents did fifty years ago. In total, parents spent 70 minutes per day on childcare in 1965, compared with 163 minutes today. In fact, working parents today spend as much time on childcare as full-time moms did in the 1970s.[21]

According to the *Washington Post*, parents today are providing "around-the-clock devotion of attention and resources to children's free time, emotions and behaviors."[22] Known as "intensive parenting," this includes carefully monitoring kids' school and after-school activities; attending their athletic games and practices; arranging and supporting their other extracurricular activities; chauffeuring them from school to activities, parties, and more; finding ample opportunities to play with them and talk with them about their feelings, opinions, and thoughts; vacationing with them; and in general grooming them to be accepted into the finest college possible and to compete successfully in a cutthroat global economy.

In her memoir, *Sharing the Work*, Myra recounts how she was pressured into providing "intellectual stimulation" for her two-year-old daughter and three other toddlers:

> *Just as I begin teaching my new course at Berkeley, I get a phone call from a neighbor who would like [my two-year-old daughter] Liz to join a playgroup she is forming. I like the idea of Liz's joining a playgroup. She's too young for nursery school (no school will take her until she's three) and I think it would be great for her to have some playmates.*
>
> *[My neighbor explains to me that] . . . they're thinking of twice weekly meetings, two hours for each session, rotating among the four kids' homes. That all seems fine, I say, but since I work, [my babysitter] Margie would need to entertain the kids when they play at my house.*
>
> *"Oh, no, no [my neighbor says], that wouldn't work at all. . . . We want this playgroup for the children's intellectual stimulation, and we're counting on you to be there when the kids come to your house."*
>
> *My heart sinks. What am I going to do with four two-year-olds for two hours twice a month. . . . I ask Margie to help me, and she and I*

supervise an art project that I discover in a parenting magazine at the pediatrician's. I buy colored paper, and Margie and I cut it into the prescribed patterns. Then the kids glue the pieces into three-dimensional objects—pumpkins, witches, ghosts, etc. What a mess. Glue all over the tables and chairs. Glue all over the floor. Glue matting the kids' hair. Margie finds all of this hilarious and is good natured about cleaning things up, but it's the least favorite part of my week. . . .

After several months of these sessions, my patience runs out and I make a deal with Liz. She can have swim lessons instead of playgroup. She's happy. . . . But I'm even happier, having regained the equivalent of a half workday every month. And I'm no longer searching parenting magazines for art projects.

Although intensive parenting began as a middle- and upper-middle-class practice, recent research finds that intensive parenting is valued by mothers and fathers across the income spectrum.[23] However, parents are not equally capable of making investments in their children's cognitive and extracurricular development. Annette Lareau, who coined the term "intensive parenting," worried that inequality of intense investment in children would only serve to worsen the social class inequality of children's education—and ultimately their earnings. Her concerns remain apt.

Like so many evolving norms, intensive parenting is likely a reaction to previous parenting norms that didn't factor in the development of the whole child. However, as well intended as intensive parenting may be, it may not benefit children as much as parents hope. Overscheduling children, even with diverse and stimulating activities, has been shown to lessen children's critical executive functioning skills (planning, problem-solving, decision-making, and self-regulation).[24] This is especially notable because in adulthood, these skills are important to success.

While the intensity of today's parenting may be unnecessary

and even counterproductive, there is a prisoner's dilemma aspect to it. Even if individual parents would like to stop their intensive parenting, they may feel that doing so would disadvantage their children, and so they continue to behave like the parents around them.

Even the strongest, most independent-minded parents among us find it challenging to buck the trends and go it alone when it comes to setting standards for parenting, particularly when those parameters don't mirror the groupthink of the day. Changing the intensive parenting culture takes a concerted, enduring effort within and between communities.

We've heard positive stories from parents of middle school–age children who band together and take the Wait Until 8th pledge, agreeing to delay giving their children smartphones until they're fourteen years old or in eighth grade. Wait Until 8th understands the prisoner's dilemma nature of parenting and does not consider the pledge "active" unless ten or more families from the same grade and school sign it.[25] Only then do they publicize the pledge within the group of families who signed it and empower them to share it with others.

WHEN TO HAVE A CHILD

Medical innovations ranging from the pill to in vitro fertilization (IVF) have given us greater freedom and control about when to have a child. However, the realities of fertility are often complex and uncertain. The question of when to become parents is also complex because there is no single best time. There are costs and benefits of having children at a younger age and other costs and benefits of having them later.

At younger ages, there are biological and physical benefits.

Fertility and energy are higher, congenital abnormalities are less frequent, and there is more time to address any fertility challenges that arise.[26] At older ages, income and savings are likely higher. Since careers may also be more established, negotiating additional work flexibility may be easier. Given that people are waiting longer to settle into long-term relationships, having children later makes sense because it provides more time to find a mate.

However, waiting until age thirty-five or later can have drawbacks, as Cami, a highly paid executive, discovered. When she and her husband married, Cami was thirty. Since her income was significantly higher than that of her photographer husband, they decided to delay having children until her career was more fully launched. Five years later, when she began trying to get pregnant, Cami had three consecutive miscarriages. The experience was traumatic, but finally, at age thirty-nine, she gave birth to their son. She went back to work soon after giving birth, and during the next two years she had two more miscarriages. When she turned forty, Cami began IVF treatments, but she stopped because the procedure proved so painful. She and her husband considered adoption but ultimately decided against it. They were heartbroken when they realized they would only be a family of three.

Miscarriage is more common than many people realize; as many as one in four pregnancies ends in miscarriage.[27] And the chance of miscarriage increases over the age of thirty-five.[28] As Cami found, the experience can be devastating, and even when the loss happens in ea[illegible] pregnancy, as it does in the majority of cases, the grief can [illegible] lasting.

[illegible]ple's fertility is determined by the age of both partners, [illegible]y declines with age. For women, fertility is highest before age thirty and declines after thirty-five. After forty-five, it is unlikely for a woman to become pregnant without assistance.[29] For men, beginning at some point between the ages of forty and forty-five, there is a decreased chance of inducing pregnancy and an increased chance of inducing a pregnancy that will end in miscarriage. For men older than fifty-five, the chance of pregnancy is further reduced and the chance of miscarriage further heightened. Older men and women also have a greater chance of giving birth to a child on the autism spectrum.[30]

The success of IVF is also age dependent. A woman under thirty-five who undergoes IVF has a 39.6 percent chance of having a child. For a woman over forty, the chance decreases to 11.5 percent.[31]

Sometimes external factors help people decide when to have a child, as this couple experienced:

When we found out our daughter [had] special needs, we had to have some discussions on how to ensure that she was getting what she needed to hit her delayed milestones. One of those decisions was deciding when to go for a second child. Ultimately, we wound up waiting too long and it became too difficult for us to have baby number two. We continued to realize that our daughter would need extra help and more attention for the rest of her life rather than for her first few years.

A second couple shared the following:

We decided to have our first kid because we both wanted a family. We figured there would never be a perfect time, and the sooner the better! About a year after the first was born, my mom was diagnosed with Parkinson's and we decided to have our second baby sooner than we'd planned, so that my mom would be able to fully enjoy grandparenting for as long as possible.

It's very common to want to have a child sometime in the future but never quite feel ready, even if you have a partner, some career success, and other key pieces of the equation. Abby discovered this when, nearing her two-year wedding anniversary with Ross, she found herself in a job that wasn't a good fit and wanting to start a family. She wondered whether she should first seek out a better job or have a baby:

Needing to get out of my own head, I hired a career coach, and I worked with her for four months to try to sort out my feelings and what my approach should be. I was terrified that if I wasn't in a job I loved when I got pregnant, I wouldn't want to go back to work after having a baby, which would penalize me financially (as I had learned in Myra's class) and make it harder to find a job once I had a baby.

In the meantime, to get a better sense of my cycle for when Ross and I would be ready to start actively trying to conceive, I stopped taking birth control pills. Since my parents had difficulty conceiving, I was prepared for a long road ahead. As life would have it, I got pregnant about halfway through the coaching engagement (woman plans, God laughs!). From that point, my work with my coach became less about answering the question "Should I have a baby or look for another job?," which I later realized was a false choice, and more about "How might I make this job work until I go on maternity leave?" Ultimately, I decided to make peace with staying in the job because I had already answered the baby question. And lo and behold, once I stopped holding so tightly to my career angst, my dream job came along.

During the first few months she was grappling with this decision, one of Abby's mentors told her, "There's never a good time to have a baby. . . . If you think you want one, the time to start trying is now." That advice—plus her work with her coach—helped

Abby detach from the need to identify a perfect sequence of events. She and Ross welcomed their first child about a year later, and she started her new job when their baby was four months old.

Of course, this advice is clear-cut only if you have the necessary resources to have a child. Without that cushion, the calculation is far more complex. You may still decide to have a child, but in that case, do what you can to prepare for the likely difficulties ahead, which may include seeking out the ongoing support of friends and family members.

ADOPTING A CHILD

In 2015, Americans adopted 53,500 US-born children.[32] (To put that number into perspective, in that same year, almost four million children were born in the United States,[33] and almost 112,000 children were in need of adoption.)[34] Of all non-stepparent adoptions, 59 percent are from the foster child system, 15 percent are from voluntarily relinquished American babies, and 26 percent are from other countries.[35] In recent years, for various reasons, including political ones, South Korea, China, Russia, Guatemala, and Ethiopia, the major countries from which Americans have adopted children since 1999, have all curtailed or closed adoptions to the United States.[36] In 2019, there were only 2,677 international adoptions, 42 percent of them from China.[37]

The cost of adopting a child varies significantly, depending on the specific case. Currently, the cost of adopting from the foster care system is low, and if the adopted children have special needs, the adoptive parents may qualify for some financial aid. Private adoptions tend to be far more expensive.[38] International adoptions may also cost more, especially after travel costs to the foreign country are included. Regardless, adoption tends to be stressful, time-consuming, and lengthy. Typically, a domestic adoption will take two years,[39] and international adoptions tend to take longer.[40]

If you want to consider adoption, you will need to make several decisions: Do you want to adopt a newborn or an older child? Would you consider adopting a sibling group together? Would you consider a child with special needs or one who was exposed to drugs or alcohol? Are you prepared to adopt a child of another race or religious background? How much contact do you want to have with the child's birth family?[41] If you live in a state that restricts adoptions for same-sex couples, would you consider moving to another state with different policies?

The degree of contact between a child's adoptive and birth families is a matter for negotiation between the two parties, but with the advent of DNA testing services, it is virtually impossible to have an adoption where the child's birth family remains secret forever. And with research that shows that there are benefits for all involved when there is an open arrangement, more and more families are opting for some contact between birth and adoptive families.[42]

Abby's parents had her when they were thirty-six, which was considered ancient at the time. They wanted another child and eventually opted to sign up with several adoption agencies. After years of waiting, they got a call from an agency about a baby boy from Korea. Abby was a little older than five when he arrived. She still has vivid memories of going to John F. Kennedy International Airport to meet her three-month-old new sibling.[43]

Abby's parents were intentional about incorporating aspects of her brother's Korean heritage into their family life. They celebrated Korean holidays such as Chuseok (Korean Thanksgiving) alongside Jewish and American ones. Abby's mom learned how to cook Korean foods (Chap Chae, a noodle dish, was a family favorite). And when Abby and her brother were in high school and middle school, respectively, their family made a pilgrimage to Korea along with other families with adopted Korean children. While their experience was positive, transracial and transnational adoption is complex. Even the most intentional parenting does not erase the issues of "race, power, privilege, and oppression" that come up for transracial adoptees.[44] All are important issues to consider when exploring whether this option is right for you.

HOW MANY CHILDREN WOULD YOU LIKE TO HAVE?

According to a *New York Times* poll, 64 percent of people who said they had fewer children than their ideal number cited the expense of childcare as the reason, and 54 percent cited the desire to have more time with the children they already had.[45] How many children to have is often a negotiation—sometimes a tense one—between partners.

> *My husband wanted one child, so as not to overpopulate the planet and to keep our relative freedom. I wanted three kids, to make up for my lonely childhood with just one glum older sibling and wretchedly unhappy parents who split during my high school years. I wanted a house full of noise and affection. So, my husband and I met in the middle and decided to have two kids. But right after I gave birth to my second child, I knew I wasn't finished. My husband and I then spent two tense years (during an otherwise warm and loving marriage) in a standoff about whether to "break" our deal and make another human. He argued that a deal's a deal; I argued that feelings change. Deep*

down, I knew he was right. But I eventually pleaded to get my way and won, and in having that wonderful third child, I learned that I needn't have had him to have the warm, loving family I always craved (and he's an essential part of the team anyway). And that my husband is an incredibly generous person. And that it's totally weird to bargain about making humans. To think that our third might not have made it into this world and made our family complete and what it is today—it's such a strange existential weight.

After her public speaking engagements, Myra will sometimes be approached by a woman in the audience who shares her difficulty in combining career and family after having a third or fourth child. "I was fine until my youngest was born, and then it all fell apart" is an all-too-common refrain. In some cases, the woman simply couldn't figure out how to organize childcare and after-school activities for so many children while meeting the demands of her career. At other times, the last child had unanticipated special needs and the woman had left her career to attend to that child as well as the several children who were older.[46]

If you're considering having a child after you've had your second, taking a clear-eyed approach can be especially important. When she was expecting her third child, one of our survey respondents was surprised to learn that this third child was, in fact, twins. She had this to say about the experience of going from two to four children:

I don't think anyone can say it better than the comedian Jim Gaffigan: "You know what it's like having a fourth kid? Imagine you're drowning. And then someone hands you a baby." So true. And those people who say that once you get to three kids it's all the same, as you've already gone from "man to man" to "zone defense" . . . I doubt they have more than three kids! I swear, if any one of my kids is not there, it is twice as easy as having all four of them together. Even the oldest. Just fewer fights, disagreements, and egging each other on into all sorts of mischief.

While there are certainly examples of women in high-powered careers who have more than two children (Susan Wojcicki, chief executive officer of YouTube, who has five children, comes to mind), combining a demanding career with multiple children is exceedingly difficult. Most women who succeed have the financial resources to hire a lot of help, enlist the help of their families, or both.[47]

HAVING A CHILD ON YOUR OWN

Kim was thirty-eight when she decided to have a child on her own, using artificial insemination and the sperm of an anonymous donor. After confirming that her mom, who was divorced and living alone, was excited about becoming an active grandmother, she uprooted her life to move to Los Angeles, settling in a house a few blocks from her mom. Over the past fifteen years, she, her son, and her mom have been a close-knit family. Her son is thriving, and Kim feels that her decision to go it alone was absolutely the right one for her.

Having a child on your own is a gigantic decision. Not all mothers or other relatives are as enthusiastic and energetic as Kim's mom, and some who are initially enthusiastic don't or can't follow through. If you're having a child on your own, be sure to build a sturdy "village" of available caretakers and other forms of support. Know also that there may be extended periods of time when you are truly on your own. Prepare for that as best as you can, but be sure to also relish the pleasures of parenthood.

Getting Life Insurance

However you become a parent, consider purchasing life insurance. Even financial advisors who recognize that life insurance is not a particularly good investment nonetheless recommend that new parents purchase life insurance.[48] For most new parents, a term life policy, for which the premiums are less expensive, is more appropriate than a permanent life policy. However, if you have a large estate and may be liable for estate taxes when you die, you may want to consider a permanent life policy.[49]

USING THE 5Cs FRAMEWORK: BECOMING A PARENT

Deciding whether to become a parent is yet another intensely personal and emotional choice that will have long-term ripple effects on love, money, and lifestyle. Even more than choosing a mate, becoming a parent—assuming total responsibility for a new life, or several—is a lifelong responsibility as well as a source of deep and abiding love, fulfillment, and joy. Whatever expectations you may feel from family, friends, and society, know that there is no right choice, nor is there any perfect time or perfect number of children to have or adopt. By using our 5Cs framework, you can feel more ease and confidence, ready to embark on a journey that is sure to transform you and your life, knowing that the decisions you make are rooted in *your* authentic goals and desires.

Step One: *Clarify*

Why do you want a child? Why don't you? In her book *Workparent: The Complete Guide to Succeeding on the Job, Staying True to Yourself, and Raising Happy Kids*, Daisy Dowling includes an extensive list of pros and cons related to this topic. She suggests reading through them all and seeing which ones resonate the most with you as a way of clarifying your thinking.[50]

Guided self-reflection can also help you resolve the yes/no and push/pull dynamics that many people feel when deciding whether or when to have children. One lesbian couple enrolled in a course to gain clarity. Knowing their journey would be long and would involve IVF, they wanted to be as certain as possible before pursuing motherhood. After several introspective months taking the course, each independently decided that they did indeed want a child. Even without a three-month course, it's worth spending time on self-reflection rather than skipping this step or brushing it off. The exercise at the end of this chapter is designed to help, and it can be done at different points in your thought process.

Keep in mind that deciding how many children to have may be best postponed until after you have had at least one child. Unless you grew up in a large family, you are likely to underestimate what it takes to raise numerous kids. And even then, it's difficult to have an accurate picture of the time and effort that will be required of you as a parent. On the other hand, if you are relatively sure that you want more than two children, you may want to start having them in your early or mid-thirties to avoid possible later difficulties with fertility.

Step Two: *Communicate*

Once you've gained some clarity, talk openly with your partner, if you have one, about what each of you wants. If you don't have a partner, talk with key people in your life who are likely to play a caregiving role, as Kim did with her mom.

Carve out dedicated time for these conversations when you and others are feeling good (not too tired, hungry, or stressed). Like most of the topics we address in this book, the question of whether and when to have children is an emotionally charged one. Since it is such a significant issue, many couples need multiple conversations to make a decision. Returning to the topic repeatedly can be productive, but it can also encourage talking in circles. Remember, fertility decreases with age. Waiting too long can translate into letting biology make the decision for you, which may mean that by the time you're ready for children, you're no longer able to have a biological child without ongoing, often costly, interventions that can't guarantee success.

Finding a Time and Place to Connect

Every couple has their own best times and places to have talks about intense topics like this one. Often, it's a good idea to get out of your normal environment and do something together. This may mean taking a hike or a long nature or beach walk, having a casual picnic, or something similar. Whatever the setting, be sure it's a time and place you both agree on for having the conversation without disruption from people or technology.

More often than not, it's best to avoid "springing" this kind of conversation on the other person during, say, a date night, when you're out to have fun. Let those times be about you two as a couple, in the moment, enjoying each other.

Even when the conversation is a scheduled one, try to arrive with minimal expectations for how the conversation will go. First and foremost, these discussions should give each person the opportunity to reflect and share thoughts and feelings openly and honestly, even when that means disappointing the other person.

Step Three: Consider a Broad Range of *Choices*

What would you like to do in your life with children? What would you like to do in your life if you don't have children? Are there nieces and nephews or children of friends you could help raise if you decide not to have children of your own? If you wait to have children and then need to explore alternative options such as IVF or adoption, will you be okay with educating yourself about those options by speaking with your doctor and conducting additional research? Are you interested in taking a workshop to learn new skills and mitigate possible negative effects on your relationship with your partner or spouse?

Step Four: *Check In*

During the check-in part of the process, seek out people of various ages who have decided to have children, perhaps including your own parents, as well as those who have decided not to. Which perspectives resonate more? If you're facing particular challenges, such as infertility or a partner's illness, talk with people who have faced similar situations and learn whether and how they overcame them. Also spend time alone with children, whether by babysitting, volunteering, or another route. Keep in mind, however, that it's impossible to feel the love you'll feel for your own children when you care for somebody else's.

Step Five: Explore Likely *Consequences*

How do you think a child might affect your relationship? How might it affect you, your career, your family, your finances? Having a child is one of the few decisions in life that can't be undone, so do your best to consider various consequences. Research has shown that people's biggest regrets tend to be about things they *didn't* do, so that little voice inside pulling you in one direction or the other may be more significant than it initially seems.[51]

CHAPTER FOUR EXERCISE:

How Will You Decide Whether and When to Become a Parent?

This exercise is designed to help you CLARIFY your feelings by tapping into your reactions to the CONSEQUENCES of different scenarios. Choose one of the following options, depending on the decision that's most top of mind for you. Find someone with whom to complete this exercise. If you have a partner, you may want to complete it with them, but you also may deliberately want to complete it with a friend instead.

Option 1: If you are trying to decide whether to become a parent.

Pretend that you have decided to become a parent. Share with your person all the reasons why you have decided to pursue parenthood. What are you excited about? What are you relieved about? What are you concerned about? Note how you feel in your body when you are taking this position.

Now, pretend that you have decided ***not*** to become a parent. Share with this same person all the reasons why you have decided against pursuing parenthood. Answer the same questions you did before.

Reflect on this exercise. Recall how you felt when you took each position. Which position felt more natural to you? Ask the person with whom you shared which position sounded more genuine coming from you.

Option 2: If you know you want to be a parent and are trying to decide when the best time will be to become a parent.

Pretend that you are expecting a child right now. What are you excited about? What are you relieved about? What are you concerned about? Note how you feel in this situation.

Now, pretend you have made the decision to put off becoming a parent for at least three years. Answer the same questions you did before.

Finally, pretend you have found out you cannot have a child without significant intervention. Share the alternatives you would be willing to pursue (consider adoption, foster parenthood, IVF, surrogacy, and not having a child). Note how you feel in your body when you think about each of these alternatives.

Reflect on this exercise. Recall how you felt in each scenario. Which scenario felt more natural to you? Ask the person with whom you shared which scenario sounded more genuine coming from you.

FIVE

LET'S MAKE A DEAL

Dividing Housework and Home Management

As soon as Luis came home from work, he decided to do something he'd never done in twenty years of marriage to his wife, Rosa. He walked into her studio, where she was busy painting, and said words he'd once never imagined saying. "I feel guilty," he began. "We've been married all these years, and I've never helped around the house. I want to make amends now that you're going to work. How about I start doing the laundry?" Expecting to be showered with gratitude, Luis was instead shocked by her reaction. "Oh, no," Rosa replied angrily. "You can't start with the laundry. Doing laundry is a skilled job. You need to know how to separate the colored clothes from the whites, what temperature to use in the washer, and what can go into the dryer and what can't. If you want to help, you'll have to start at the bottom. You can start by cleaning the toilets!"

As in most traditional marriages of their generation, Luis and Rosa had always worked under the assumption that it was his job to succeed at his career and hers to manage their home and family. Luis had never done any housework, and Rosa had never voiced any objection. With their older children now in college and their youngest in high school, however, Rosa had gotten a teaching job. Luis wanted to show his support, particularly since her income would help with tuition bills. However, he was unwilling to clean toilets, and he withdrew his offer almost as soon as he'd made it.

As old-school as Luis and Rosa may sound, this gender-based approach to managing housework has had surprisingly long-lasting ripple effects. As recently as 2018, studies found that women were still primarily responsible for the "second shift"—cooking, cleaning, and childcare—even after working and getting paid for the same long days as their husbands.[1] In 2020, as schools and offices closed because of the coronavirus pandemic, managing childcare and educational activities fell disproportionately on mothers. They responded by leaving the labor force entirely or reducing their hours of employment.[2] Among essential workers and those who worked at home, almost half reported difficulties in combining work and family. Essential workers who were mothers found it challenging to meet home obligations, and mothers who worked at home found it difficult to care for their children and complete their work simultaneously.[3]

How many couples, like Luis and Rosa, still struggle with who does what at home? This issue can exist for any couple, of course, but research indicates that an imbalance in housework is most prevalent among heterosexual couples.

Inequality in the division of household labor, whether gender based or not, isn't inevitable, of course. There are other ways for cohabitating and married couples to address what is both a simple commonsense issue and, often, an emotionally supercharged one.

GENDER NORMS AND THE PATH OF LEAST RESISTANCE

Even couples who value equality may surprise themselves by defaulting to stereotypical gender roles in housework and caregiving, as this man and his wife experienced:

When we were first married, the home management tasks were undertaken in a very joint manner. Whether it was finances, cleaning, or home repairs, we did much of it together—even if one of us was more of a leader in a given area. Almost as soon as kids came, we started to divide and conquer. And we did it in a way that was highly specialized. I vacuumed and did dishes. My wife did the laundry. We would very rarely switch roles. It also became more traditionally gender based. I (the husband) did finances and most of the home repair. I think it was part survival and part slipping into social norms.

This kind of shift isn't inherently negative, but it can be helpful to understand the cultural influences at play. In September 2021, the online humor site McSweeney's Internet Tendency published a satirical piece titled "This Is Your Kid's School and Even Though the Emergency Contact Form Lists Your Husband, We Need You, the Mom."[4] A clever commentary highlighting how much of the moment-to-moment workload of parenting is put on moms, it quickly attracted attention from women who could relate all too well.

In their early days as first-time parents, Abby and Ross decided that he would manage the kids' doctor and dentist appointments. After listing Ross as the primary contact, they assumed that was all they needed to do, especially in a progressive city like San Francisco. However, time after time, their pediatrician's and dentist's offices called Abby, not Ross, about appointments. She repeatedly asked them to contact Ross, but still they continued to contact her. This is incredibly common, and it is just one of many examples of how ingrained the traditional gender roles have become in our society.

Another reason couples resort to gender norms regarding chores is that one partner insists on micromanaging how the other partner completes household tasks, as this man discovered:

After taking Professor Strober's class, and reading "Getting to 50/50," I had every intent of divvying everything up 50/50. However, my wife wanted to handle things more organically. This unfortunately devolved into her doing more than me, because "organically" we chose the traditional male and female roles. We've gone back and forth a bit on different approaches, and we have settled into a pattern of each doing what we feel more strongly about or do better (e.g., I wash all the dishes and do the taxes, she manages outsourced help and social calendars). Net, she still does meaningfully more than me (60/40?), especially when it comes to mindshare [also known as the "mental load"], which we're trying to tweak. An additional factor here is that my wife regularly makes meaningfully more money than I do.

Interestingly, women who earn more than their partner may be *more* likely to take on the lion's share of the housework and childcare. In the 1980s, Arlie Hochschild interviewed couples and found that some wives who took on the heavier load of housework and childcare did so because they thought their husbands felt threatened by their career, their salary, or both.[5] Hochschild also found that in some cases, the wife was so grateful that her husband "allowed" her to work outside the home that she rewarded him by making fewer housework demands. Hochschild named this the "economy of gratitude."[6]

Again, this dynamic seems remarkably resistant to the changing tides of time and culture. In a 2019 article in the *Atlantic*, Aliya Hamid Rao, author of the 2020 book *Crunch Time*, noted that in heterosexual upper-middle-class families, "the more economically dependent men are on their wives, the less housework they do" and that "even women with unemployed husbands spend considerably more time on household chores than their spouses."[7] In stressful situations such as a husband's unemployment, wives may be particularly reticent to bring up controversial issues like renegotiating household work.

If you do set out to create a nontraditional division of labor, keep in mind that your arrangement may seem strange, even confusing, to people who adhere more closely to conventions, as this woman and her husband experienced:

Growing up in the Midwest, it was sort of assumed that the husband in the relationship would be the breadwinner and the wife would run the house. After college, my then-boyfriend, now-husband and I moved to California together—him for grad school, me for a corporate job. As it turns out, I really like working, and he really doesn't. It became pretty clear from early on that I was going to build a career and he was going to run the house.

I still contribute to things like laundry and picking up around the house, and he still works at a low-maintenance job . . . but things look a lot different from what I had originally imagined. And I think that's because I wasn't imagining at all. . . . I was only seeing what was, not what could be. I hadn't yet dared to imagine a different life for myself and my future family.

The truth is, I'm a terrible cook, I hate paperwork, and I'm not a natural teacher. He is. Everyone is much better off (happier, healthier, and more stable) because we dared to reverse the normal roles of a heterosexual couple and embrace a more honest, fulfilling life.

This was shocking to some, especially relatives in Indiana, who couldn't fathom a man not wanting to "provide." But providing in my house means making sure everyone's butts are wiped, mouths are fed, and all the doctor appointments are attended.

Remember, your relatives, friends, neighbors, and colleagues do not live your life. What matters is that you and your partner are satisfied with the arrangement you have.

A PRACTICAL BUT PIVOTAL ISSUE

In a 1970 landmark article, "The Politics of Housework," Pat Mainardi emphasized that housework seems like a trifling subject but in fact has enormous psychological, political, and economic implications. In the years since, a cacophony of voices have reiterated that insight. Wives have told their stories of trying to get husbands to do their fair share. Others have authored articles, tweets, and cartoons about the "mental load" and "emotional labor" of household management; scholars have underscored the ill effects on women's careers of shouldering the primary burden of housework.

Housework is critical and relentless, undervalued, invisible, and often boring. Within couples, satisfaction with the division of chores leads to satisfaction with the relationship and promotes a sense of well-being.[8] On the other hand, dissatisfaction with the division can cause anger and resentment, which, if left to fester, can slowly erode the fabric of a relationship or suddenly explode, as it did with Luis and Rosa.

In the same way that a budget reflects your priorities, the way you divide housework speaks volumes about your values, your relationship, and how you see your partner. After all, if you regularly watch sports while your partner cleans the toilets you both use every day, whose time do you value more, yours or theirs? Whose quality of life matters more to you, yours or theirs? In her book *Fair Play*, Eve Rodsky explores how resentment builds up in couples (or between cohabitators or roommates) because of the belief that "men's time is finite and women's time is infinite."[9]

This statement is held up by research, which finds that same-sex couples divide household tasks more equally than heterosexual couples. One recent study across seven countries also found that female couples divide chores more equally than male couples and that in more gender-egalitarian countries, such as Norway, there is less difference in the division of household tasks between male and female same-sex couples.[10]

Resorting to a gender-based division of labor in which the woman does the most housework can sometimes feel like the path of least resistance, but it comes with considerable long-term risk. In addition to the tension it may cause within a relationship, women who perpetually shoulder the heavier load of housework may also be prone to burnout, which can contribute to stress-related health problems. To avoid still greater challenges down the line, it is important to initiate the conversation about how work is divided sooner rather than later, even if it initially causes some friction.

The US Bureau of Labor Statistics divides housework into seven categories: food preparation and cleanup; interior cleaning; laundry; household management; lawn and garden care; interior maintenance, repair, and decoration; and exterior maintenance, repair, and decoration. In 2019, women spent an average of 2.16 hours per day on these seven categories of work, while men spent about two-thirds of that, an average of 1.39 hours per day.[11] In the five-year period prior to the pandemic, although employed mothers of children under the age of thirteen spent about 25 percent fewer hours in employed work than fathers, they spent about double the amount of time in housework and direct childcare as did fathers of young children.[12]

The pandemic highlighted just how much work is involved in running a household. One survey respondent noted that without work trips and dinners out, "the constant burden of cooking and cleaning made us realize just how much there is to be done." This may be a silver lining, since its increased visibility provides an opening for greater respect for housework and greater communication about the distribution of chores. Some enterprising parents with older children were even able to turn this reality into a teachable moment.

When we were no longer able to have our cleaning person come into our house, my husband and I decided that we all would clean. My husband is far better than I am at cleaning, so I asked him to come up with a plan of what the tasks were, and then I divided them between the four of us (including our two fourteen-year-olds). What surprised me most is how well everyone pitched in and just accepted this new norm. My kids often push back on new work around the house, but they just picked up what we asked them to do, and do their quarter of the housecleaning every week without comment or complaint.

Of course, this story is notable because it's an exception—not all households distributed the added workload so evenly.

AWARENESS OF THE TERRAIN

In the early years of Myra's course, she realized that many of her students had little understanding of how many tasks are involved in running and maintaining a household. When her students were growing up, many of their mothers had managed the household rather invisibly. As a result, few of them had much experience in completing household tasks. After creating a role-play exercise to give students a sense of the number of important household chores, as well as some experience of negotiating with a partner, she was delighted to see how many students found it both educational and enjoyable. A version of that role-play appears at the end of this chapter, and we suggest you begin by using it.

In her book *Fair Play*, Eve Rodsky includes one hundred cards, each one listing a "daily grind" task that needs to be done often, like washing dishes, as well as others that can be done less frequently, like planning vacations. As a first step, Rodsky encourages couples to define the set of tasks that they value as a family. Couples should discard any cards they don't value (writing thank-you notes, for example, or enrolling kids in extracurricular activities) and then "deal" the remaining cards until the distribution feels fair.[13] You can buy a set of actual cards on the book's website or create them yourself.

Before you broach the topic with your partner, however, take some time to think about your particular situation. What influences— in your family of origin, your culture, or your socioeconomic class, for instance—might you and your partner have internalized about the way household tasks are divided? One woman noted, "Being from a Latin traditional family influences you. You grow up seeing your mother do everything and no one says anything. It's in your subconscious." After marrying someone from a different country who grew up in a culture where it's the norm to outsource most household tasks, she found herself in a situation that was different from yet similar to that of the women she'd grown up with. "He was accustomed to a different lifestyle where you have at least five employees—a driver, a gardener, a nanny, a housekeeper, and a cook. It's not that he doesn't want to help; it just doesn't occur to him." Identifying these kinds of background influences, which can be conscious or subconscious, can help to create a common ground of mutual understanding.

BE HONEST—WITH YOURSELF

Housework is an interesting topic, too, because it can sometimes feel taboo. After all, we're adults, right? Fighting over who cleans floors and buys toothpaste sounds petty, even childish. As a result, it can be hard for people to admit, even to themselves, just how angry, resentful, or fed up they feel about how, when, and by whom the work at home gets done. Even confessing the intensity of your emotions about this issue to friends and family members may be embarrassing or unsatisfying if they brush it off with "What's the big deal?" Left without any healthy outlet for these emotions, people may simmer silently until one day when they, like Rosa, suddenly boil over with the emotions they'd previously stuffed down. Needless to say, falling into this pattern doesn't support you, your partner, or your relationship.

If you're feeling charged up about how the housework is handled in your home, stop and notice what you're actually feeling—not just about the tasks themselves but also about the current division of labor. Do you feel valued by your partner? Do you feel that your time matters as much as your partner's? How would your partner answer those questions? If the current division of labor feels unfair, does this imbalance pervade other parts of the relationship, or is it exclusive to household chores? What kinds of changes would help you create a more egalitarian partnership where you both feel appreciated?

As you consider these issues, also keep in mind that your emotions on this topic may be influenced by past experiences. If you watched your mother work herself into a nub, week after week and year after year, you may subconsciously look for faults in your partner when, for example, they forget a task. Conversely, if doing housework feels demeaning because you weren't expected to do much of it when growing up, you may feel justified in pushing aside chores because other demands on your time seem more important. Whatever your situation, be honest about the emotions this topic awakens in you and their intensity. Then take some time to release those emotions, ideally before broaching the topic with your partner.

Are You Negotiating or Talking It Over?

Some couples don't like to call their discussions negotiations: "I negotiate with my boss; I talk things over with my partner." Call these conversations what you will; the reality is that you and your partner will need to make numerous decisions about who does what and figure out how to resolve your disagreements.

HOW TO DIVIDE THE WORK

There are different ways to figure out the division of labor. First, you can decide whether to use a *top-down* or *bottom-up* approach. With the top-down method, you first come to agreement on your targeted overall distribution of household labor (50/50? 80/20?) and then divide the individual tasks. In the bottom-up scenario, you divide the tasks first and then see if you like the resulting distribution. Either way, you need to answer three questions:

1. What are the tasks, and who will do each one?
2. Does the overall division match the type of relationship you are seeking?
3. Do both of you think the overall distribution is fair?

As you begin this process, don't assume you're identifying a permanent solution. Dividing household tasks and management is an ongoing activity. You will likely refine your major decisions hundreds of times as you revise your sense of fairness, as your jobs and family change, and as life happens, as this couple experienced:

When I returned to work [after having a baby], we made a list of every single task that we collectively need to do each year, from the routine, like cooking, cleaning, laundry, to the ongoing, like home or car maintenance, to one-off and emotional labor tasks, like remembering and preparing for holidays or family occasions, and then assigned each task to either of us. Over time, as I have been pregnant and breastfeeding through two kids, we've adjusted which tasks each of us does at any given time. During more intense parenting periods, my husband has done significantly more than 50 percent of the home chores.

For the first go-round, focus on agreeing to an initial distribution, and then try it out. Remember, assigning household tasks is the practical side of whatever relationship you are striving for. If you want a relationship where both partners are career oriented, the distribution of labor at home has to facilitate that. If you want an equal parenting relationship and one of you travels a great deal, you will have to be creative in dividing parenting tasks (although an increasing number of tasks can be done online from anywhere, as anyone who has logged in at 9:00 a.m. sharp to sign their kids up for summer camp can attest).

The easy part of dividing tasks is telling your partner which tasks you like and hearing their preferences. One couple reported that they divided chores "Montessori style, observing each other's natural inclination toward home management." If you both like to cook, for instance, you can each take a turn. But what happens when neither of you wants a particular task, or when one says they like to cook but the other doesn't like the dinners that result? Outsourcing and having your children help with chores are options we discuss later in the chapter, but for now, let's just say that figuring out how to improve one's cooking (or any other skill) or accept what your partner prepares is an ongoing aspect of sharing your life with someone.

Be aware also that excessively broad categories can be misleading. For example, a category like "food preparation" includes at least three individual tasks: identifying what to make, shopping, and cooking. Each has its own appeal, requires its own set of skills, and can be further subdivided or coupled with related tasks, such as cleaning up. Cooking includes daily meals, weekend meals, holiday meals, baking, and so forth, and each can be split by day, week, month, or season (as in "I'll be in charge of weekend meals in the summertime, when I can use the outdoor grill, but let's take turns packing school lunches"). Every other task can be similarly subdivided. For instance, helping with homework might be apportioned by subject matter so that, for instance, the parent who doesn't enjoy math isn't tasked with checking in on algebra homework.

In *Fair Play*, Rodsky points out that most tasks have three components: *conception*, *planning*, and *execution*. Problems tend to arise when these components get separated from one another and assigned out of context. Abby's sister-in-law once asked her husband to buy shrimp for a recipe, and he came back from the grocery store with a shrimp cocktail, which seemed perfectly logical to him—it was the only type of shrimp he'd ever bought—but wasn't what she needed for her pasta dish. Rodsky recommends keeping the conception, planning, and execution portions of the same task together, when possible, to avoid these kinds of snafus.

There's also a fourth component: *decision-making*. This can be simple, depending on the couple and their inclinations, as one interviewee noted: "I disdain process conversations, so when I own something, it means I have full authority to make and execute the decision, without input of any kind." While this might work when it comes to, say, school forms, other categories, such as discipline and screen time, might warrant regular discussion and agreement prior to decision-making, even if one partner technically owns the task.

IT'S NOT JUST WHO DOES WHAT; IT'S ALSO HOW AND WHEN

When you're figuring out the division of labor, be clear about any strong preferences you have for when and how housework gets done. For example: "I like when the dishes are washed and loaded into the dishwasher right after a meal is finished. When I come into the kitchen and see a sink full of dirty dishes, it stresses me out. On the nights when you do dishes, are you okay doing them right after dinner?"

Notice that this list of preferences begins with an "I" statement: "I like when. . . ." It doesn't say "There's only one way to do dishes, so please do them that way." As Sharon Meers and Joanna Strober (Myra's daughter-in-law) suggest in their book, *Getting to 50/50*, when you discuss division of housework with your partner, be direct but not directive.[14] You don't need to make alternative ways of doing things wrong; you just need to say that you personally don't like the alternative ways. The way you say something (in this realm and all others) is just as important, or perhaps more important, than what you say. Nobody likes to feel bossed around or have their work endlessly nitpicked.

Couples who successfully divide chores with minimal frustration and haggling tend to agree that the partner not doing the chore should not micromanage the other. Often, however, that rule works only after much discussion and at least some trial and error. For example, it may be that the person with the higher standards for housework will need to do more of it, while their partner shuttles the kids to events and appointments. Or the partner who doesn't see the crumbs needs to have them pointed out a few times and will then begin seeing them. In *Fair Play*, Rodsky introduces the importance of agreeing upon a "minimum standard of care" for each task. Agreeing that the person in charge of emptying the dishwasher should do it before the next meal so dishes don't pile up in the sink goes a long way toward preventing subsequent arguments. Sometimes, lowering the bar on the minimum standard of care can be helpful. Abby remembers hearing her friend sigh with relief after learning from the pediatrician that his toddler needed a bath only twice a week instead of nightly.

All that said, it is important to get comfortable with the way your partner does chores. If they are in charge of shopping and you don't like the produce they bring home, consider offering to go to your favorite market on the weekend and bring home exactly what you want rather than criticizing your partner's choices.

REVIEWING YOUR DIVISION OF LABOR

Many couples review and revise the distribution of household work quarterly or at least every six months. Some of this review will occur because your original distribution doesn't work. For example, one of you may feel left out of discussions with your child's doctor, especially if any serious health issues arise. At other times, you may get sick of overseeing a task and want to take a break, which Abby experienced after years of supervising her children's writing of thank-you notes. Life changes—your child goes through a difficult period, one of you switches jobs or takes on increased responsibilities for a friend or family member—can also prompt these reviews. In the renegotiation process, remember to be flexible. There is nothing sacred about the original distribution you created. Plus, you may need your partner to be flexible on the next go-round.

Abby and Ross have periodically used a checklist of about fifty tasks they found on a website to review their division of labor. They each evaluate their own satisfaction with each chore by giving it a rating from 1 to 5 and then compare their lists. Number 1 means

"We've discussed the issue and have come to a comfortable decision about who should handle it." Number 2: "We've fallen into a routine and it's okay with me." Number 3: "We've fallen into a routine and it's not okay with me." Number 4: "We're in the process of settling this point." And number 5: "We are fighting about this issue." The directions encourage couples to see how many 3s, 4s, and 5s they have and try to shift them through conversation.[15] Abby and Ross's total score has decreased over the years as they have been more explicit with each other about their preferences and made changes to address perceived imbalances.

HOW MUCH, IF ANY, HOUSEWORK SHOULD YOU OUTSOURCE?

Some couples who can afford it outsource some of their housework, such as interior cleaning, lawn mowing, and more. The cost of having others do this work ranges widely, depending on where you live.[16] From a purely economic perspective, if you can afford it, you can hire a house cleaner, landscaper, or similar help, knowing that the time you're not spending on these tasks you can use to do paid work. If you spend the time that's freed up to pursue a leisure activity or connect with friends and family, you're effectively deciding that your quality of life and well-being outweigh the cost of outsourcing.

That sounds straightforward enough, but as we've seen in earlier chapters, when love is involved, decisions that seem to be about money can get complicated. One guest speaker in Myra's course enlists her children in Saturday morning family cleanups. She and her husband have been proud of the values and skills these sessions pass on. "I don't want my kids to have their first apartment and not know the basics about cleaning toilets or washing windows. I'd say I'd failed them if that happened."

Research on families supports this point. Summarizing their work on the value of giving children chores, Wendy Klein and Marjorie Harness Goodwin wrote that "the consistent effort to involve children in housework may be crucial to their development of life skills, independence, and responsibility."[17]

Myra started her children on household chores early on and had a chore sheet on the refrigerator so the children could check them off once they were completed. One of her friends saw the chore sheet and asked what would happen if the children didn't do the chores. Myra joked: "No chores, no food." Her children laughed, but they did their chores.

Just as it's critical that adult partners know exactly what, when, and how household tasks are to be accomplished, it's important when assigning tasks to children that everyone understands what, when, and how they are to be done. The chore sheet on Myra's refrigerator worked well because the tasks and their timing were crystal clear, and the children could easily review what they were supposed to do. And they liked checking off the items on a daily basis. The "how" part of the chores was harder, often requiring multiple sessions of teaching, and the scheme didn't always work well. But when it did, there was no haranguing and no arguing, which felt like a victory in itself.

THE ETHICS OF OUTSOURCING

Every year, one or two students in Myra's class voice passionate objections to paying people to clean house and do other domestic tasks, arguing that it's per se oppression. However, others feel equally strongly that if you pay people well and treat them fairly and respectfully, there's nothing wrong with outsourcing cleaning and other household chores. If you have children, you may want to help your kids understand (in an age-appropriate way) why the people who typically clean houses are disproportionately people of color.

Even more popular than outsourcing cleaning is outsourcing cooking—ordering takeout or eating at a restaurant.[18] In an article titled "The Slow Death of the Home-Cooked Meal," the *Washington Post* reported that in 2014, less than 60 percent of suppers served at home were actually cooked at home, and many people are concerned about the health implications of eating food, especially fast food, that is not prepared at home.[19]

Cooking is an especially important skill to teach children. If time is tight during the week, consider cooking with your children on the weekend. If you yourself lack these skills, try learning a few dishes alongside your children. Having the whole family learn to cook can be enjoyable and gratifying.

USING THE 5Cs: DIVVYING UP HOUSEWORK AND CAREGIVING

As you proceed through the framework to divvy up housework, remember that each new agreement is essentially temporary, changing as different parts of life ebb and flow. Also keep in mind that this topic, however mundane, doesn't always have to feel serious. When both people in a relationship feel valued, it's always possible to lighten the mood. We know one woman who has always hated matching her husband's white socks, partly because, as she says, "he owns a million of them!" On more than one occasion, rather than getting annoyed about matching his socks, she's started a sock fight. It may not be the most efficient method for getting the task done, but it has added levity and enjoyment to an otherwise tedious task.

Step One: *Clarify*

Before discussing and dividing tasks, first take time to get clear on which tasks you feel are important and how they could be divvied up in a way that feels fair and causes the least consternation in your relationship and disruption to you and your partner's lives and schedules. Once you have some clarity, you're ready to move forward.

Step Two: *Communicate*

Once again, before bringing up the topic, think ahead of time about how to approach the conversation. At times, it may be helpful to explain why you're raising (or re-surfacing) this topic. When Luis walked into Rosa's studio and made his offer, she had no idea that he'd been thinking about this topic for some time because of conversations he'd been having with his work colleague Myra. If Rosa had understood the *why now* of their conversation, the two of them might have been able to have a better first conversation on this topic.

Some may want to approach the discussion like an appointment: "Things have been feeling extra busy lately. Can we figure out a time to discuss how we're dividing housework?" Whenever possible, find a time when you and your partner feel ready to engage in a focused discussion. Research conducted by Nir Halevy suggests that in potentially confrontational situations, it may be best to begin communication by email. However strange it may seem to email your spouse or partner about a personal issue, it can give both of you time to be thoughtful about your words and responses before hitting Send.[20]

With that said, make sure that scheduling a time to discuss housework with your partner or spouse doesn't feel rigid or transactional. Instead, strive for a loving and lighthearted atmosphere (even if you have different perspectives) and try to reach an outcome that strengthens your ability to see each other's point of view. That way, regardless of the particular outcome, your partnership will feel stronger.

Ideally, you will be able to have the conversation calmly, since it's generally easier to get things straight when neither of you is frustrated, exhausted, hungry, or distracted. If frustration does arise, try to avoid attacking your partner.[21] As in all tough conversations, begin with "I" statements: "I feel frustrated because I have been cooking every meal." Then propose a solution: "I would appreciate it if we could divide the cooking more equally."

Over time, one or both of you may become dissatisfied with the overall division of labor, and you may have to keep written track of who does what for a week or so. Research shows that people tend to remember the chores they do and overlook the chores their partner does. If you feel you are doing "everything" and your partner is doing "nothing," more communication is in order. Is your partner really slacking, or are you feeling overwhelmed for reasons having nothing to do with housework? Or does your overall distribution of tasks need renegotiation? Certainly, renegotiation is in order when there are fundamental changes in your life, to avoid feeling like this survey respondent:

> *Prior to my moving in with my partner, we had a frank discussion about household chores. One of them was laundry. He asked me if I would do his laundry, and I flat out said no. Things nicely fell into place; sometimes we took turns doing the dishes (but I would*

say I did them more regularly), he took out the trash, and since we could afford it, we had a housekeeper who helped us keep the rest of the house in order. But I have to say, after having a child, I do think there is more on me to keep the house in order. We still each do our own laundry, but now I do my child's laundry too. And now there are more dishes to do and toys to pick up. I just feel like more falls on my shoulders.

To address the frequent, necessary changes in the division of housework and childcare, some couples, like Abby and Ross, review their upcoming calendars together each weekend. This allows them to anticipate likely sticking points during the coming week. Other couples prefer to text each afternoon to see how they will handle whatever is on tap. The *New York Times* featured one family that used this method, making domestic decisions "in passing."[22] After realizing that their casual approach was putting a strain on their relationship, they adopted office management tools to help them regularize their interactions and decision-making. Some of these tools included Sunday "huddles," mid-week "brain dumps," and computer platforms to help them keep track. Whatever strategies you may borrow from the corporate world, keep in mind that the goal of dividing and completing childcare and housework is to create a loving, well-functioning home and family life. Toward that end, it's important to infuse these conversations with mutual understanding and appreciation.

Step Three: Consider a Broad Range of *Choices*

After you have your initial session to determine the overall distribution of tasks, and then try out your plan for a week or two, you will want to refine your arrangement. Are you both satisfied with the overall distribution? Are you satisfied with what you are responsible for? Are you satisfied with your partner's contributions?

It is most unlikely that everything will go as you hoped. You will almost surely need to keep talking and changing.

The initial conversation works to decide *what* you each do. But sticking points are likely to arise concerning when and how you do it. Maybe the person in charge of cleaning bathrooms thinks a once-a-month scrubbing is sufficient, but their partner wants more frequent and intensive cleaning. Maybe the person not in charge of vacuuming is frustrated by ever-present crumbs under the kitchen table but their partner doesn't even see the crumbs. All of these wrinkles can be ironed out. Some tasks may need to be divided into subtasks (meal planning, grocery shopping, and cooking, for example) and others reassigned. There are many different ways to divvy up the load, so be open to new ways of approaching old problems.

Step Four: *Check In*

As in other matters concerning love and money, checking in with friends and colleagues about housework and family responsibilities is useful. How do they make decisions about who does which tasks? Are they satisfied with their decisions? How do they renegotiate when things aren't working well? How did things change for them once they had children? What can you learn from their experiences? After Abby heard a couple talk on a panel about their annual review process, she and Ross implemented an annual check-in, similar to this one described by a survey respondent:

> *When we got married, we created a process for evaluating decisions and talking through key questions. We do a retreat one or two times a year. During that retreat, we discuss:*
>
> *What has changed since the last review?*
>
> *What's true about our lives today?*

What's our joint purpose?
What is on our stop-doing list?
What are the new things that we are doing well?
We also check in on goals, marriage, kids, legal (will, guardians), house management, and finances.

Spending dedicated time away in a nice setting (away from the usual piles of laundry and dishes) can help couples reconnect on a deeper level. This time away allows you to focus on enjoying each other, reminding you both why you got together in the first place and how to relate to each other in ways that feel less clinical and more intimate. The trick is to remember the positive feelings you felt when you were away once you're back at home with all the usual predicaments.

Step Five: Explore Likely *Consequences*

The notion that the modern family with children needs to be "run" like a small firm has become increasingly popular. In chapter three, we cited Lori Gottlieb's idea that being married with children is akin to running "a very small, mundane, and often boring nonprofit business." She's not alone; Emily Oster titled her book on raising young children *The Family Firm*.

Even though managing your life as a family is in some ways like running a small business, your household is not a business, and efficiency is not a primary end goal. Love, connection, fulfillment, education, enjoyment, unscheduled time, and so much more are vital to creating a satisfying life for yourself and your family. As a result, to create a rich and rewarding home life, some adults may need to unlearn behavior that works well at school or at the workplace.

Take cooking with a six-year-old. If you were primarily interested in saving time and being efficient, you wouldn't cook with a six-year-old. Done as a joint activity with a child, cooking takes longer, requires more cleanup, and likely results in a lower-quality product. But that's not the point. You cook with your child to spend quality time together and, hopefully, teach them a skill.

This caveat applies to sharing breadwinning and caregiving responsibilities as well. There are always *consequences* to your approach. In the short term, letting the higher-paid worker do all the breadwinning and the more experienced cook do all the cooking may be maximally efficient. However, near-term efficiency can, at times, result in long-term unhappiness that erodes the relationship it's meant to serve. Take these potential consequences into account as you negotiate (and renegotiate) the division of labor at home.

As challenging as the topic of dividing housework can be, know that change is possible. After Luis and Rosa had their initial, tense exchange about his desire to help with laundry, they used Myra's division of tasks exercise to move beyond their stalemate. It quickly opened Luis's eyes; he was amazed at the number of tasks to be done, even in a household with older children. The conversations about housework that followed led to conversations about money. Realizing they could allot some of Rosa's income toward housecleaning, they outsourced that task. Rosa then taught Luis how to do laundry, and Luis slowly began to develop his cooking skills. Much to his surprise (and Rosa's delight), he now cooks dinner several nights a week.

CHAPTER FIVE EXERCISE:

How Will You Divide Housework and Home Management?

The following exercise—which will help you CLARIFY what you want and examine your CHOICES—can be completed in two ways (if you do it with a partner, it's also a way to COMMUNICATE).

Option 1: If you have a partner, children, or both, you can discuss who currently has responsibility for each of the household and child-related tasks (if you select "Outsource," be sure to note who will oversee the task). Make sure to talk not only about how the tasks are divided but also how satisfied you are with the arrangement. If things feel imbalanced or one or both partners are dissatisfied, how might you redistribute tasks to address this?

Option 2: If you don't have a partner or children, you can discuss this exercise with a friend or roommate or even complete it on your own as a theoretical exercise. If the latter, how would you want to divide these tasks with a partner to ensure the arrangement works for you?

HOUSEHOLD TASKS	PARTNER A	PARTNER B	OUTSOURCE (A OR B)
Shopping for food			
Cooking			
Meal cleanup			
Laundry			
Cleaning (vacuuming, cleaning bathrooms)			
Yard work			
Home repairs			
Managing money			
Managing social calendar			
Errands (dry cleaning, pharmacy)			
Car maintenance			
Paying bills			
Managing household help (cleaners, etc.)			
OVERALL			

CHILD-RELATED TASKS	PARTNER A	PARTNER B	OUTSOURCE (A OR B)
Feeding children			
Playing with, trips to the park			
Driving to and from activities			
Taking to doctor and dentist			
Caring for when sick			
Meeting with teachers			
Helping with homework			
Purchasing clothing and toys			
Coordinating play dates/ social events			
Managing care for			
OVERALL			

Some questions for consideration after you've completed the exercise:

Does income make a difference in how tasks are divided? How much?

____

What percentage of work done by your partner is sufficient for you to feel comfortable and not resentful?

____

How often might you want to revisit this list to ensure you're comfortable with your distribution of tasks?

____

SIX

THERE'S NO PLACE LIKE HOME

Deciding Where to Live and When to Move

Annie Dillard reminds us that how we spend our days is how we spend our lives. *Where* we spend our days is, to some degree, also how we spend our lives. The location question looms large over many of us, especially now as we reassess our priorities individually and en masse in light of the evolving pandemic and its effects on our culture. Decisions about where to live and when to move inspired more comments from our survey respondents than any other topic.

Where we live affects a wide swath of other choices—economic choices, people choices, lifestyle choices, and practical choices. How much will we spend for housing? Whom will we see in person regularly? How much time will we spend commuting? How good are the schools we'll send our children to? How walkable will our neighborhood be? The answers to these questions shape our lifestyle, the quality of our life, and our social interactions. Unlike some of the other decisions discussed in this book, where to live is a decision we confront repeatedly at various times and stages in our lives. In this chapter, we examine how to approach decisions about where to live, what type of housing to choose, and when to move.

WHERE TO LIVE—LOVE AND MONEY BOTH PLAY A ROLE

According to a survey by the Pew Research Center, prior to the coronavirus pandemic, the top reason for moving was job or business opportunities, with educational opportunities following closely behind.[1] In fact, those with college or professional degrees are much more likely than those with only a high school education to live farther from their parents.[2] Economic issues such as affordability of housing and rates of income and property tax have also traditionally been important factors people analyzed when looking at where to live or whether to move.

While these all remain critical considerations, our survey respondents made clear that deciding where to live is as much about identity, culture, and lifestyle (including climate) as it is about money. At the same time, because technology and the pandemic have created new options around how and where we work or attend school, it remains to be seen whether commute times and the availability of public transportation will become less important drivers of decisions about where to live. For many, locations that were never considered before are now realistic choices.

PROXIMITY TO FAMILY

Many who move away from their hometowns for education and jobs later realize how challenging it is to raise children without family nearby. "It takes a village" is a truism that we tend to ignore until we're in the throes of needing that village. After Abby's father was offered a significant promotion to a role in New York City, her parents left Wisconsin for New Jersey a few months before Abby was born. While his success was welcome, his new job required frequent travel. Abby's mother, a librarian, had decided to stay home full-time after Abby was born, but she underestimated how lonely and isolated she would feel as a new mother living nine hundred miles away from her hometown. After Abby herself became a mother (while living three thousand miles away from her parents), she asked her mom how she had coped that first winter in a new city with an infant. "I cried a lot," her mother responded. Eventually, Abby's mother built new networks, but it took time, and she often had to pay people to care for Abby, which quickly got expensive.

The notion that parents can—and should be able to—meet all of their children's needs without help from other caregivers is unrealistic, and it is evolutionarily impossible. Anthropologists agree that without shared caregiving networks—called "alloparents"—it's unlikely humans would have survived as a species.[3] This understanding was reflected in some of our survey respondents' decisions about where to settle down after becoming parents.

> *We decided to move from the [San Francisco] Bay Area to Colorado to be closer to my family. It was a challenging decision, as work opportunities for both my husband and me are much stronger in the Bay Area. We spent a lot of time trying to figure out how to quantify what we were gaining and losing with the move to get comfortable and found it challenging, but ultimately useful, to figure out how to weigh the value of closeness to extended family (especially with a young child) after a decade-plus away from family and mostly prioritizing our careers.*

Sometimes the trade-offs involved in moving closer to family are significant, as they were for this couple:

My husband and I . . . raised our first son for the first two years in a foreign country, away from both [sets of] parents. When we were expecting our second son, it was clear to us that we didn't want to be away anymore. It wasn't a matter of practical difficulty being away, since we were in a country where good help and childcare were abundant and affordable. It was rather a matter of our children's emotional well-being and sense of community. We thought that they would have a more well-rounded life close to their grandparents. The decision to relocate home was abrupt and had a long-lasting career impact on both of us, but more so [for] my husband. He left a high-paying, high-growth job after eight years in the company, and he never found a remotely similar career in our home country. What surprises me even more is that every time we revisit this decision and I bring up the idea of moving away again for better career prospects for him, we end up deciding against it. Somehow it is not as important anymore as it was before we had children.

In these examples, proximity to family took priority over other aspects of life, including career prospects. This became increasingly common during the pandemic, when living closer to family became a primary driver for many who moved. According to a Pew Research Center survey in November 2020, one in twenty adults in the United States (5 percent) said they moved either permanently or temporarily because of the COVID-19 outbreak.[4] Seventeen percent of those who moved said they did so to be near family; the true percentage is likely higher, however, because another 14 percent moved because college campuses closed (likely going back to live with their parents), and an additional 33 percent moved for financial reasons (potentially moving back in with family).[5] While some of these people may eventually move back, many may appreciate the benefits of living close to their family and end up staying.

IDENTITY AND LOCATION

Identity can also influence our choice of location. Race and ethnicity, sexual orientation, religion, and other factors can be reasons to cross out some locations as options and highlight others. One interviewee told us, "As an LGBT person, my choices [about where to live] were narrowed much earlier in life. Teach for America recruited at my college. I was planning on applying—but then they told me that that while applicants can preference cities, TFA has the final say in where you're going to be. I ultimately didn't apply because I knew [my chance of] meeting my soulmate in a rural place was slim."

A different interviewee—a Filipino woman married to a Black man—explained how the couple's identities informed their decision: "I had my sights set on living in Oakland for a very long time (since undergrad). . . . Oakland is a mecca for multiracial families. There's a comfort there. My kids see other Black and Filipino couples. We picked this place very intentionally, and there's a lot of value to me."

For others, where they're from feels virtually inseparable from who they are, as this woman realized while on her first date with the man who would eventually become her husband:

> *My husband is from Hawaii, and it is a very strong part of his identity. He told me at the end of our first date that he would return to live in Hawaii in the future and if that was an issue for me, we shouldn't go on a second date. We proceeded to live post-college in Washington, DC; North Carolina (coordinating to attend grad school together there); Hawaii for a year; [and] DC again for a prenegotiated five-year period that both of us thought would benefit our careers; and [we] now have lived in Hawaii for the past eleven years and are raising our children here. Each of these moves have been joint decisions with consideration about what's best for*

our jobs and family. We revisit our current decision to live in Hawaii periodically to make sure it's still what both of us feel is best.

THE ROLE OF CULTURE, MINDSET, AND VIBE

Geographies often have dominant industries, which shape the contours of life in those places. In his book *Who's Your City? How the Creative Economy Is Making Where to Live the Most Important Decision of Your Life*, economic geographer Richard L. Florida goes further and suggests that there are connections between regions and the dominant personality traits of people who live there. Using zip code information from people who completed a survey of personality traits, Florida mapped the "Big Five" dimensions of personality—openness to experience, conscientiousness, extroversion, agreeableness, and neuroticism—against urban regions. His book includes a series of maps showing, for example, that neuroticism is concentrated in the New York metropolitan area and the midwestern heartland, while agreeable and conscientious types cluster in the eastern Sun Belt area.[6] His point is that "regions, like people, have distinct personalities," and "most people will be happier and more fulfilled in regions that match their personalities."[7]

During their second year of business school, Abby and Ross had several conversations about where to look for jobs. Given the fields they were both interested in—finance and social impact roles in corporations—New York City made a lot of sense. However, Abby had lived there before attending Stanford Graduate School of Business. After experiencing firsthand how all-consuming the work culture was there, she told Ross, "Sure, we'd have great jobs, but we'd never see each other." He agreed, and they decided to limit their respective searches to the San Francisco Bay Area. They had both lived and worked in the Bay Area previously and valued the emphasis on life outside of work, as well as the proximity to hiking trails. While the decision would likely narrow their job prospects, it was a trade-off they were willing to make.

Sunita and her husband had lived in Washington, DC, since college graduation and their marriage a few years after that. While they were happy there, they observed that so much of people's lives and conversations revolved around policy and politics. Since neither was planning to go into politics, they'd begun to wonder whether the city fit them and their goals. Both children of Indian immigrants, they were getting ready to have children and wanted to raise their children in a city with a large Indian population. After ruling out several major cities for one reason or another, they began to consider Dallas–Fort Worth. It had the added advantage of being the largest hub of American Airlines, a plus given her husband's consulting work. After settling there, they enjoyed reconnecting with college classmates, who, they were pleased to learn, had many other interests besides politics.

WHAT TYPE OF HOUSING SHOULD YOU LIVE IN?

Picking a location is, of course, just one part of the decision to move. Next, you need to decide what type of dwelling you want. In many ways, it's a cyclical conversation, since the costs of living and housing correlate with salary, and all of it may vary from one location to another. The *New York Times*'s Real Estate section has a weekly "What You Get" column, which shows what a given amount, say $500,000, will get you in three different places across the country. The differences are so dramatic that it routinely makes Abby and Ross wonder why they chose to settle in the San Francisco Bay Area.

The amount you spend on housing can have a significant impact on your lifestyle, as well as on your other choices. One of our survey respondents noted, "The most important advice I got was to not upgrade when everyone else is upgrading just to upgrade. When everyone else is getting the next big house, try to keep your costs low so you and your partner can keep job flexibility." Another respondent summed it up this way: "All of these choices are tightly coupled—to live in a certain house, education choices, spouse choices, car choices—those lock me into certain job choices. If I change the nature of those first choices, the other choices [also] change." Because housing costs tend to be one of the bigger expense line items, it's worth asking a few additional questions as you search for and select your dwelling.

How Much Space Do You Need?

There has been a dominant narrative in the United States that bigger is better when it comes to housing (witness the McMansion trend in the 1980s), and the pandemic certainly fed that narrative. A survey in January 2021 found that in 60 percent of households with children, those children were doing distance learning, and nearly half of households had someone else in the household working from home who hadn't worked from home before the pandemic.[8] With houses suddenly needing to be schools, offices, gyms, restaurants, and movie theaters all at once, it's no wonder that this same survey determined that "COVID-19 has amplified the role of the home as sanctuary."[9] And who wouldn't want a bigger sanctuary?

Ron Lieber, the *New York Times* money columnist, wrote an article in October 2020 with the controversial title "Make Your First Home Your Last: The Case for Not Moving Up."[10] With detached suburban housing prices at a premium, he encouraged readers to consider all the ways they could spend the additional money (e.g., fund retirement savings or 529 plans, donate it, use it to fund travel or a vacation home). He also cautioned against viewing your home as an investment vehicle and noted that it's difficult to know the "psychic return on the extra space," especially if you haven't lived bigger.

A study in the *Journal of Environmental Psychology* examined the actual amount of space per person (a metric known as density) in families with young children and then surveyed participants about their perceptions of how crowded or spacious their home felt and how well their families got along. Interestingly, it found that "how individuals perceive their home environment has more of an effect on family functioning than actual home characteristics."[11] That is, the way people see their space matters more than the actual square footage per person. While having enough space per person helps families get along more harmoniously (so that five people aren't constantly fighting over one bathroom), there are diminishing returns, and in fact, perceptions of being too distant from others at home can make families feel disconnected and less close (especially for those with boys).

As you consider your space needs, think about who else will be using the space besides your family. If you value having an in-law unit for a live-in caregiver or visiting relatives, it can make sense to invest in this additional space up front as a critical element of what will help your family work. As one survey respondent shared, this consideration figured prominently into her housing wish list:

> *I was born in Europe and my family still lives there. When my wife and I chose a house to live in, we thought about the fact that my family will be here for weeks at a time. I'm glad we thought ahead. Having that separate space has reduced friction when family's here because we're not on top of each other. Because they live so far away, it's beautiful for our kids to spend time with grandparents in a way that's intense, when they're around for all phases of the day.*

Not everyone can afford to invest in additional space, but everyone can take a hard look at how they are using the space they have. Clutter can make a space feel smaller. A 2021 survey found that during the coronavirus pandemic, the most popular activity people were doing more of in their homes than they were before the pandemic was "decluttering and organizing" (46 percent of respondents reported that they were doing more decluttering—compared with 38 percent who were eating more meals, 30 percent who were exercising more, and 25 percent who were working more).[12] It turns out that part of what's driving our desire for more space is the fact that as a society, we are really bad at getting rid of things—and the more space we have, the more things we acquire and the more time we need to spend organizing.

The Japanese brand MUJI has a design philosophy that can help to inform your decision about how much space you need and how to arrange it. "MUJI" is short for Mujirushi Ryohin, which in Japanese means "no-brand quality goods."[13] MUJI's products are designed to get the job done—and nothing more. The brand's stated goal is for customers to see a product and say, "This will do." MUJI's approach is similar to the Swedish concept of *lagom*, or "just enough." Instead of buying an item for every possible use, you focus on what will suffice most of the time. For example, rather than buying a large dining room table to seat your entire extended family at Thanksgiving dinner, buy the smaller table you will need regularly and then set up a temporary additional eating surface on Thanksgiving.

The idea of designing for everyday use is espoused by architect Sarah Susanka in her book *The Not So Big House*. Her rule of thumb is to design smaller houses (about one-third smaller than her clients' original goal), eschewing rooms designed for others—such as formal living and dining rooms that rarely get used—and instead spending her clients' budgets on layouts tailored to their daily activities and thoughtful design details that make the space feel bigger. While most of us won't have the luxury of building our dream homes from scratch, we recommend Susanka's book to anyone considering the amount of space they need.

Should You Buy or Rent?

Deciding whether to buy or rent is about affordability, as well as factors such as stability, but often it's also a personal, emotional decision. Given that the answers to the practical questions—affordability, stability, and so on—don't always mesh with the answers to the emotional side of the equation—renting may feel like a "failure," for example—it can be helpful to parse out the practical questions from the personal ones.

Looking first at some practical questions, consider issues such as these: Does it stress you out to think about your rent getting hiked significantly or, worse, getting kicked out of your place because your landlord is moving in? How much do you value your ability to renovate a property or fix something that goes wrong without relying on a landlord? Even though you can't predict the future, do you anticipate staying put for more than five years (which is the general rule of thumb to make sure you recoup the transaction costs involved in buying)? Are you feeling stable in your job and relatively certain that your income will continue at the same level or be higher in the future? If you value flexibility, buying a home can work against that. One survey respondent, a first-time home buyer, remarked, "I have definitely felt more tied down to my job long-term after experiencing the high up-front costs of closing on my house and the large monthly mortgage payments!"

The more personal, emotional side of deciding whether to rent or buy a home is due, in part, to American folklore that painted home-ownership as a quintessential part of the American dream and buying a home as an important indicator of success. Increasingly, this pressure to own is waning, especially for younger generations living with credit card and school debt and dealing with stagnating wages as well as underemployment and unemployment. People younger than thirty-five are more likely to rent than any other age group, with two-thirds of this age group renting, compared with 42 percent of those aged thirty-five to forty-four and 32 percent of those aged forty-five to fifty-four.[14] Homeownership also varies widely by race and ethnicity, with about one-quarter of households led by non-Hispanic White adults renting, compared with 58 percent of households headed by Black adults, nearly 52 percent of Hispanic- or Latino-led households, and just under 40 percent of Asian-led households.[15] Homeownership is also correlated with income levels, although systemic discriminatory practices such as redlining have also contributed to the lower homeownership rates among non-Whites.

More recently, built-to-rent homes, which are single-family homes built specifically for renters, are making renting more appealing to some. Often located on the fringes of "America's second-tier cities," the number of these homes grew by 30 percent from 2019 to 2020 and is expected to continue to increase.[16] In some ways, these properties give occupants the best of both worlds, providing the quality of new construction, the privacy of single-family living, and the flexibility of a rental while eliminating the stressors of maintaining one's own home. According to one survey, renters show a slightly higher level of community satisfaction than homeowners.[17] With remote work enabling newfound geographic flexibility for a growing number of knowledge workers, it remains to be seen whether people will continue to place a premium on owning a home.

Should You Renovate Your Current Place or Move?

While moving and renovating can be stressful, 77 percent of people surveyed reported that they'd prefer to renovate rather than move to a new home.[18] There are ample online resources to help you determine whether it is more cost-effective to renovate your current residence or move to a bigger home. You can even find questions and flowcharts to help you assess some of the nonfinancial considerations involved in answering this question, such as how emotionally attached you are to the community and what your tolerance is for living in a construction zone.[19]

Before embarking on a remodel, also consider whether you are a maximizer or a satisficer. The term "satisficer" was coined by economist Herb Simon, who studied organizational decision-making, winning the Nobel Prize in 1978. He introduced the term in his 1947 book *Administrative Behavior* to describe someone who settles for an option that is satisfactory rather than searching for the optimal solution. Psychologist Barry Schwartz built upon this concept in a 2002 article where he and other researchers suggested the idea that maximizers (people who relentlessly seek optimal solutions) tend to be less happy than satisficers.[20]

When you tackle a home renovation, even a relatively small one like upgrading a bathroom, there are endless decisions to make. There's the overall design and layout, and then there are numerous product decisions (color, shape, and size of the tile, the hardware finishes, the fixtures, and more). If you tend to want the "best" option, consider whether you enjoy researching the many available options. Abby and Ross both have maximizer tendencies and found the task of renovating a bathroom exhausting. Ross's sister, however, is a satisficer. She was virtually undaunted while managing the renovation of an entire house in the months leading up to the birth of her second child. Knowing where you fall on the maximizer–satisficer spectrum can help you determine whether to renovate or move.

Should You Live in the Suburbs or the City?

Again, this question points to priorities. The clearer you are about what those are, the easier it will be to answer this question, as this survey respondent experienced:

My priority is to live in a good school district for my children and have a short commute in case I need to be back home quickly because of an emergency. All decisions regarding where to live are based on these criteria. I've always been a renter in order to afford to combine these two criteria. With COVID, the commute time criteria suddenly disappeared, and we desperately needed more space to accommodate four people on Zoom simultaneously. I recently purchased a house in a much farther suburb . . . with great schools, hoping that I won't have to commute to the office more than a few times per week in the future. I had always planned to make that shift when the children were older, but COVID accelerated the process. My parents helped me with the down payment to make it possible.

While many people choose to prioritize the suburbs for schools *after* they become parents, this survey respondent and his partner took a proactive approach:

We were living in San Francisco when expecting our first child. My wife worked in the suburbs, in an area with a good school system, and wanted to keep working after childbirth. We decided to prioritize making her working life as easy as possible, so it would be more sustainable. I worked in San Francisco at the time but decided [that] between the two of us, it would be better for me to commute. Thus, before our first child was even born, we'd moved to the burbs, bought a house, bought a minivan (needed another car anyhow), and settled in. We were glad we did so, as it made the first few years [of parenthood] much easier.

This other couple made a similar move, but with different results:

We decided to move to the suburbs in 2015 shortly after my first child was born. We felt cramped in our space in the city, and I wanted to be in a community where my child would grow up. I wish we had stayed in the city longer. I still miss it, and because of the schooling choices we made, my older child didn't make friends within the community until she started elementary school many years later.

Having a child involves a significant identity shift even before introducing a major life change, so relocating to the suburbs without a strong community in place shortly after becoming a parent can be doubly alienating. If you're considering a move to the suburbs, you would be wise to ask yourself what you're really solving for and get clear on what you'd be gaining and what you'd be losing with this move. Remember, this is a decision that can be undone. Abby knows a couple who lived in the suburbs until their children moved out of the house, and then they promptly moved back to the city. They haven't looked back since.

WHEN SHOULD YOU MOVE?

This is a thorny question with no clear answers. Given how costly and time- and energy-intensive moving can be, in the absence of a specific force, like a new job in a different city, dictating the timing of a move, many succumb to the pull of inertia. Others, however, take an enterprising approach:

After living in New York City for almost a decade, I decided to move by myself to Denver, Colorado. I always thought I'd leave NYC for a partner or a specific job, but ultimately, I had been ready for a change of pace for several years and made the decision to move based solely on my own desire. While scary and a bit overwhelming to start a new life and build a whole new community in a new city in my mid-thirties, it has 100 percent been the right move.

If one partner gets a job opportunity in a different city, the couple should consider the impact on the other person's career. Skipping this step can have long-lasting implications, as it did for this couple:

When we decided to move from San Francisco to Austin, we made my husband's job the focus of our decision-making. . . . I didn't realize that not having a professional reputation in Austin would make it hard to network, to find jobs, and to transfer my nonprofit fundraising career successfully. It sounds so obvious now, but my career really took an unexpected hit from this move. I ended up effectively working in the Bay Area consulting remotely and via travel for about three years before transferring my career to Austin, and now, over eight years later, I am still professionally more tied to the Bay Area than I am to Austin. This is definitely a major life decision that I'd go back and do differently, if we could do it again!

Some women in heterosexual couples hesitate to prioritize their career over their partner's, especially if they grew up in a culture that values men's careers above all. This discomfort doesn't fade easily, as this woman realized:

I sought professional counseling to understand the intense feelings I felt about asserting my professional aspirations "over" a man's. This was very much against everything I had seen modeled for me as a girl.

Some couples are able to solve the "which job to prioritize" question by taking turns choosing their location, as this couple did:

My partner and I both went to graduate school; he was two years ahead of me and so was on the job market earlier. He got a job in Boston, which is the center of gravity for his industry. Although I would have preferred to move to another city, I decided to look for a job there so that we could be together (going against my deeply feminist instincts!) on his promise that when we changed jobs again, it would be my turn to lead. Three years later, we just moved into our new home in New York (my choice).

Regardless of whose career leads, it takes conscious effort and a commitment on both sides to ensure that a move isn't detrimental to one partner's career. Couples who work as a team and view these as joint decisions seem to realize the best overall outcomes:

My husband and I have been committed to our careers. Based on industry, he will be the breadwinner, but we consider both careers and our upward trajectory before making any moves. In fourteen years of marriage, we have made four moves, and aside from the initial move, the last three have been what we consider to be perfect storms. One of us has been the recipient of a quality opportunity and the other has been able to leverage an opportunity in the same area to make it a possibility. In order for our marriage and family to work, there are a lot of factors that have to align, and we work as a team to advance our careers on a timeline that works best for us.

If you have children, especially older ones with established friendships, an important consideration is how the move will affect them. Yes, children are resilient, but moves take a toll on everyone. One survey respondent, whose children are now grown, reflected on the impact a cross-country move had on her children, who were in elementary school at the time.

We moved back [to California] with our two kids, who were entering second and fourth grade at the time. Our younger daughter (age seven) refused to change her clock to West Coast time because that was not "real time." Our older daughter (age nine) seemed to take the move well, but later we realized that it was very hard for her.

Having children is not a reason *not* to move, but do consider the consequences for them and do your best to mitigate the disruption to their lives as well as yours.

HOW CAN YOU BE HAPPIER WHERE YOU ARE?

While moving can sometimes add some initial excitement, and hopefully also bring you closer to your goals, considering how you can be happier where you currently are is a valuable life skill. Moving is costly and often stressful, and it's probably not something you'll want to do every time life begins to feel dull.

While we may enjoy the exhilarating newness of a move, the uptick in our happiness is relatively fleeting. Being the remarkably adaptable creatures we are, over time our happiness tends to return to its natural level (or "set point") regardless of our circumstances. One study found that eighteen months after winning the lottery, the winners weren't any happier than those who didn't win.[21] Similarly, people may overestimate the permanent happiness boost that might come from moving to a bigger house or a new town with better restaurant options. Psychologists call this effect the "hedonic adaptation" or "hedonic treadmill." Sure, you may revel in your bigger home at first, but over time the novelty will wear off and you'll stop noticing and valuing the extra space.

But there's good news: antidotes to hedonic adaptation do exist. According to one study, variety and appreciation may help sustain happiness increases over time.[22] By changing up how you experience something, you can trick your brain into prolonging the novelty of it. Rearranging your furniture from time to time can help you continue to value the extra space in your new home by forcing you to move through the space in different ways. This idea can apply to anything—your neighborhood, for example, might feel new again if you go on a mindful walk where you engage all five of your senses, really tuning in to the details of your environment. Are there aspects of your home or neighborhood that you have become habituated to (and thus are overlooking) but that contribute to your happiness?

USING THE 5Cs: WHERE TO LIVE AND WHETHER TO MOVE

Deciding where to live involves trade-offs; no place is perfect. The trick is making sure you're clear about what's important to you in a place (both in a city and in a dwelling) so that you're trading off the things you don't care about to get more of the things you do. Using the 5Cs framework can help with that.

Step One: *Clarify*

Do you want to live close to family? Are you intent on living a location-specific lifestyle (e.g., where you can go surfing or skiing easily)? Do you have a health condition that might improve in a particular climate? Are you seeking more space for pets? (Abby and Ross have friends who moved from California to Montana because of their dogs.) Your answers to these questions can anchor the decision-making process.

Ron Lieber suggests conducting a "values audit" of potential places to live to "figure out what a community really stands for and whether you would want to be friends with any of the people who live there."[23] According to Lieber, this involves eavesdropping on conversations on the sidelines of children's soccer games as well as scanning the titles in the local library. But before you can determine whether a community shares your values, first you must determine what *your* values are.

Some find it helpful to create a rubric that lays out high-priority values and location attributes that they then rate or rank one by one. Your rubric can be simple or more detailed. Media innovator and entrepreneur Alexis Grant and her husband created an elaborate spreadsheet to determine their current home base. It included a dozen factors, each with a different scoring system (her husband is a developer who specializes in Google Sheets).[24] For most of us, keeping it simple works best. Begin by using the exercise at the end of this chapter as a starting point, and embellish it later, if you like.

Once you're clear on which places—whether dwelling types, neighborhoods, cities, or regions—best fit your values, go visit them. Conducting an in-person assessment of each place that ranks high on your list will ultimately give you the most valuable "data" about where, when, and whether to move. How does each place measure up to your highly ranked values and attributes? Keep in mind that the rubric is merely a guide, and your gut may ultimately be your best resource. As Alexis aptly puts it, "a spreadsheet can provide insight, but what feels right trumps all the numbers."

Step Two: *Communicate*

If there's someone else who will also be affected by the decision—your partner, or family or friends you're moving closer to or farther away from—be sure to communicate with them. How do they feel about the choice? If you're considering moving back to your hometown so your parents can provide childcare, are they planning to stay where they are for a while, or are they also considering moving? If you're moving away, how will your loved ones cope in your absence?

The question of where to live or whether to move is one you may revisit from time to time. However, asking these kinds of questions continuously can drive you crazy. Couples may find value in scheduling conversations on the topic at regular intervals or at an annual retreat, as this man did with his wife:

> *We had a vague sense that one day we wanted to live in Vancouver, where I grew up. Our careers were going so well in San Francisco that it felt like it would be sometime in the quite distant future. But . . . reflecting and dreaming together really helped us get the courage to do it. We had an annual couple retreat where we'd evaluate our happiness across several categories. We did worst-case and best-case scenario analyses about moving there, and over time our timeline got sooner and sooner until we realized that we wanted to do it. The only things keeping us in San Francisco were career and money. Everything else was worse there than it would have been in Vancouver. Once we decided to do it, it was still a two-year process (meeting with an executive coach for two years, my wife getting permanent residency, lining up dual citizenship for our two kids, me getting American citizenship, tax planning, my wife leaving her job, me clearing it with my business partner, buying a house in a different country), and we finally did it last November. It was one of the scariest, and best, decisions we ever made.*

Step Three: Consider a Broad Range of *Choices*

Technological advances and lifestyle changes forced upon us by the pandemic have changed the game in many ways, potentially creating new and viable options about moving (or staying put). If you're considering a career-related move (e.g., to take a specific job), you may want to ask your prospective employer whether moving is even necessary. Many employers that previously required new hires to relocate to a certain location are now rethinking that requirement. If you're moving to get a bigger space, consider how you may be able to get more space without moving. If you've found yourself working out of a makeshift home office and are considering upgrading to a bigger space, perhaps you could instead rent a nearby apartment or office space. If you own a single-family lot, perhaps you might build an accessory dwelling unit (an additional space that is independent from the primary living quarters, also known as an ADU) on your property.

Step Four: *Check In*

Do you know people who live in the place or places you're considering? Can you reach out to those who have moved away from where you live currently? If so, what was their experience like? Are there others who have considered a similar move but stayed put? Talking to people who have had different experiences with moving can open your mind to new options and help you adjust your expectations. That's especially important because expectations can profoundly affect our experience. One survey respondent expressed her regret about not taking the time to check in with more people before making a big move. When she took a new job in a midwestern city, her son was nine months old. Moving to a new city where her family knew no one proved more intense than she'd imagined. Over the next three years, she and her family tried to adapt to a different climate, culture, and community, but the transition proved challenging. Eventually, she was presented with another job offer in the West Coast city where they had lived, and she jumped at the chance to move back. She shared:

> *I can't say I wish we had never done it because we gained so much, yet it also came at an intense price. It makes me really hesitate to put us through that again. I have much sharper criteria for us to follow if we ever do. I feel the weight of that decision and the extremes we experienced together, and I hesitate. Going into our move, I didn't know any-*

> *one who had done it before, and I wonder if it would have helped set my expectations if I had.*

Step Five: Explore Likely *Consequences*

Determining the likely consequences of a move can be challenging because it's not always possible to foresee how the process will play out. If the opportunity arises, you can try living in a new location for a week or, if possible, a month or two. This family did a trial relocation for one summer and found it helpful:

> *A couple of years ago, we reconsidered moving back to the United States as interesting opportunities kept coming up, and we decided to "prototype" the idea by spending a whole summer in California. In an interesting turn of events, my youngest (who was three at the time) had a massive health crisis while there (she's okay now), and the whole experience convinced us that we were very happy in our current country. [Our experience in the pandemic] confirmed again that this was the right decision.*

Whatever you decide, it may be helpful to give yourself a certain time frame—perhaps a year or two—when you won't consider changing anything, even if you hate it. One friend of Abby's who initiated a move from the city to the suburbs with her family said she was "in shock" for at least six months. Eventually, the shock wore off, and she came to enjoy her new home.

Putting down roots in a new place takes time and demands deliberate attention. Try joining different local organizations and getting to know people in the area. If you later decide to reverse the move, you'll do so knowing you gave your new home a fighting chance.

CHAPTER SIX EXERCISE:

How Will You Decide Where to Call Home?

This exercise focuses on how well possible CHOICES meet your top priorities (note: knowing these involves the CLARIFY step of our 5Cs framework). Complete this exercise with those who will be living with you in your potential home (you decide whether to involve children; we suggest limiting participation to adults).

What are your top priorities in a potential home (could be a specific city, neighborhood, or dwelling)? Bonus points for listing these in order of importance to you.

1. ______________________________

2. ______________________________

3. ______________________________

4. ______________________________

5. ______________________________

What are the top potential homes (e.g., cities, neighborhoods, dwell-ings) on your short list?

____

____

____

In the table, list your top priorities in the first row and potential homes in the first column. Adjust the scoring criteria if desired. Then, assign each potential home a score according to how well it stacked up against your criteria. Add scores to get a total. How do you feel (e.g., relieved, disappointed)? Does your "gut" agree with the winner?

	Priority 1	**Priority 2**	**Priority 3**	**Priority 4**	**Priority 5**	**Total Score**
Scoring criteria	**High=3 Medium=2 Low=1**	**H=3 M=2 L=1**	**H=3 M=2 L=1**	**H=3 M=2 L=1**	**H=3 M=2 L=1**	
Potential Home (PH) A						
PH B						
PH C						
PH D						
PH E						

SEVEN

MAKING IT WORK

Combining Career and Family

Figuring out how to combine paid work with parenting is one of the most complex money/love decisions people make. The topic involves numerous moving pieces, especially for dual-career couples, and has high stakes that demand constant attention. The questions that arise can seem endless. Will both partners continue to work full-time? Will one partner leave the workforce entirely? Will one or both work part-time or look for a job with more flexibility? What type of childcare is best? How do household tasks fit in once childcare responsibilities are added to the list?

How you answer these questions is personal and financial, logical and emotional. What's more, the decisions you make will impact almost every other aspect of your professional and family life and determine the distribution of every one of your resources—money, time, energy, and attention. The good news is, with forethought and consideration, the give-and-take these choices demand can feel purposeful and satisfying.

THREE TYPES OF COUPLES

Couples tend to fall into one of three groups when it comes to returning to their jobs after having a child. The first group is engrossed in their work and eager to find ways to pursue their careers while also raising children. Neil and Prisha exemplify this group. As soon as Prisha was pregnant, they got on a waiting list for a childcare center. As Neil explained:

We wanted to be super-prepared. Prisha has an MBA and loves her career, and my mother had always worked, so I fully supported her wish to go back to work as soon as her maternity leave was up.

Since they had settled in an area with a high cost of living, they also knew that two incomes would be necessary to meet their budgetary needs. They were concerned that taking more than a few months away from work would also likely result in financial penalties, especially for Prisha. That concern is well-founded; according to data gathered before the pandemic, women who leave the workforce for a short period typically face an earnings penalty of 4 percent once they find a new job; for those who are out of the workforce for more than one year, the penalty almost doubles, to 7.3 percent.[1]

Some couples who fall into this first group are also forced into maintaining their careers by circumstances beyond their control, as this couple experienced when their child was diagnosed with a serious health condition:

It took several months for our doctors to diagnose our son with the rare disease of Williams syndrome, which is associated with medical and developmental problems, including heart disease and learning challenges. I extended my maternity leave to care for him, but it was clear to both my husband and me that neither of us could stop working permanently. We needed both incomes to survive in New York City. And we couldn't move elsewhere because our jobs were tied to the city.

Neither of our families lived nearby to help us with childcare, so I spent my extended maternity leave researching programs we could apply to for assistance with our son's care. I returned to work when he was a year old, and for the past ten years we have had amazing care five days each week. A nurse picks him up in the morning, takes him on the subway to a special school far from our apartment, and brings him home in the late afternoon. If my husband or I had stopped working and devoted ourselves to raising our son full-time, we never could have provided him with the help we get from professionals with an understanding of his developmental needs. My husband and I struggle every day, and our son has had many setbacks, but for now, he is okay and our marriage and jobs are intact.

The second group of couples is already prepared to live on one salary, like Amanda and Christopher, who knew that Amanda would be a full-time parent once they had a child. As Amanda explained:

I knew I didn't want to continue working full-time once we had a baby. My mom had worked full-time, and I had always craved more attention from her and felt guilty when I was sick and had to stay home from school and inconvenience her. Christopher agreed with me. He had enjoyed having a stay-at-home mom when he was growing up and wanted our child to have one too.

The Rise of the Stay-at-Home Dad

The overwhelming majority of stay-at-home parents in heterosexual couples are female, but stay-at-home dads have been on the rise in recent years; in 2016, dads made up 17 percent of stay-at-home parents.[2] For some, having one partner at home can feel comforting, as it did for this woman:

I was the main breadwinner for the first decade of our firstborn's life. I held a full-time job at a corporation and my husband held more flexible part-time gigs. This allowed him to take care of our firstborn the first year after I went back to work. Back then, I couldn't imagine dropping off a four-month-old at a day care or leaving him with a just-hired nanny. I felt so fortunate he could be at home with a loving dad.

The third type of couple is often undecided about how to combine work and family, as Jasmine and Mia were:

When our first child was born, Jasmine was already unsure about staying with the company she'd been with. She hadn't gotten the promotion she deserved, and her boss had cut her no slack during a very tough pregnancy. I thought Jasmine should go back despite these things, but then we had a lot of trouble finding childcare. My mother was going to watch the baby, but my dad got sick, and she suddenly had a full-time job taking care of him. It took us a long time to decide what to do.

Since couples like Jasmine and Mia have more fluid priorities, their decisions about whether to stay in the workforce after having a baby can be powerfully influenced by external factors, such as the views of their families, and by their ability to find affordable, high-quality childcare. This isn't inherently negative or positive, but it is something to be aware of, since others' priorities may not always serve your family's needs and goals.

STAGGERED SCHEDULES

Some couples who wish to have two paychecks but want their children to be cared for only by themselves stagger their schedules to accomplish these dual goals. This couple created a hybrid solution so their children would always be cared for by one of them:

> *Our discussion around how we raised our children included not having them in day care. My parents volunteered to take care of our firstborn so I could return to work, but unfortunately, three weeks after his birth, my parents both were diagnosed with cancer and couldn't take care of him. Our decision was for me to leave my job. After I approached my employer, he wanted me to stay, so we worked out a part-time arrangement and my husband took the second shift on his job so he could be home with our son. It was a difficult first year, with both my parents being sick and passing away and my returning to work. We had two more children after this and worked opposite shifts until our children were grown. Fast-forward to today and we are glad we made the decisions we did. They enabled us to keep our careers and also raise our family. It wasn't easy being on different shifts, but it was worth it! We learned that the quality time spent with your children is what they remember.*

It is not clear exactly how many couples use this strategy. (In 2004, it was estimated that about 11 percent of employees worked a nonstandard schedule, but in 2014 it was estimated that about 25 percent of employees worked a night shift.)[3] For many years, scholars have argued that children could be harmed if a parent worked a nonstandard shift, particularly in single-parent families and lower-income families.[4] But one recent study of shift work in two-parent families found a complicated pattern where some children experienced behavioral problems and others experienced behavioral benefits.[5] Keep in mind that the best solution may not meet everyone's every need perfectly, but by meeting the most essential needs of all involved—the children as well as mom, dad, *and* their relationship—the entire family benefits in the long term.

When Nothing Goes According to Plan

Even when couples agree on how to combine work and family, external circumstances and personal preferences can change unexpectedly. The economy may weaken, job satisfaction may shift, one parent may become sick or disabled or discover more joy in baby care than they ever imagined. Or perhaps the world wakes up one day to discover a once-in-a-century global pandemic has begun. Monkey wrenches like these can feel unsettling, but the disruptions they cause sometimes lead to positive outcomes. When unforeseen obstacles appear in your family's path, take them as a prompt to reflect on your priorities as a couple and as a family. The exercise at the end of this chapter may also help you (and your partner, if you have one) reevaluate your work and family plans.

DECIDING TO PAUSE PAID WORK

One reason some couples choose to have one parent stay at home full-time is to reduce family stress, as this woman explained:

> *While we were both in good positions to work outside the home and earn money, it felt like our "compensation" as a family was increased with highly specialized roles. With my husband working and me handling basically everything else, we had enough income to cover basic costs, and used my forgone income to essentially "buy" other things we valued like flexibility, reduced stress, more free time, less friction, and less negotiation on "who does what." We informally revisit this arrangement regularly, but as the sole operators and customers of this family firm, this arrangement continues to maximize our utility.*

Money, or lack thereof, is another important factor in family decisions about who works. Having the option to live on a single salary is a luxury. But one way to increase income is to reduce expenses, so some families who would like to have one parent stay at home with their children but cannot afford it consider moving to an area with a lower cost of living. Keith and Alice took that route when they moved from New York City to Boise, Idaho, where the lower cost of living made it possible for their family to get by on one income. Then, as their children got older, Alice ramped up the consulting she'd done on the side to bolster their children's college savings fund.

Sometimes the decision to leave the paid workforce is more of a Hobson's choice—not really a choice at all. During the first year of the pandemic, as childcare centers and schools closed, forcing children back into the house, more women than men quit their jobs because they found it impossible to balance working for pay with caring for their children and helping them manage remote school. Since most women earn less than their husbands (wives outearn their husbands in only 30 percent of heterosexual married couples), in the majority of dual-earner families, it made financial sense for mothers to leave the workforce rather than fathers.[6] It's also still socially acceptable for mothers to leave the workforce to care for a child but less acceptable for fathers. This survey respondent's experience was atypical only because it didn't result in additional financial stress for her family:

> *When the pandemic struck, my job was eliminated. It coincided with my husband's small business doing well, so we decided that it was a perfect time for me to leave my job and focus on the kids during a very challenging time of distance learning and homeschooling. I felt fortunate that we could afford that and make the kids our number one priority during that time.*

In 2019, prior to the pandemic, more than 70 percent of all mothers of children under the age of eighteen were in the labor force. This was a remarkable increase in mothers' employment. Forty years earlier, only 56 percent of mothers were in the workforce.[7] The pandemic erased much of those gains, and it is unclear when and whether mothers' labor force participation rates will return to prepandemic levels.

Other external factors can force decisions about leaving work, as this family experienced:

When our second daughter, Chara, was about two, we learned she was on the autism spectrum. My wife had a successful law career at the time, but she decided she could not give Chara the attention she needed and continue her high-pressure job. We had already noticed that Chara's development was much slower than we remembered from our first daughter's early years, and my wife wanted to spend her time helping Chara in any way she could.

She became an expert on how to help a child with autism and worked at it for sixteen years. Losing her income was a severe hit for us. We moved to a smaller home and economized in every way we could. But we know we made the right decision.

The diagnosis of a child can be hard on a marriage, but that was not our experience. Over the years, my wife and I became closer than we had ever been as I watched her help Chara and learned from her how I could help too. Chara did well in high school and was recently accepted to her first-choice college. My wife is now planning her second career—probably something related to supporting kids with autism.

Factors That Affect the Decision to Return to Work After Having a Child

The more education a woman has, the more likely she is to return to work after becoming a mother. In 2019, 70 percent of mothers with a college or professional degree who had given birth in the previous twelve months returned to work, but only 50 percent of new mothers with some college or an associate's degree, and 40 percent of those with a high school diploma or less, resumed their careers.[8] This makes good economic sense. Women with a higher level of education generally earn more, so their opportunity cost of staying home is greater.

Still, in couples who can afford to get by on one salary, the higher-earning partner will often deflect and say that the decision to leave the workforce is the other partner's alone: "Whatever you want, honey." This is shortsighted. If one member of the couple fails to return to work, the cushion that having another earner in the family provides is gone. As a result, the higher earner may face noticeably more stress. It's like an airplane. While technically it can fly on only one engine, doing so puts a lot of pressure on that single engine not to fail. As one survey respondent put it, "Having two people working is a great insurance policy, as well as a great way to deal with life's inevitable ups and downs. Usually, you don't both change jobs at the same time or have incredible highs or lows at work at the same time. That's a good thing!"

The decision to work for pay or take on more of the unpaid work at home is fluid for some families, with one or the other parent leaving and returning more than once. A parent may return to work after having their first child, then leave for a time after their second (or third). Or they may work steadily until they reach a point when they feel the weight and time intensity of parenting with the greatest force—such as their child's teen years, or when their child receives a diagnosis—and then decide to leave their job or career for a time.

Although the question of whether a parent should work for pay or work at home is usually described as a decision for new parents, a family may revisit that decision when children reach their teens. That was the case for Stella, who had been a professional musician and music teacher before her son was born. After becoming a mother, she continued to teach privately, working mostly after school and on Saturdays. When her son turned twelve, she realized that her work hours were precisely when her son needed more of her attention. Wanting to provide activities alternative to the ones he was finding for himself after school, she stopped teaching and didn't resume until he left for college.

If Mom Works, Do the Kids Suffer?

We have good news for parents who wonder whether their children will suffer in some way if there is no full-time parent at home. A recent study that surveyed more than one hundred thousand parents across twenty-nine countries found that daughters of moms who worked full-time when they were growing up felt as happy with their lives when they became adults as the daughters of stay-at-home moms. However, the daughters of working moms performed better in their careers than the daughters of stay-at-home moms. The research also concluded that sons of full-time working moms were more likely to hold gender-egalitarian attitudes, more likely to marry a woman who works after she has children, and more likely to put in more hours of housework in their adult family.[9]

THE RIPPLE EFFECTS OF WOMEN LEAVING WORK

The decision to leave the workforce is a personal one that primarily affects the woman who leaves and her family (we focus on women here because they are more likely than men to leave the paid workforce after becoming parents). However, when a successful woman leaves the workplace, it can also have a ripple effect across the entire organization. With fewer senior women in their midst, junior women have fewer models of how to successfully combine career and family. When they see the dearth of senior women in their organization, they may conclude that they, too, will need to choose between work and children. Moreover, when senior women leave, junior women have fewer senior women to draw on as mentors, and since the #MeToo movement has discouraged some senior men from mentoring junior women, the loss of senior women mentors is even more concerning. It is important for organizations to promote ways to retain senior women.

Deloitte was one of the first companies to recognize the costs of women opting out of paid work after motherhood. The company developed a program that allows employees to leave for a time or move into less demanding jobs and—here's the key—return, whenever they are ready, to jobs on the trajectory they were originally on. In effect, Deloitte did away with the so-called mommy track, where women who return to work or seek to reduce the demands of their job are given secondary status for the rest of their career at that firm, with lower pay and decreased opportunities for promotion. Deloitte's approach is called Deloitte Flex and has been working successfully for years. Instead of a linear organization, the company talks about career paths organized on a lattice.[10] The firms Booz Allen Hamilton and Ernst & Young have also been pioneers in providing flexibility and what economist Sylvia Hewlett calls "on-ramps" to help former employees who are women return to work. Other professions have much to learn from these businesses about how to create opportunities for women to combine work and family without incurring penalties.

What's Happening in the Professions?

The lack of support for working women who are juggling childcare will likely become an increasingly significant problem, given that women in the United States now constitute more than 50 percent of those with bachelor's degrees, master's degrees, and doctoral degrees.[11] Women make up slightly more than 50 percent of those receiving an MD degree[12] and 54 percent of those getting JD degrees.[13] In thirteen of the top twenty law schools, as ranked by *U.S. News & World Report*, women also constitute the majority of students.[14]

Doctors and Surgeons

In recent years, within six years of completing their residencies, about 23 percent of women physicians worked part-time,[15] and about 17 percent left medicine entirely.[16] Depending on the medical or surgical specialty, it takes between eleven and fifteen years to train a physician, and that training costs more than $1 million.[17] Although gender harassment and gender bias in compensation and promotion explain part of the exodus of women from medicine, its major cause is work/family conflict. Elena Frank, a researcher at the University of Michigan Medical School, argues: "Until system-wide reforms are made within the institution of medicine to better support women in their roles as mothers and physicians, significant gender disparities in physician retention . . . will persist."[18] The difficulties facing women surgeons who are moms are particularly acute, given the long residencies and demanding work schedules.[19]

Lawyers

A recent study by the American Bar Association (ABA) found that 58 percent of experienced women lawyers cited caretaking commitments, and 46 percent cited difficulties with work/family balance, as their reason for leaving their firm.[20] The report explains: "When senior women lawyers leave firms, the firm's relationship with those lawyers' clients suffer, there is a reduced range of legal talent to offer clients, a narrower base for firms and businesses to develop robust client relationships, a diminished ability to recruit and retain skilled women lawyers at all levels, and, ultimately, serious challenges to the firm's future growth and revenue. It is evident that current policies and practices will not be enough to close the gender gap."[21]

Women lawyers who responded to the ABA survey favored a formal work-from-home policy, paid parental leave, a formal part-time policy for partners, and clear and consistent criteria for promotion to equity partner. The ABA report concludes: "What is holding senior women lawyers back is not a lack of drive or commitment, a failure to promote themselves, or an unwillingness to work hard or to make substantial sacrifices. Simply put, women lawyers don't need to 'lean in' any more than they have already done. What needs fixing is the structure and culture of law firms, so firms can better address the needs of the many women they recruit and seek to retain."

The report also points out that having policies on the books is only part of the solution. Making sure managers are trained to support employees who are interested in flexible options is also necessary. And providing incentives for lower-level managers to implement the policies is critical.

Academics

In academia, it is virtually unheard of to have a part-time position on the tenure track, and with rare exceptions, faculty who leave their positions to raise children take themselves out of the running for future tenure-track positions. There are many part-time positions to be had in academia, but they are adjunct positions—low paid, impermanent, renegotiated from year to year, and often without benefits or opportunity for promotion. Women are more likely than men to be in adjunct positions.[22]

ROUTES TO EMPLOYMENT FLEXIBILITY

Working Part-Time

Working part-time may initially seem like the ideal way to combine work and family. The Pew Research Center found that in 2012, 53 percent of married mothers and 36 percent of unmarried mothers with children under eighteen said they preferred part-time work to full-time work or leaving the workforce entirely.[23] However, working part-time has numerous downsides, especially for knowledge workers. Most employers aren't seeking part-time knowledge workers, which makes desirable part-time work hard to find. Typically, employers also view part-time workers as "not committed." As a result, even if you succeed at finding part-time knowledge work, you're likely to work more hours than you sign up for (typically without additional compensation) and unlikely to receive plum assignments or promotions.

Moreover, part-time workers are paid less per hour than full-time workers. A study of wage data from 2003 to 2018 found that part-time workers were paid 23.9 percent less in wages per hour than full-time workers with similar demographic characteristics and education levels.[24] After controlling for industry and occupation, the wage penalty was still 19.8 percent. Dissecting the data along gender and race lines shows that White men faced the highest wage penalty (a whopping 28.1 percent), followed by Black men (at 24.6 percent). The penalties for Black women, White women, Hispanic men, and Hispanic women ranged between 17.2 percent and 12.3 percent (data on Asian men and women were not included). The study points out that the "racial gap in part-time wage penalties likely reflects a combination of Whites' advantage in wage rates at their full-time jobs along with a shared disadvantage when they are in part-time jobs." The wage penalty has increased over time (six percentage points for women and four percentage points for men since a 2005 study using data from 1992–2002). No matter how you slice it, part-time work comes at a high cost to the worker.

In her memoir, *Becoming*, Michelle Obama recalls some of the difficulties she experienced as a part-time lawyer with a young child. Her tips for making part-time work successful include the following: from the beginning, negotiate clear parameters around what parts of your job you will do and what parts you won't; arrange your schedule so you are unavailable on certain days; and finally, be sure to keep track (in writing) of how many hours you work.[25]

The hard truth is, to get a part-time professional job, you often have to prove yourself as a full-time employee first. When Jada had her third child, she had just been made a partner at a prestigious law firm. She used her new status to ask for a four-day workweek at four-fifths pay, and the managing partner approved the request. "I need to have Fridays off so I can catch up with my life," she explained. The arrangement worked out, but not perfectly. As time went on, she did work on some Fridays, usually about one Friday out of every four. It was a reality she was willing to accept because of the freedom it gave her. "Nobody expects me in the office on Fridays. If I'm there, I'm seen as being a team player and that's a real plus. If I'm not there, nobody complains. For me, the trade-off in lost salary is more than worthwhile." This scenario is not uncommon among those fortunate enough to negotiate part-time work, as echoed by another part-time worker:

> *People always ask me, "Doesn't working 80 percent mean that you just get paid less to work the same amount?" My reply is this: "Do I sometimes work on Fridays? Yes. But do I work 80 percent of the hours that I would work if I were 100 percent? Also yes." If I work half a day on Friday, I rarely work on nights or weekends. So, it feels more sustainable. I've always chosen demanding jobs that have surprises and wouldn't*

want a classic 9 a.m.–5 p.m. job. Working 80 percent at jobs with long hours is a way to get the kind of work I enjoy in a way that's sustainable.

However, there are no guarantees that part-time work will be available, even after you've proven yourself with an employer, as this woman discovered:

Although I made twice what my husband made when we first met, I was down [in salary] by the time I was pregnant, so when our son was born, I was the one to step off the gas. I asked my large, well-off hospitality company if I could stay on part-time after maternity leave, and the answer was a flat, disdainful "No." So I quit and spent the next twelve years cobbling together project work and getting a master's. I felt smug when my friends had to hire au pairs or keep their infants in day care until 6 p.m., while I was making homemade baby food and going to toddler music classes at 10 on a Tuesday. But our kids are in elementary and middle school now, and those mom friends who stayed full-time at work through their kids' baby and preschool years are enjoying flourishing careers, being interviewed by the news as field experts, or having their names on law firms, while I'm just now getting back to full-time work that is much more menial than my age and life experience might dictate. Things would be so different now if my manager had been willing to let me have a part-time schedule. I know I could have made it work.

As this story showcases, there is a need for a collective effort to incentivize approval of part-time work for trusted employees. Since these decisions are typically made by an immediate manager, top management needs to create an environment where managers who approve part-time employment are rewarded for retaining talent. The economic rationale is compelling: part-time opportunities within a company not only eliminate the cost of finding a replacement but also position the company to successfully recruit talented women. Workplaces that become known as good places for women to work are widely sought after, not only by women but also by capable men interested in playing a significant role in their children's lives, and by people who may be playing a caregiving role for a sibling or older relative.

Part-time careers that do not penalize people provide an ideal way for families to raise children and pursue a demanding career. Given the continued increase in longevity forecast by demographers, it is likely that over time the retirement age will be close to eighty. With so many more years in the workforce, allowing for part-time work during the years of intensive child-rearing makes even more sense.

OTHER ROUTES TO EMPLOYMENT FLEXIBILITY

Moving to Easier Assignments

Moving to an easier assignment, perhaps with less travel or as an individual contributor (or a manager with fewer employees to supervise), is another way to create greater flexibility at work. However, a decision to take on less may mean being judged as less committed to the organization or less capable of simultaneously managing multiple moving pieces. If you are permitted to somehow slow down at work, you're likely going to have to work hard to prove your commitment and competence.

Becoming Self-Employed

Another way to gain greater flexibility is to become self-employed by starting your own business or consulting practice. Among self-employed women, almost one-third work part-time.[26] Several of Myra's former students have gone this route. Some find they can control their hours without needing to tell anyone that they work part-time. As one reported: "None of my clients knows how many other clients I have. When I'm stressed, I just reduce the number of my clients, or take clients with less complex assignments, and nobody's the wiser."

Nonetheless, self-employment does come with its risks and demands on your time and energy. You may not get as much work as you need, or you might end up with more work than you can reasonably handle at a given time (sometimes called the feast-or-famine nature of self-employment). While the opportunities to succeed can be significant, as a self-employed person you're entirely responsible for paying your own taxes and benefits, including funding your retirement.

Some who opt in to self-employment because of what they assume it is—a chance to work "whenever you want" and to forgo having a boss—are disappointed to discover how intense it can get. In reality, your schedule will likely be *extremely* demanding at times, sometimes for extended periods of time, and at least some of your clients likely will be too, becoming a kind of de facto boss. Before deciding to go this route, use the 5Cs framework, making sure to research the pros and cons by connecting with newer and more experienced self-employed people. Find out what they love and hate about being self-employed, what kinds of challenges they've had to overcome, and how they did it.

Staying with One Employer

Another way to slow demands at work and make it easier to combine work and family is to stay with one employer instead of job-hopping for advancement. If you're already a valued employee, the management team, as well as co-workers, may be more flexible when you need to attend to family matters. However, you may trade off other benefits, such as salary increases, since studies find that women who change jobs tend to get higher-percentage increases than men overall.[27]

> *I graduated from business school when I was twenty-eight and started a job with a new employer. Then, between the ages of thirty and thirty-five, I had three kids. At several points I seriously thought about leaving, which arguably would have expanded my experience and increased my salary. But, thanks to excellent on-site day care from my employer, I stayed with the same company—albeit in several different jobs—through those years (and am still there, over ten years after graduating B-school).*
>
> *It turns out that, through a combination of hard work and good luck and opportunities, my career is doing great, and I think likely better than if I had changed employers. While there has been a lot of turnover around me at my organization, I have emerged as someone with great experience and the ability to see my projects and initiatives through to completion. As a result, I have been able to move up the ranks. My conclusion is that for parents (moms especially) who want to "stand tall" rather than "lean in" during the young child years, professional stability can be a good thing both on the home front and at work. I think of this career path as different from the typical "rapid ascent" MBAs pursue out of school; instead, it is about treading water and building experience and power in the early years (with young kids), so that you are ready to move up quickly when the time is right.*

Abby's experience working at Gap Inc. for nearly a decade during her own kids' "young child years" echoes this survey respondent's perspective. Finding an employer that will enable you to advance your career without checking your identity as a parent at the door is essential. For her, working in a supportive culture that offered her career stability was worth the "cost" of temporarily releasing her fantasy of rapid ascent within an organization.

FINDING CHILDCARE

Availability, Affordability, and Quality

Whether you work full-time, part-time, for yourself, or for someone else, working when you have young children is predicated on finding available, affordable, quality childcare. That combination has long been hard to find, but it became increasingly out of reach when the pandemic struck and many day cares were forced to close. That may change over time, but regardless, finding the childcare arrangement you need is often an arduous undertaking that may need to be done repeatedly as your child grows and other circumstances change.

Although day-care centers are the most common type of care for children under the age of five (35 percent of children and 16 percent of infants), they are not the only viable option. According to the most recent US Census Bureau data on childcare arrangements, grandparent care was the second most common arrangement, providing care for 32 percent of kids (slightly higher for infants). Family day-care homes provide slightly less than 8 percent of care for all children under five and almost 10 percent of care for infants.[28] Care in a child's home by a babysitter or nanny, which can offer convenience but at a high cost, was relevant for only 5 percent of children.

Regardless of what type of childcare arrangement you choose, there will come a day when you need backup care. If your child gets sick, they can't go to a childcare center or family day-care home (and now they will likely need proof of a negative COVID-19 test to return). If your child's grandparent or nanny gets sick, has a medical appointment, or has travel plans, they won't be able to provide care. As a result, it's a good idea to consider plan B and C options at the same time you make your plan A. One couple Abby knows discusses who's "on deck" as backup childcare in their weekly planning sessions. That kind of strategizing can go a long way toward minimizing chaos when your child wakes up with a fever.

Prisha and Neil shared the ins and outs of their search for childcare. Like many couples, they were astonished by how complex the process can get:

Since Neil's mom ran an in-home day care for most of his childhood, we decided we were "day-care people," that either center care or care in a neighbor's home would work for us, and we got on waiting lists when I was ten weeks pregnant. We were due in late July, and I planned to go back to work in October. We initially were told we would have a day-care spot (at our second choice) starting in November, so we arranged for our moms to come help in October.

My mom was able to stay for about half of October, and then we found out that our second-choice day-care center spot wasn't going to be available in November, but that a spot at our first-choice place might open up in January. So, I ended up taking our son to a woman who was retired from running an in-home day care (which my friends' kids had gone to) but was willing to take our son four days a week. On Fridays, I attempted to work while he napped, and Neil's cousin (who was in college nearby) came for a few hours.

By December, it was clear that that arrangement wasn't working out. The baby cried a lot, and Neil's cousin wasn't interested in caring for a crying baby. As the month wore on, it looked more and more like the January spot might not happen either. However, the daughter of the first-choice spot reached out because she was thinking about opening her own day care, and she wanted to know if we'd be interested. She had to find a house in a difficult housing market, get all of the supplies, and get licensed, in a little less than a month over the holidays, so we were skeptical. But she actually offered to nanny for us until they were up and running. She couldn't nanny full-time, though, so she split the schedule with her friend from church.

Eventually it was clear that the new day care wasn't opening, and they didn't want to be long-term nannies, so after six weeks, we ended up finding a nanny share, which we were in for six months before a day-care spot opened up—when my son was thirteen months old. We'd been on the waiting list for nineteen months. All in all, my son had five care-takers in his first six months. For our second son, we went straight to a full-time nanny (no share) for his first year, and he got his day-care spot when he was eleven months old, after we'd been on the waiting list for five months (and that was with sibling priority!).

While Prisha and Neil's search was challenging, they were the lucky ones; they could afford quality childcare. Moreover, unlike 51 percent of residents of the United States, they didn't live in a "childcare desert"—defined as "a census tract with more than fifty children under age five with either no childcare providers or three times as many children as licensed care slots."[29] As a result, childcare options were more plentiful for Prisha and Neil than they are for millions of Americans trying to combine work and family.

Because of the shortage of childcare slots and problems with quality and reliability, parents often need multiple childcare options to cover their needs, as this family discovered:

When our son was first born, my parents moved in with us for close to a year, and then we found a nanny, who we've been blessed to have since [pre-COVID]. I traveled for work internationally four times a year, and domestically several times a year as well, and my wife works East Coast market hours, so whenever I traveled, we needed childcare coverage starting at 5:30 a.m. Our nanny didn't necessarily want to work that early. It would have made for a really long day for her. We were able to manage only because we found a few high school kids and other nannies who wanted extra hours to help us out.

Other couples outsource more non-childcare-related tasks to fill in the gaps:

> *In Professor Strober's class we had a panel with alums, and the couples where both parents chose to work at demanding jobs said they had to outsource everything. I told my wife about that, and we followed suit. We outsource housecleaning, gardening, home repairs, and so forth. Some of our friends have weekend nannies, but we've tried to reserve weekends to spend time with our two young boys.*

These families are undeniably privileged, which grants them access to options that are financially out of reach for most families. This is a massive issue that needs and deserves attention and resources so that more parents can go to work knowing that their children are being safely and capably cared for.

Returning to Paid Work

Economist Sylvia Hewlett conducted two national studies of women who left the labor force to raise their children full-time. She found that most sought to return at some point and succeeded in doing so. Approximately 90 percent sought to return, and three-quarters of them were successful.[30] Of the returnees, 40 percent took full-time jobs, about one-quarter took part-time jobs, and approximately 10 percent became self-employed. (The number of self-employed may have increased in recent years.)[31] Pamela Stone and Meg Lovejoy's smaller, more recent in-depth longitudinal study of forty-three upper-middle-class professional women who left work and sought to return found a higher degree of success than they had in the careers they paused.[32]

There are many reasons to return to the paid workforce. While having one parent at home can be helpful when children are younger, the arrangement can come with its stressors, as this woman explained:

> *During the pandemic, I decided to take a full-time job, twelve years after having my first child and going to very part-time work. The new job is nothing to particularly admire, pay or status wise. I took it to provide backup to my husband in case he loses his job. He works in an industry where cuts are being made right and left, and it's scary to think of my housewife self with my apron on, anxiously wringing my hands as my husband searches the job boards. And I also wanted to afford my husband the freedom to quit and find a new role or career after twelve years of supporting our family if he would at some point like. Until I took the new job, I didn't realize the low-level guilt I had felt this whole time, of asking my husband to carry almost the full financial load for a family of five. He never complained, but I know that put a lot of pressure on him.*

In Hewlett's initial study, about 60 percent of those who wished to return cited financial reasons: they missed having an independent income, they viewed their families as being under financial pressure without their incomes, or both. Many also missed the intrinsic satisfaction of pursuing a career.

Almost one-quarter of the women in Hewlett's study who sought to return to work had altruistic motives, wanting their work to be a way to give back to society. Work was a way to add fulfillment and meaning to their lives and, in the process, create a legacy. In many cases, this translated into women who had worked in male-dominated jobs prior to pausing paid work later seeking female-dominated positions when they returned to the workforce. The female-dominated positions were lower paying, incurring a wage penalty of 18–38 percent,[33] but offered unique benefits, including schedules more conducive to raising a family. To some degree, this trend toward changing to female-dominated jobs may explain a portion of the wage penalties exacted upon women who pause their careers to raise children and return years later.

Great Resources for Returning to Work

In recent years, numerous companies have sprung up to help women return to the workforce, such as iRelaunch and The Mom Project. They help women develop new skills, particularly technical skills; they provide a peer group of others seeking to return to work; and they consciously work on increasing women's self-confidence. Some have developed a network of companies with open roles. In addition to preparing women for job interviews, they set them up with potential employers.

If you are seeking to return to work, remember that the success rate is high and maintain your confidence. It may take a while to find what you are looking for, but you are at an exciting place. Think about it as starting a whole new chapter.

TAKING CARE OF YOURSELF

Raising a family while working for pay can leave little time for anything else. One way to ensure that priorities outside of work- and child-related ones aren't neglected is to schedule them, just like you schedule meetings and doctor's appointments. Make sure regular exercise, meetups with friends, dates with your partner, and time for creative pursuits that nourish you make it onto your calendar alongside your work meetings.

You're probably wondering how on earth you're supposed to do that. It's not easy, but when it comes to finding time for these activities, we encourage you to be creative. Go on a lunch date with your partner when school or day care is in session. Use some weekend childcare time for physical activities you can do as a couple. Schedule time with friends to run errands together and catch up.

This is the part where we are supposed to encourage you to schedule adequate sleep, too, since the short- and long-term ill consequences of chronic sleep deprivation are well documented.[34] But we also want to be realistic. We know very few people combining paid work and care work who feel like they consistently get adequate sleep (yes, this is a problem). Technology plays a big role in this, as does the "always on" culture of too many workplaces. Try to harness technology to help you get more sleep: turn off the "autoplay next episode" feature within Netflix; schedule your Wi-Fi router to turn off after a certain time; and buy a basic alarm clock so you can leave your phone outside of your bedroom.

USING THE 5Cs FRAMEWORK: COMBINING WORK AND FAMILY (ESPECIALLY AFTER A PAUSE)

Finding a new job after a work pause is a major endeavor, especially if the pause has been lengthy. Rest assured, if you're willing to persevere, your odds are favorable. Using the 5Cs, you can structure the decision and the process in ways that add some ease for you and your family.

Step One: *Clarify*

Before deciding to reenter the workforce, clarify your goals by answering two key questions: Why do you want to return? And what kind of work do you want to do?

Keep in mind, clarifying what you want can be an ongoing

process. Changes in overall economic or societal circumstances, as well as industry and job requirements, often create a need to reassess what you want. Keep asking these questions as you move forward in the process. And remember that changing your mind is a normal part of the process.

Step Two: *Communicate*

Talk to your partner or spouse, if you have one, about what you want, how your home and family might function differently if you were working, and any concerns you may have about the job hunt. In two-parent families, each person's decisions affect the other even if both members are currently in the workforce. For example, if one parent is considering a promotion that entails longer hours or more travel, talk about whether the other will be able to step up at home. If you're returning to work and your child doesn't get a spot in the after-school childcare program, how will you cover those hours? If your child hated summer camp last year, should you see if you can negotiate a reduced schedule over the summer, or ask your parents who live in another city if they might be interested in caring for their grandchild this summer? If you have older children and intend to return to work, how do they feel about it? Remember, as the parent, you can hold firm in your decision while addressing any concerns others may have. Speaking your mind—and listening to what your loved ones have to say—are essential for healthy, balanced communication.

Step Three: Consider a Broad Range of *Choices*

Whatever your work life used to be, stay open to new and different options. For example, if you've never considered self-employment, remember that risk is unavoidable even in full-time employment. Some people successfully turn their favorite hobbies into businesses. Maybe you could, too.

The job search process may also require some creative maneuvers. If the traditional route isn't getting you the attention of employers, consider other ways to improve your chances of getting hired. Some volunteer positions, for instance, can be helpful. Jordan, who'd had a career in finance, volunteered for her city while she was out of the workforce, helping to plan a new building. When she was ready to return to work, she broadcast her desires far and wide. The news of her job search reached a board member of a nonprofit looking for an executive director. Impressed with her financial volunteer work, the board member facilitated an interview, and she got the job. While her new nonprofit position earned a good deal less than her former finance job, she loves her new work and is "more than okay" with the pay cut.

Creative teamwork can sometimes make the dream work. After twelve years out of the workforce, Ishita felt ready to go back to work, but only part-time. In the course of talking about her desires everywhere she went with everyone she encountered, she met a woman who was also looking to return to a part-time job. They teamed up and searched for an employer who would hire them both so they could share a job. It took them two years of searching, but they found their dream job.

Step Four: *Check In*

Whom can you contact about your desire to return to work? Networking can help you decide whether to pursue paid work and, if so, how to get a job you want. Seek out experts in the industry you are interested in. Talk to the people in your network about their work, as well as how they combine work and family. Talk to your neighbors, to the parents of your children's friends, to people at your place of worship or in an extracurricular group. Ask questions, tell them what you are looking for, and be open to suggestions.

This same openness to checking in is often necessary whenever you're considering a change in how you combine work and family. When Myra's grandson was having trouble reading in grade school, her daughter-in-law, Joanna, shared that she was considering leaving the workforce so that she could help her son. Joanna's mother provided a different perspective. "How are you going to help him by staying at home?" she asked. "Why not continue to work and use some of your earnings to hire a professional reading tutor?" Joanna realized the wisdom of her mother's thinking and did just that. Checking in with her mom was crucial to her decision.

Step Five: Explore Likely *Consequences*

As you make the myriad ongoing decisions about how to navigate work and family, try to anticipate the likely consequences of your various decisions. For example, if you decide to send your child to her grandparents' because she hated summer camp, what might that mean for your overall relationship with your parents or in-laws? Will you feel judged if you hear bemused comments about how few foods your child will eat or how your child hasn't learned basic manners? Or will you be grateful for the help, regardless of the comments? Might the experience even bring your family closer? You probably won't know the answer for sure, but you can make a good guess based on what you do know.

Hopefully, your life and your career will be long. If you find yourself not liking the way you're currently combining work and family, remember that you have agency to make changes. Few things in this world are final.

CHAPTER SEVEN EXERCISE:

How Will You Combine Career and Children?

This exercise focuses on the CLARIFY and COMMUNICATE steps of our 5Cs framework. Do some self-reflection on the following questions and then discuss them with your partner, if you have one.

1. How certain are you that you want to continue working full-time after you have children? Which of the following three statements suits you best? Why?

___

A. I know in my bones that I want to continue working full-time after I become a parent. My professional identity is very important to me, and I'll do everything I can to preserve it.

B. I see advantages to continuing to work full-time after I become a parent, but I also see some drawbacks. If the stars align for me to continue working full-time, great, but I'm not making any promises.

C. My career is important to me, but my children are more important. I would like to pause my career or downshift somehow to spend more time with my children, at least for a time.

2. Which of these statements about childcare suits you best? Why?

___

A. As long as my child is safe and being cared for by a skilled caregiver, I'm comfortable with having someone other than a family member provide care.

B. I can see benefits of having my child cared for by a family member, but if we found the right caregiver or day-care setting, I could be convinced that it could work for our family.

C. It is very important to me that my child is cared for full-time by a family member, ideally a parent.

3. Do you think the way you answer these questions might change over time? How?

____

If you have a partner, share your answers to questions 1–3 with them, explaining why you selected the answers you did. Listen actively to your partner while they share the same explanations with you.

4. Did your partner's answers surprise you? What implications does your combination of answers about career and care have for your family?

____

5. If you both chose A for question 1, discuss how you will decide whose career will take priority. Will that change over time, and if so, how will it change?

____

6. If you both chose C for question 1, discuss whether or how you will sequence this and how you anticipate the arrangement will work for your family financially. Will you need to make any changes to your lifestyle or the place where you live?

____

7. If you and your partner chose different answers for question 2, how will you resolve this difference?

____

EIGHT

CHOPPY WATERS

Facing Relationship Challenges (and Ending a Marriage Gracefully)

On an airplane flight from New York to California, Myra's first husband, Sam, told her he was unhappy with their marriage. The news came as a shock; in the eighteen years they'd been married, he had never said that before. Alarmed, Myra suggested they go to couples therapy, but Sam said he preferred to see a therapist by himself. A month later, he asked for a trial separation and moved out. Soon thereafter, he asked for a divorce.

While divorce is certainly not the outcome in all relationship challenges, being mindful of ways to anticipate and address relationship speed bumps can be enormously beneficial to any partnership. Knowing how to strengthen your bond with your partner and manage the rough patches can improve your relationship. And if someday you do divorce, those same skills can allow your separation to be as amicable as possible.

ALL COMMUNICATION IS NOT CREATED EQUAL

Most people are aware that communication is the mainstay of any healthy relationship. Yet the core question—*what is good communication?*—is rarely addressed in any meaningful way. Myra learned the importance of good communication in the school of hard knocks. She and Sam talked regularly and rarely fought. Their conversations were about politics, their jobs, and their children. They regularly shared the details of their work, and there appeared to be mutual interest and respect between them.

Years passed before Myra began to understand why their communication fell short. Her second husband, Jay, a psychiatrist, introduced her to the idea that *intimate* communication is what nourishes a marriage. He defined intimacy as "into-me-see." To communicate with your partner in an intimate way, you must let your partner into your feelings *in the moment*, including how you are feeling about your marriage. It's important to trust your partner with those feelings and not be afraid that your partner will leave because you have them. Paradoxically, by making yourself vulnerable to your partner, you preserve your marriage and make it stronger.

Although fighting is often viewed as a negative—which of course it can be, if it's misused—productive fighting is better for a relationship than poor communication. John Gottman, who, along with his wife, Julie Gottman, is an expert on how couples communicate, finds that couples who fight for the purpose of solving problems are much more likely to stay together than couples who fight to prove their partner wrong, shame their partner, or stonewall their partner's ideas.[1]

Communication is, of course, a two-way street. In addition to talking about your feelings, you must also be a careful listener. In fact, good listening—characterized by empathizing and commiserating, *not* suggesting solutions—is more than half of good communication. People who feel heard are much more likely to continue sharing their feelings. Communicating well means engaging fully, believing your partner's statements (rather than assuming your partner will come around to your point of view), and trusting that, as a couple, you can eventually come to agreement.

For a marriage to flourish, both partners must feel that the compromises they reach are fair. While it's often impossible to resolve every issue to both people's complete satisfaction, overall, over time, there must be a mutual feeling of evenhandedness. When the bridging of differences feels unfair, the bridge eventually destabilizes and becomes a weak foundation for the partnership to move forward.

PRESERVING ROMANCE AND PHYSICAL INTIMACY

Keeping the romantic spark alive between two people over many years and through life's ups and downs requires time and effort that may be in short supply as careers, kids, extended family, and more enter the picture. This can result in a noticeable, even significant, decline in romantic and sexual intimacy. At times, this lack of physicality may lead to infidelity, but infidelity often has other causes. Sexual interest can diminish with time and age, but even when sex declines, all is not lost; tenderness, affection, and warmth can act as important substitutes for periods of time.

Many couples schedule regular date nights to stay connected beyond their normal daily interactions. Many also try to schedule a weekend away when they can. However, date nights and occasional weekends away aren't enough to sustain a marriage over many decades if the benefits of these "couple time" activities don't carry through to everyday interactions. Somehow, each partner must remember why they married the other and work to rekindle at least a small flame that burns consistently. Loving glances, touches, and real kisses (not just pecks on the cheek) are needed as well as private time to talk and laugh.

The nonprofit organization AARP surveyed couples over the age of fifty and found that the happiest couples found multiple ways to keep romance and intimacy alive in a marriage.[2] On the basis of the survey responses, three experts weighed in with advice. Some of their suggestions are simple: don't be reticent to hold hands or kiss in public; tell your partner you think they are great and be sure to tell them every day that you love them; sometimes have sex even if you are not in the mood right then; exchange passionate kisses at least once a week and have a date night with your partner at least twice a month. However simple, these suggestions can seem daunting to achieve when kids are young or when you're going through a stressful time (such as, say, a global pandemic). So don't panic if you haven't had a date night in a while or your sex life is going through a dry spell. The goal is to commit to investing in your relationship despite everything else going on, so that your relationship can be something that sustains you rather than adds to your stressors.

IT'S ABOUT (A LOT) MORE THAN SEX

The amount of romance and sex in your life is relative to whatever else is happening in your relationship. This also makes nurturing the deeper bond between you and your partner essential, including supporting each other's dreams and desires. Making sure both partners feel seen, heard, and supported allows the romantic and sexual side of your relationship to thrive. This is similar to the research showing that couples who share housework equally have sex more often.[3] When both people feel valued, intimacy, laughter, and joy come more easily.

Esther Perel, a couples therapist, author, and podcaster, describes the paradox of wanting both adventure and security in a monogamous relationship.[4] She also notes the difficulty of having erotic interest, which thrives on mystery, and at the same time having intimacy, which requires honesty, the opposite of mystery. Having all of these elements at once with the same person is a tall order, especially since life expectancy today is far longer than it used to be, and sex is no longer just about childbearing.

According to Perel, couples who have been together for a while should not expect sex to happen spontaneously. Instead, she recommends scheduling it. She also advises couples to prepare for their scheduled sex by changing their mindset to include imagination and lightheartedness. Couples focused on raising children, pursuing careers, managing a home and social life, and keeping finances on a sound footing can fall short on fostering novelty and playfulness. But, Perel argues, it is precisely those qualities that are key to good sex.

On Infidelity

Discussions of sex and marriage inevitably bring up the topic of infidelity. According to the 2010–2016 General Social Survey, 20 percent of men and 13 percent of women said they had sex with someone other than their spouse while they were married.[5] Other research estimates that the prevalence of extramarital affairs ranges from 20 percent to 40 percent.[6]

While some do manage to work through infidelity issues (especially with the help of trained professionals), couples therapists view affairs to be "one of the most damaging problems couples face and one of the most difficult problems to treat."[7]

WHEN MONEY ISSUES LEAD TO DISTRUST

When Hana's maternal grandfather died, she inherited a substantial sum. Hana's mother explained to her that the money belonged solely to her, that inheritances are not community property. However, with three young children and, as she put it, "no head for numbers," Hana asked her husband, Sean, to manage the money for her. They never talked about how Sean was investing the inheritance, but after a few years, it became clear that the funds were gone. Sean had lost them in a real estate "deal" that failed. Hana's trust in her husband evaporated. Soon thereafter, she filed for divorce.

Disagreements about money are a major cause of marital discord and divorce, especially when they are combined with poor overall communication. While Hana and Sean's situation was particularly dramatic, disputes about finances can be lethal for a marriage even when the amounts involved are smaller and the clashes more quotidian and ongoing. Some people are savers; others are spenders. Some like to buy on credit; others want the whole amount in hand before they make a major purchase. Some want a lavish house, even if it's a budgetary strain, while others want to live more simply to build a financial cushion that allows them to sleep more soundly. If you are married to someone who approaches finances differently from the way you do, you will need to spend more time and energy working through those differences.

One way that couples deal with contrasting financial philosophies is to keep their finances separate. They each put some of their money into a common fund while also maintaining separate accounts. A recent study by Bank of America suggests that more couples than ever are keeping separate bank accounts. The study found that 29 percent of millennial couples had separate bank accounts, as compared with only 13 percent of boomer couples.[8]

Even couples with similar financial philosophies may appreciate having a combination of joint and separate accounts, as we discussed in chapter two. Abby and Ross have used this approach since moving in together after graduate school. While the percentage of their income that's contributed to their shared account has increased over time, having individual accounts allows them each a simple, guilt-free way to pay for things such as weekend trips with friends and gifts.

WHEN CHANGE ROCKS THE BOAT

During a marriage, partners inevitably change their ideas, goals, views, and more. Inevitably, at least some of these changes happen simultaneously, at different speeds and in different directions. When long-term couples are interviewed about their marital success, they often talk about the importance of negotiating these shifts. These inflection points, many say, can be pivotal moments in their relationship. Some recall with pride how one or the other worked to accommodate, compromise, or retool in response to their partner's shifts.

Change can be scary, but couples who have a history of talking frequently, listening mindfully, and believing what the other is saying eventually grow more confident in their ability to manage change in themselves, each other, and their relationship. Their fear becomes less overpowering because of their past success. For newer couples, one of the challenges, then, is not to let the fear of change overtake their willingness to engage with each other to figure out what's changing and how it impacts their relationship and life together.

In her book *Couples That Work: How Dual-Career Couples Can Thrive in Love and Work*, Jennifer Petriglieri defines three transitions couples make in their work/life journey.[9] Making these transitions successfully brings deeper intimacy, while failing to navigate them can lead to discontent or divorce.

In the first stage of marriage, success requires that couples figure out how to combine two busy lives and, often, young children. They need to find individual success at work and success as a couple at home.

As time passes, one or both partners may begin to wonder whether they want to stay on the path they've forged. The question "What do I really want?" takes on new meaning, and they may experience what has come to be known as a midlife crisis. Traversing this crisis in a way that enables each partner to feel content is critical to the ongoing success of their marriage.

Margaret and Evan met in college and married soon thereafter. Evan went to law school right out of college, and Margaret, after working as a secretary for a few years, focused on raising their children and managing the household. When their youngest son entered high school, Margaret realized she wanted to attend business school, both because she wanted the challenge and because she wanted to contribute financially. Knowing how much this dream meant to his wife, Evan encouraged her to apply, assuring her that he would take on half of the childcare and household responsibilities. He delivered on his promise, and Margaret eventually became the chief executive officer of a large nonprofit organization. They recently celebrated their sixtieth anniversary.

The third transition Petriglieri identifies comes later in life, sometime in one's sixties, seventies, or eighties. This time, couples ask, "Who are we now?" Both mates have undergone significant physical change; their bodies are far from the ones to which their partners were initially attracted. Their children, if they had any, are independent or almost so. Their work may no longer be a central part of their identity; their parents may require caretaking or may have died. Friends, or they themselves, may face serious illness. Close friends may have passed away. "Now what?" they ask themselves.

Evan and Margaret had more difficulty navigating their third transition than their second. Evan retired from his career long before Margaret was ready to leave hers, and while Evan wanted to travel to a long list of countries he had never visited, Margaret became even busier working on a book. They decided to see a couples therapist. Fortunately, after many years of good communication and compatibility, they crafted a travel plan they could agree on and a volunteer activity they could do together—mentoring high school students. Neither has everything they want, but they both have what they want most: a loving relationship with frequent time together.

As Margaret and Evan found, a neutral third party—in this case, a therapist—can be instrumental in helping resolve problems related to any of the potential derailers we mention. If your partner proposes going to one and you disagree, oblige your partner and give it a try. It can be a surprisingly good decision, as this woman experienced:

> *We always kept separate finances and shared the bills 50/50 until 2020, when (in the midst of considering a divorce) my business collapsed. It took a lot of courage for me to ask my husband for his financial support, and initially he was hesitant. But the marriage counselor we saw taught him that giving that support was part of marriage, and this support, which he gave (and gives) without question, now is one of the main things that has patched up our marriage.*

A couples therapist can be helpful in a time of crisis and also in times of connection, when you both may be more open to improving communication and proactively addressing issues. An experienced couples therapist can watch couples talk with each other and pick up patterns and make suggestions for change "in the moment."

Couples therapist Vanessa Katz likens the work she does with couples to going to the gym and exercising emotional muscles.[10]

However beneficial, therapy is expensive, although with a wide range that varies by the therapist's location, experience level, education, and reputation. Unlike individual therapy, which is now required by federal law to be included in most insurance plans, couples counseling is often not covered by insurance. Some lower-cost alternatives include meeting with a clergy member or choosing a book on relationships to read and discuss together. There are even free or low-cost twelve-step programs for couples that focus on recovering from addiction or other issues. Whichever avenue you pursue, one key to successfully working through hard times is making sure you and your partner are willing to engage in an exploratory process with the goal of repairing and strengthening your bond.

DECIDING TO DIVORCE

After speaking at a national conference, Myra met a graduate student named Irina, who asked if they could have coffee. After they sat down at a private table, Irina explained her situation. She and her husband, Leonid, both originally from Russia, had grown up in the United States and met while attending graduate school in New England. They had been married for three years before he left to do research for his dissertation in a rural part of Russia, where he had no internet connection and phone service was unreliable. Although they had agreed to write to each other every week, they had both fallen down on the job and had not corresponded for two months. Meanwhile, Irina had been spending more time with a man in her graduate program and found herself increasingly attracted to him. "Do you think I should write to my husband and tell him I want a divorce?" she asked.

"Slow down," Myra said. "You are talking about divorce awfully quickly. You just told me you got married not that long ago, and you lived happily together for several years. Surely you two have a lot to talk about before you consider divorce. And you have a lot to think about yourself before you talk to him."

Myra asked Irina if she wanted to stay in her marriage. Irina said she thought she did. Deep down, she still loved Leonid, but she was furious with him, first for choosing to do doctoral work in rural Russia with sparse internet and phone service, and second for not writing to her regularly. She thought telling him she was considering divorce might get him to be a better correspondent. Also, she really did like the man in her graduate department.

Being neither a marriage counselor nor a psychiatrist, Myra urged Irina to try to separate her anger at her husband from her desire to stay married. Also, she suggested that Irina carefully consider whether she wanted to take steps to preserve her marriage. That also meant keeping her relationship with the other guy on a friendship-only basis until she was clear about what she wanted from Leonid.

Many couples experience times like this when one or both partners have to decide whether to call it quits on the relationship. Having these thoughts isn't in itself a bad sign, but it does indicate a need to explore what's happening inside each person and within the relationship. While some couples are well served by doing the work and staying together, parting ways leaves others happier and healthier in the long run, even when the divorce process itself proves to be challenging. Whatever your situation, know that these tough times can, and often do, end up proving beneficial.

When Myra divorced, in the early 1980s, the divorce rate was at its peak. It has since fallen, and so far, millennials are advancing this trend by divorcing at a lower rate than prior generations. Still, an estimated 40–50 percent of today's marriages will end in divorce.[11] And in recent years, the divorce rate has increased among couples over the age of fifty. Interestingly, when Myra asks her students if they think their current or future marriage will end in divorce, everyone says no. While this is a good sign in some ways—it suggests people remain optimistic about marriage—in other ways, it may encourage complacency and denial. In addition, feeling immune to divorce may prevent people from considering what a "good" divorce looks like, including how to manage the complex emotional and financial decisions inherent in the dissolution of any couple's joint life.

How Divorce Affects Children

Every year, about 1.5 million children in the United States experience their parents' divorce. According to research, most children do not suffer from serious problems at the time of their parents' divorce or later as adults (although about 15 percent do).[12] One predictor of serious problems for children is ongoing bitterness between parents during or after the divorce process. However, an intact but acrimonious marriage can also have ill effects on children, which suggests that parents are not necessarily helping their children by staying in a bad marriage.[13] In the end, the most troubling factor for children may be the discord between their parents, not merely whether they're married or divorced.

Sometimes divorce is less disruptive to the family than parents imagine, as was the case for this woman:

I had thoughts about getting divorced before, but I always had a reason why it was okay, why things weren't that bad. I'd wonder how I would manage the kids and manage financially. The idea of being a single parent, even with shared custody, seemed pretty overwhelming. . . . I stayed longer in my marriage because I was uncomfortable with the idea of my ex-husband taking care of the kids. But ultimately, I didn't fight him on having 50 percent custody. Overall, it has turned out better than I expected.

Some individuals or couples decide to wait until after their youngest child has left for college before they divorce, thinking that once a child is older and perhaps no longer living full-time at home, getting used to a divorce will be easier for them. The literature seems to suggest, however, that while the immediate effects of a divorce may be different for older children, it is not necessarily easier for them to adjust, and that, like younger children, they need parental assistance in navigating their new family situation.[14]

DIVIDING ASSETS

Division of assets is often a major source of contention in divorces and can lead to lasting bitterness. Ninety percent of divorces are settled out of court, but when cases do come to trial, they generally concern money—child support, division of assets, and alimony—and, in some cases, child custody as well.[15] In both community property states and so-called equitable distribution states, assets are generally divided equally between the two partners and litigation is not necessary.

Myra has served as an expert witness in four high-profile divorce cases where the equitable distribution of assets was an issue. In each, the question was how to value the unpaid labor of the wife, who had been a full-time homemaker throughout the vast majority of a long-term marriage. Myra concluded that statistical methods for finding market equivalents for a homemaker's activities or guesstimating what the homemaker would have earned on a paid job are seriously flawed. Rather than bicker about the value of unpaid labor or use these flawed methods to estimate it, she recommends viewing a long-term marriage as a 50/50 partnership that was based on mutually agreed-upon terms.[16] Seen through this lens, a divorcing couple, from an economic perspective, becomes a unit that made investments in themselves and in each other throughout the duration of the marriage so that when the full-time homemaker cooked, cleaned, and grocery shopped, or the breadwinner left home to perform paid work, each was working to support their joint existence. As a result, at the time of a divorce, assets should arguably be split equally, and the equal split should not be viewed as a gift to the partner who earned less, nor as related to economic need. Rather, it should be viewed as both partners' return on their investment in the marriage.

Minding Your Tax Bills

Even in relatively amicable and straightforward divorce cases, it's advisable to seek counsel from tax attorneys, since tax laws change frequently and the potential pitfalls of overlooking tax implications can have significant financial consequences for both partners. In more complex cases, additional experts may need to weigh in.

When dividing assets, considering tax liabilities can get complex. For example, even when the values of two properties are currently equal, if they were acquired at different times and have unequal bases, their value will not be equal after the taxes owed are paid. Also, be sure to remember that if a spouse receives a pension plan (or part of one), that person will need to pay the taxes on it. And while we're on the subject of taxes, remember that divorcing couples with children need to agree on which of them will get the childcare tax credit when filing their tax return.

ALIMONY, CUSTODY, AND CHILD SUPPORT

Alimony, child custody, and child support are additional hot-button issues between divorcing spouses. Coming to agreement on these matters can keep your case out of court and potentially allow you and your children to settle into your new life more easily and quickly. Using a mediator, rather than opposing attorneys, may help you come to an agreement without unduly antagonizing each other, as this couple experienced:

> *What we both did well is try to put our kids first. As much as you can, do that. One of the things our mediator said to us is that one person is always going to be the instigator of the divorce. That person needs to be sensitive and compassionate to the other person. As the instigator of the divorce, I wish I had been more sensitive and compassionate at the time.*

Child Custody

Custody arrangements for children have two facets: *legal custody* determines who has responsibility for the children's welfare, including their health and education; *physical custody* dictates where the children live.

In most states, parents have *joint legal custody* after divorce, and if the case goes to court, judges generally award *joint physical custody* so that children will be in regular contact with both parents.[17] Needless to say, joint custody works much better if there is relatively little conflict between parents.

While courts historically gave mothers sole physical custody of their children, particularly children under five, that has been changing. Advocacy by fathers' rights organizations and increased parenting by fathers have increased the likelihood that judges will award joint custody or at least significant visiting privileges to dads,[18] as one of our respondents learned:

Initially, we thought we could get a mediator, share custody of our twins, split our assets quickly, and be done. We both found it was much harder emotionally and financially than we anticipated. I thought I would keep the house and have my daughters with me most of the time because I had always been the primary caretaker, but my now ex-husband decided he wanted the house and 50/50 custody, which was shocking.

Joint physical custody can be tough on older children and teenagers, who may rebel, unwilling to split their time between two homes. These disputes can sometimes be resolved by having time with one parent most of the time and the other during the summer or vacations. However, in other cases children may simply want to stay where their friends are.

When Karen and her husband, Jeremy, divorced, they assumed they would have joint physical custody of their son, but thirteen-year-old Edward balked. He wanted to stay in the same house and be near his friends. Karen and Jeremy originally planned to split their assets in a way that would allow Karen to keep the house, but after Edward rejected the idea of moving back and forth, Karen made a difficult decision. She proposed to Jeremy that they split their assets in a way that would allow Jeremy to keep the house and have Edward live with him. Not being with her son on a daily basis was extremely distressing, but, as she explained, "If Jeremy has primary physical custody, I'll see Edward multiple times a week . . . if *I* have primary custody, Jeremy will rarely visit. I want Edward to have a relationship with his father. That comes first."

Karen found a new place to live and after many months became used to the custody arrangement. Edward and his father got along well and bonded further over learning to cook. Thirty years later,

Karen feels good about the gift she gave her son, but she still tears up when she thinks about the five years she missed out on living with him.

Some parents approach the problem more creatively and turn the equation inside out, having the children stay in the house full-time while the two parents move back and forth between the house and their separate apartments. It takes considerable means to be able to fund three residences, but if you're able to, this solution may provide more stability for the children and minimize the number of physical transitions they need to make. However, this arrangement also requires that the two parents agree on how household work is divided and how and when it is done. During times of elevated tension, these additional discussion points may pile unneeded stress on to already heated debates.

Child Support and Alimony

The purpose of child support payments, which generally continue until the child is eighteen, is to allow children to live at the same economic level they had before the divorce. Spouses may also agree to continue child support payments until college graduation, but states vary in their rules about whether support for postsecondary education is required.[19]

If one parent has sole physical custody, they may be entitled to child support payments from the noncustodial parent. But even when there is joint physical custody, the parent with the lower income may receive child support payments. In addition to differences in income, the dollar amount of child support payments is affected by differences in the time each parent spends with the child, expenses involved in maintaining each home, number and age of children, cost of education and childcare, and any special needs a child may have.[20]

The fact that child support is awarded doesn't mean it will be paid in full, or at all. The US Census Bureau reported in 2018 that only about two-thirds of custodial parents who were owed child support received some child support payments from the noncustodial parent, and only 44 percent received the full amount.[21]

The purpose of alimony is quite different. Alimony is no longer seen as a permanent stream of payments to allow the less affluent spouse to maintain his or her former lifestyle. Nowadays, its purpose is to provide interim payments so that the spouse with the lower income has time to do what is necessary (e.g., get additional education, find a new job) to become self-supporting. The amount of alimony that is awarded depends on numerous factors: the income of the higher-earning spouse, the plan that the lower-earning spouse proposes to follow, the length of the marriage, the age and health of each spouse, the economic and noneconomic contributions each spouse made to the marriage, the generosity of the higher-earning spouse, and the two spouses' negotiating skills.[22] If the spouses cannot come to terms by themselves, the amount will be determined by the preferences of the judge who rules in their case.

Divorce in Our Changing Times

During the coronavirus pandemic, when stress peaked, the divorce rate spiked. It's not surprising that the added stress for couples led to more divorces, but it will be important to see whether that trend continues. Still, in the long run, the divorce rate may rise again with the projected increase in life expectancy. The authors of *The 100-Year Life* concur, pointing out that "being in an unhappy marriage when you are 70 and expect to live to 100 is very different from being in the same situation when life expectancy is 75."[23]

USING THE 5Cs FRAMEWORK: MANAGING TOUGH TIMES IN YOUR RELATIONSHIP (AND ENDING IT WHEN NECESSARY)

Relationships invariably have their ups and downs. During the low points of your relationship, if ending the relationship or marriage feels like an option you need to consider, the first thing to do is slow down. At times like these, it can be easy to get swept away by the idea of another life or another partner. However, these are often fantasies—escape routes that in a time of uncertainty and vulnerability may seem more appealing than they actually are. Instead of rushing toward what's new, try to slow down and consider at length whether ending the relationship is truly the right solution for you. If one (or both) of the partners in a relationship or marriage is unhappy, seek help from professionals, if possible. Above all, do whatever you can to reach a point of clear-eyed certainty before proceeding with dissolving your relationship, since this decision will have far-reaching consequences.

Step One: *Clarify*

Since ending a relationship affects multiple aspects of life, it can be helpful to consider the different elements one at a time. First, you may want to look at the love part of the equation by asking yourself questions such as the following:

> *How unhappy am I? Would I be happier alone? Do I want to find another mate? How will I feel about breaking the vow I made to stay together for life? What will be the effect of my decision on my spouse, whom I still care about? How will I feel about my spouse dating or marrying again? What will our custody arrangement be? What will be the effects of divorce on my children? What will it be like for me not to live full-time with them?*

Regarding money, consider questions such as these:

Can we afford to sustain two households? Can my spouse eventually support themself? What will our divorce settlement look like from a financial perspective? How do I feel about winding up with approximately half the assets I have now? How do I feel about giving (or receiving) child support? Do I think my spouse will honor child support agreements?

Given that this is only a partial discussion of the issues involved in deciding whether to end your relationship or pursue divorce, it's important to invest significant time and energy in this early part of the process—clarifying what you want, what you need, and what you're willing to endure and sacrifice.

If your relationship does seem to be ending, look at how to have the least acrimonious divorce possible while still creating a fair division of assets. When Gwyneth Paltrow and Chris Martin divorced in 2016, they worked with Katherine Woodward Thomas, a marriage and family therapist and the *New York Times* bestselling author of *Conscious Uncoupling.* This type of process can lay the groundwork for a future where former spouses maintain a friendly relationship, which benefits them, their children, and their eventual grandchildren.

You can also create this kind of amicable environment without professional help, although the process may take longer. After Myra and Jay were married, Jay suggested that they invite their former spouses to Thanksgiving dinner. Myra appreciated the benefits of allowing their family to come together in its new and expanded form, but she wasn't yet ready to participate. "Ask me again in five years," she replied at the time. When, five years later, he made that same suggestion, Myra agreed. By then, her ex-husband, Sam, had also remarried. Sam's new wife and young child came, in addition to Jay's ex-wife. The families have now celebrated holidays together for more than twenty-five years; Myra and Jay's grandchildren know no other way.

Step Two: *Communicate*

We've already underscored the importance of good communication in marriage; it becomes even more crucial in unwinding a marriage. Make sure you're clear about how and when you'd like to communicate. It can be helpful to set up guidelines about when to call, text, or communicate in person. Be mindful of when *not* to communicate, too. There are times when biting your tongue and saying nothing may be the better option. The trick is to think carefully before you speak. Remember that you can't take back what's been said, but that generally (although not always) if you are silent at one point, you will have an opportunity to speak about the issue later.

Step Three: Consider a Broad Range of *Choices*

As we've noted, many choices are involved in deciding whether or not to divorce, including how to divide assets and share custody of children. As you consider those choices, keep your intention in mind. Even the most conscious uncoupling may involve choices that could feel suboptimal at best and unfair or hurtful at worst. If you keep your overall priority in mind as you move through the process, it may help ease the sting of each individual choice.

Sometimes, people considering divorce decide to have a trial separation first to see what it feels like to live on their own, thereby broadening their range of choices.[24] But trial separations are unlikely to fix troubled marriages. It is estimated that about 80 percent of trial separations are followed by divorce.[25]

Step Four: *Check In*

Before you get too far into the process, it may be helpful to check in with others who have navigated divorce and ask them what they learned as a result. Their perspectives might surprise you and cause you to think differently about the outcomes of decisions related to divorce. You may also want to check in with close friends and confidants—not only for their perspectives but also because they will be crucial members of the support system you'll need during and after the process.

Step Five: Explore Likely *Consequences*

As you're making your decision, look at the short- and long-term consequences of splitting and of staying together. Either way, there will be consequences related to money, love, happiness, lifestyle, and children (if you have any). Again, take your time. Think this through at length. By making your decisions about divorce in a thoughtful way, you may be able to minimize rancor and be in a better position to move forward.

Sometimes seemingly awful consequences have a silver lining. When Myra's first husband, Sam, left her, he told her that one day she would see that he was doing her a favor. Too distraught to agree, she assumed that day would never come. However, within a year, Myra took Sam to lunch and thanked him. "You did, indeed, do me a favor," she told him. Later, when she remarried, she took him to lunch again. Marriage number two was so much happier than marriage number one!

CHAPTER EIGHT EXERCISE:

How Might You Strengthen Your Relationship?

This exercise is a form of CHECK-IN—a self-assessment of your relationship at a point in time. Select a number to indicate how much you agree or disagree with each statement. Write the number next to each question; then add all nine numbers to get a total score. To go further (and add the COMMUNICATE step), consider asking your partner to complete this exercise from their perspective and then compare responses.

Strongly Disagree 1—2—3—4—5—6—7 Strongly Agree

COMMUNICATION

1. We fight to solve problems rather than to prove each other wrong or shame each other.

   ____

2. We discuss the state of our relationship regularly, sharing how we feel honestly.

   ____

3. We listen to each other actively, empathizing and commiserating instead of criticizing or leaping to suggesting solutions.

   ____

ROMANCE AND SEXUALITY

1. We have date nights and find quality time to spend with just the two of us.

   ____

2. We are both satisfied with our sex life.

   ____

3. We tell each other we love each other and show affection consistently.

   ____

MONEY

1. We have a way of combining our finances (or not) that is working for both of us.

___

2. We are on the same page when it comes to our spending and saving habits, or we've found a mutually satisfactory way to resolve our differences.

___

CHANGE

1. We are committed to supporting each other, even when one of us changes our ideas, opinions, or goals.

___

2. We have a track record of successfully navigating transitions or shifts in outlook.

___

Scoring: Add up your scores; we encourage you to discuss your answers with your partner.

Score of 10–29: Every relationship goes through rough patches. Even if this one is temporary, you may want to consider couples therapy. If you're already in therapy, we encourage you to discuss this exercise with your partner and therapist.

Score of 30–49: Your relationship is strong in some areas and has vulnerabilities in others. Where did you score the lowest, and how might you prioritize those areas for changes?

Score of 50–70: Congratulations on putting in the work to keep your relationship strong. Because relationships require ongoing work, where might you want to focus in the future?

NINE

THE SENIOR YEARS

Caring for Elders

It was 10:00 a.m. on a Thursday morning in October, and Abby and Ross had just signed the papers for their first house. As they left the escrow office, they blinked in the bright sunlight, giddy with excitement and a sense of possibility. Abby looked down at her phone, noticing that she'd missed a call from her father. She checked her voice mail, expecting to hear a congratulatory message. As soon as she began playing the message, however, she stopped cold. The news he relayed was so hard to digest, she played it twice to be sure she'd heard her father's words correctly the first time.

"Hi, Abby. There's been an accident. Your mom fell on the steps when she was leaving the house this morning and hit her head. We're in the hospital now—they think she has a fractured skull. Please call me."

Abby soon learned that her mother was in the intensive care unit with brain swelling and bleeding, and her condition was unstable. In an instant, Abby's thoughts turned away from what to cook for a celebratory meal with Ross to what to pack for her trip to New Jersey, where her parents lived. Unsure of what she would have to face, she included a black dress in case she needed to attend her mother's funeral.

While she didn't end up needing that dress on the trip, the accident catapulted her into a world of difficult conversations and decisions about caring for her parents that she hadn't anticipated having to face for quite some time. It all came as a shock, as it does to many whose loved ones have an accident or fall ill. Without advance planning, these sudden changes in mobility, accessibility, and awareness for our loved ones can be more personally and financially jarring than they need to be. In this chapter, we'll look at how to anticipate some of these eventualities to minimize the challenges that come with a loved one's decline in health.

THE NEW "HYBRID" RETIREMENT

On the day she fell, Abby's mother was sixty-eight, getting ready to go to her job as a school librarian for the very last time before officially retiring the following day. Retirement is a quintessential example of a decision involving both money and love—when to retire, where to retire to, and how to finance that phase of life. This is a decision you will want to discuss with your parents and other loved ones as they approach retirement age. (This is a moving target, but for the sake of argument, let's say when they turn sixty.) For our purposes, we assume retirement is a decision your parents, in-laws, or other older adults in your life will need to make more immediately, but if you yourself are approaching retirement age, it's time for you to think about this decision as well.

If broaching the conversation about retirement with your parents and other loved ones (or even considering it for yourself) feels like something you'd rather delay, you're not alone. Retirement can be a touchy subject. One of Myra's students shared, "I had trouble talking to my dad about retirement. It felt to me like his retirement would be the beginning of his end. The dad I knew and loved was a dad who loved his job, and when he retired, that dad would be no more." Myra urged her to overcome her aversion to the conversation: "Your dad is much more than his love of work. I suspect when you talk to him, you will find that this is all more complicated than either of you thought at first. Really, there can be many rewarding years for him after retirement."

As you begin to discuss retirement with your parents, if they're not already retired, it's important to realize that today that phase of life often looks quite different from the way it did a few decades ago. In the past, retirement was an all-or-nothing proposition: either you were retired or you were still working. Until recently, retirement was like a light switch that you flipped from on (working) to off (retired) at a single moment. A better analogy for what retirement looks like now is a dimmer switch that slides up and down to allow for different levels of activity over time.

With average life expectancy lengthening (it increased by ten years between 1960 and 2015), the number of years that need to be financed from savings has also increased.[1] At the same time, fewer people have defined benefit pensions that guarantee them a certain amount of income every year. As a result, while potential retirees may want to work fewer hours, they may not be financially able to quit working entirely.[2] Also, because the labor market is now more fluid (people switch jobs more frequently than they once did, and more people are working part-time as part of the gig economy), workers who retire may well find part-time work. Finally, today's retirees are often seeking a purposeful way to spend their days, which might mean having an encore career that focuses on a cause they care about.[3]

Another factor that makes cross-generation discussions about retirement difficult is that young people today who are struggling with educational debt and unable to purchase a home may view their own retirement prospects as dim. To them, retirement is some idyllic concept that might never be possible for them. Therefore, they find it painful to discuss their parents' retirement. "Someday," they may think unsympathetically, "I wish I could have your retirement problems."

As you think about the concept of retirement, it's important to remember that giving up work is not always voluntary. Some two-thirds of people are forced to stop working before they're ready because of health challenges, workplace ageism, or other factors.[4] Whether your parents plan to retire or not, they may one day find themselves unable to work, which would have financial implications for them and possibly for you as well. For all these reasons, it's important to discuss the issue of retirement proactively with them.

When Abby's mother fell, her father had already retired from his thirty-year career at a national public health nonprofit and was serving as an independent consultant to national and international health agencies. His consulting work required that he travel for weeks at a time, sometimes to far-flung places such as India and Finland, for conferences he helped organize. He loved this aspect of his work, but when the neurologist showed him his wife's brain scans, he realized that his consulting work was no longer feasible. That evening, he emailed his clients an update, letting them know about his wife's accident and explaining why he would not be able to deliver the work they had agreed to in their latest contract. With that one accident, his postretirement plan was upended; his full-time job would now be managing his wife's care.

BROACHING THE TOPIC OF RETIREMENT

When Social Security was first enacted in 1935, retirement age was 65 and life expectancy for men was 58.[5] Currently, the average age of retirement is 64, and almost two-thirds of retirees leave their jobs between the ages of 57 and 66. But today at age 65 men can expect to live another 18 years and women another 21 years.[6]

Going forward, life expectancy will increase still further. For those born since 2000, life expectancy is anticipated to be slightly over 100 years, according to some demographers.[7] Clearly, this will require changes in the average retirement age. Retiring at 65 and expecting retirement savings to last for 35 years with no income from employment will be unrealistic for almost everyone.

Thanks to the Age Discrimination in Employment Act of 1967, it is illegal for an employer to require mandatory retirement at a particular age, although some management job categories are exempted from the law.[8] As a result, decisions about when to retire voluntarily depend on numerous factors, including overall health, the physical demands of the job, job satisfaction, and financial situation.

As you try to help your parents or other loved ones think about retirement, keep in mind the various factors that influence decisions about voluntary retirement. If they love their work, does it make sense for them to try to continue it for as long as possible? If they don't, will they need financial help from you if they retire or work less? Will they need other types of support? Is there time for them to save more for retirement?

These are questions that warrant ongoing discussion and, if possible, guidance from a trusted expert. Meeting with a financial advisor can be a good way to begin the conversation; most advisors have a list of questions that prompt their clients to consider what they want their later years to look like, and these can serve as good starters for you to discuss with older relatives.

One important, though often unasked, question is how likely they are to be bored without work. How will they organize their days when work is no longer the central activity? One of Myra's colleagues would not "permit" her husband to retire unless he had a plan for what he would do every day. She was convinced that without such a plan, he would be exceedingly bored. In her view, he had very little in his life other than his work and their relationship, and she was not prepared to be the only activity in his life.

Eventually, her prodding prompted him to begin taking courses at local colleges, and after he retired, that became his main activity. Over a decade, he took more than forty courses. After a long career in the sciences, he decided to take only courses in the humanities and social sciences. He feels his new knowledge has given him a new lease on life and is grateful that his wife pushed him to think carefully about how he would spend his retirement time.

Others may not find the idea of taking classes appealing but want to find ways to be of service. Organizations such as Encore.org help adults over age fifty use the skills they honed in their first careers to have a second act—an encore career—focused on helping others, whether it's placing retired physicians in health clinics that serve historically marginalized populations or matching seasoned professionals with social sector organizations.

Some people are happy in retirement with much less structure. They enjoy reading, playing cards or chess with friends, or going to the gym more frequently than they could when they worked. Abby's in-laws fall into this category; her father-in-law plays a mean Ping-Pong game, while her mother-in-law maintains multiple standing bridge games each week. One of Myra's friends centered his retirement on creating and leading a ROMEO group (Retired Old Men Eating Out). He realized that what he liked best about retirement was the freedom to have breakfast, lunch, or dinner with his friends, and he decided to formalize the process with three longtime buddies who lived nearby. They agreed that Monday would be "eat out" day, and they would email one another on Sunday night to see which meal it would be. Eventually, they were eating out together three or four times a week, and they decided to give their group a "proper Shakespearean name."

FINANCING RETIREMENT

Figuring out how to spend time is one top priority; making sure the financial foundation you require is on solid footing is, of course, another. Financial planners often say that $1 million is a ballpark figure of the amount needed to retire comfortably at age sixty-five; others recommend an amount sufficient to yield 80 percent to 90 percent of preretirement income for each year of projected retirement.[9]

The amount required in retirement will depend on factors including cost of living, financial portfolio performance, risk tolerance, and longevity. If that seems complicated, once your parents retire, they will need to figure out how much of their nest egg to spend at various points in time. William F. Sharpe, winner of the Nobel Prize in Economic Sciences, said that figuring out how to manage funds in retirement was "the nastiest, hardest problem I've ever looked at."[10]

To get a tailored estimate of necessary funds takes considerable financial savvy, whether it's your own or that of a trusted financial planner. Since budgets are especially paramount, be sure that your or your parents' advisor charges a fee based on the size and performance of their portfolio, not on the commission they receive on the investment products they sell.

The National Retirement Risk Index (NRRI), calculated by researchers at Boston College, found that in 2016, half of working-age households had insufficient savings to fund retirement at a level similar to their preretirement standard of living.[11]

According to the US Social Security Administration, 20 percent of married couples and 40 percent of single people rely on Social Security for 90 percent or more of their income. To put that into context, in May 2021, the average monthly Social Security payment was $1,431.[12] Social Security benefits can be claimed starting at age sixty-two, and while benefits are higher if you wait until your mid-sixties or age seventy to claim them, many people need the money earlier.

Women have a particularly difficult time financing retirement, largely because their preretirement earnings are lower than men's. Not only do women earn less than men; they also have more years out of the workforce when they are raising children. The method by which Social Security benefits are calculated penalizes time out of the workforce.

If you think it likely that you may be called upon to help your parents financially at some point, it will be helpful if you can get relevant information from them in advance. If they resist sharing details of their finances, this may be a tough assignment. Hopefully, you can prevail by explaining that you will be far more successful in providing whatever help they may need if you have some advance "warning" to do some planning yourself. If your parents will need your help in managing their finances at some point, it will be much easier for you if you have their computer passwords, the names of their accountant and attorney (if they have them), and the place in their home where they store relevant information before you have to go madly searching on your own.

WHERE TO LIVE IN RETIREMENT

Data from 2020 indicate that about half of retirees stayed in the same home they lived in when they were in their early fifties. Another 17 percent moved to a new home when they retired and stayed in that home until they died; 16 percent stayed in their original home until their eighties and then moved, sometimes to go to a retirement community and sometimes because of health changes. The smallest group, about 14 percent, moved several times during retirement.[13]

Some seniors would like to sell their home and move to a smaller home or a retirement community but are dissuaded from doing that because of tax laws. Selling a home while both spouses are alive triggers capital gains tax, which, if your parents have owned their home for a long time, may be considerable. However, if one spouse dies, the other is able to sell the home without paying capital gains tax.

WHEN TO STOP DRIVING

One of the toughest topics to discuss with your parents or other older relatives is when to stop driving. In our society, driving provides independence that is hard to replace with other types of transportation unless you live in a central city with excellent public transportation. As any teenager will tell you, a driver's license is a mark of adulthood, a pass to freedom. As we age, however, driving skills often decline, often without our conscious awareness. Even when people are cognizant of their decreased skill behind the wheel, they may not take action because they can't fathom life without their ability to drive.

Myra realized that her mother was no longer a safe driver when her preteen children reported that their grandma was "driving funny" when she picked them up from school. Myra hadn't seen her mother drive in years because when they were together, Myra always took the wheel. After hearing her children's report, she asked her mother to drive and confirmed their observations. Myra suggested to her mother that she stop driving, but her mother refused. It wasn't until her mother was stopped by a police officer for erratic driving and forced to take a driving test, which she failed, that she handed over her car keys.

Losing the right to a driver's license, that precious symbol of freedom and independence, can be a humiliating, shameful experience. People may feel devalued, as if they've been downgraded, deemed unworthy as a card-carrying adult. Not being able to drive is also a massive inconvenience. Even though ride-hailing and delivery services make it easier to give up driving than in the past, without your own car keys, independence is considerably diminished.

Perhaps one day, when autonomous cars become safe and popular, that will no longer be the case, but for now, tread lightly when you approach elders with the topic of stopping driving. Also keep in mind that drivers over the age of seventy are, on average, safer drivers than those aged thirty-five to fifty-four. They are less likely to mix drinking or texting with driving, are less likely to speed or ignore road signs, have fewer crashes reported to the police, and are less likely to be involved in a fatal accident.[14]

Jane Brody, former health columnist for the *New York Times*, suggests that older adults create an advance directive for driving in the same way they create one for medical care.[15] The document would specify the future circumstances under which they would give up their car keys and perhaps make it easier for all concerned when those circumstances become reality. It's an interesting idea that you may want to try with your family!

TALKING WITH YOUR PARENTS AND OTHER RELATIVES ABOUT END-OF-LIFE PLANNING

If talking about retirement feels awkward, raising topics related to end-of-life planning can feel downright intimidating. As a society, we avoid facing realities such as illness and death, especially when it comes to our loved ones and ourselves. One survey respondent shared that while end-of-life issues weigh heavily on her mind, "it feels like a taboo topic that we have not had much luck broaching with family." Oftentimes people tell themselves these issues are far off in some distant future, so it's a conversation they can reasonably delay.

Another respondent noted:

> *No one ever thinks they're old until something "old" happens to them. My father had a heart transplant, and he needed someone to move in with him. I had to manage that. All of a sudden, he gave me passwords and directions on where to find things. I had just started a new job. The first thing I wanted to do was prove myself in my role, but I found myself working from his hospital room so he wasn't alone the rest of the day. I had a young child, too; my son was a year old when it happened.*

End-of-life planning isn't something to push off until "someday," as many families (including Abby's) have learned the hard way. Anyone can have an accident, be in a car crash, or experience unexpected health issues at any time. Just as no one gets married expecting to get divorced, we tend to avoid facing the possibility that these life-changing events can happen to us, too. It's understandable, but denial won't help when something unfortunate does happen. Instead, it's far better to overcome our resistance and craft a plan in case the worst does happen—and once a plan is in place, hope it's not needed for a very long time.

WILLS AND TRUSTS

Nearly half of Americans over fifty-five do not have a will.[16] When someone dies without a will, the court is forced to determine the disposition of their property. This often means that their potential heirs may be saddled with costly attorney fees and even costlier family squabbles. Ensuring that everyone in your family has a will (and a trust, when advisable) can save you and your loved ones from these financial and personal burdens.

You can write a will with the help of a lawyer, or you can do it online, using suitable forms you access, usually for a fee. If you or your family own real estate or have investment accounts, it's best to consult a lawyer to discuss estate planning, since you may be best served by creating a trust in addition to a will. Creating a revocable living trust and transferring assets into the trust can save the named beneficiary time and money, not to mention making things easier should the trustor become ill or incapacitated. (Wills take effect only when someone dies.)

Wendy had an all-too-common experience when her mother, who owned the ranch she'd grown up on, passed away. At the time of her death, her mother still lived on the ranch, but she had failed to put the property into a trust. Ownership of the ranch went to her second husband, Wendy's stepfather. He subsequently married someone Wendy didn't know. When, sometime later, his health began to fail, the ranch was passed down to his second wife. To this day, Wendy is heartbroken thinking of a stranger inheriting her beloved childhood home, when it all could have gone so differently if her mother had created a trust.

As you work with family members to encourage them to write a will (and trust, when needed), be aware that they may not want to discuss the details of what these documents say. That's understandable, but you can still raise an issue that you feel deserves discussion.

Nadine was in her mid-fifties when her mother, who was in her mid-nineties, began to experience problems with her heart. Nadine lived close to her mother, visited her several times a week, called her every day, and helped her move to an assisted living facility. Nadine's older brother, who also lived close by, hardly ever visited or called. One day, as her mother was complaining to Nadine (yet again) about never seeing or hearing from her son, Nadine asked whether she'd ever considered leaving him a smaller share of her estate. Her mother became angry and told Nadine to mind her own business. A few days later, her mother brought up the topic, unprompted. She explained that if she gave her son a smaller inheritance than she gave Nadine, he would think she loved him less, and since she loved her two children equally, she could not do that. Nadine was unhappy with her mother's thinking but grateful for the conversation. After her mother died, she told Myra: "I think if not for that talk, I would be really angry with my mother. But now I'm only a little angry. And I do understand. So I'm glad I raised the question with her."

When you write a will or trust, you also need to specify the executor of your estate. That person has the legal responsibility of using the money in the estate to satisfy your existing financial obligations, such as bills and taxes, and then disposing of your property in accordance with the will. Being an executor can be a large or small task, depending on the size of the estate, the number of relatives involved as heirs, and the degree of dissension among them.

Will your parents or in-laws appoint an adult child, a sibling, a friend, or a professional as executor? A professional will take a small percentage of the estate, but if no relative or friend is willing or able to serve as executor, a professional may be necessary.

Regardless, be sure to suggest that your parents or in-laws confer with the person they want to appoint as executor and get their assent.

Your parents or other relatives also need to appoint someone who has durable financial power of attorney, which will enable them to access certain financial assets if your parents or other relatives become ill or incapacitated. The person who has power of attorney will be able to access their individual retirement accounts (IRAs) and use the funds to help pay for their care.

WHO WILL CARE FOR LOVED ONES WHEN THEY CAN NO LONGER CARE FOR THEMSELVES?

In 2018, there were 52.4 million people over the age of sixty-five, which was one in every seven Americans.[17] Although about half of Americans will need eldercare in their home or community in their later years, the vast majority will not be able to afford it.[18] Many erroneously believe that these costs will be covered by Medicare, but Medicare does not cover long-term care. Medicaid, which is basically a welfare program, does cover it, but only after you've spent down almost all of your own assets, including the value of your home and car (and you must spend them down at least five years before you apply for Medicaid).[19]

Long-term care insurance is supplemental insurance that helps cover the cost of services that aren't covered by regular medical insurance, such as help with the activities of daily living (including bathing, getting dressed, and getting in and out of bed). The Administration for Community Living estimates that at some point, 60 percent of people will need assistance with activities of daily living.[20]

Most people who purchase long-term care insurance do so in

their fifties or sixties because a policy must be in place *before* any debilitating conditions develop. It's expensive, but given the fact that the average lifetime cost of long-term care is $172,000,[21] and the average annual cost of a skilled nursing facility ranges from just under $100,000 for a semiprivate room to more than $100,000 for a private room, it can be a very prudent investment.[22]

Only about 7 percent of those over age fifty have long-term care insurance.[23] It has also become difficult to obtain long-term care insurance if you have any ongoing medical problems, because when such insurance was first offered in the 1980s, insurance companies underestimated the high cost of future payouts, and they have since restricted the number of people they're willing to cover.

Many policy makers have concluded that relying on the private market for long-term care insurance is not a viable strategy and have called for long-term care insurance to be funded by taxpayers. The State of Washington passed such a program in 2019.[24]

Another aspect of eldercare that needs public policy attention is the low wages of care workers.[25] In the summer of 2021, the average earnings of a home health-care worker were $13 per hour and $4,000 per year in overtime.[26] On average, health-care aides in nursing homes earned about $54,210 annually (about $26 per hour).[27] In part because of these low earnings, many nursing homes have difficulty recruiting and retaining staff, especially for nights and weekends, a challenge that has only been exacerbated by the pandemic.

Most long-term care for the elderly is provided by family and friends, and the majority of those caregivers are women. About two-thirds of older people with long-term care needs rely solely on family and friends to provide care, and another 30 percent supplement care from family and friends with help from paid providers.[28]

Often, students in Myra's class say that they expect to care for their elderly parents or in-laws in their own home. But they rarely have thought through the implications of such a decision. Moreover, most have never discussed the matter with their parents or in-laws, many of whom might well prefer *not* to be cared for in their adult child's home. A recent Gallup poll found that although half of adult children said they would care for an elderly parent in their home, only one-third of seniors said they would like that arrangement.[29]

Eldercare is stressful and difficult. The US Department of Health and Human Services' Office on Women's Health warns that women especially are at risk of the harmful health effects of caregiver stress. These health problems include depression and anxiety as well as physical illness.

Myra's second husband had Parkinson's disease, and in his final years he required increased care in their home. Even though she received some help from paid caregivers, she can attest to the heavy toll that caregiving exacts upon the caretaker's own health and well-being.

Hiring a geriatric care manager, who advises family members about eldercare options for their loved ones, can be helpful, especially for people whose older relatives live in another city. However, their help is also advantageous when you live in the same city as your loved one, as Myra experienced. A care manager can help you manage medication refills, doctors' appointments, and insurance company intransigence. They can also provide suggestions for enrichment activities. Perhaps most important, they can meet your loved one and help you decide whether they are best cared for in your own home or in assisted living.

A Helpful Resource About Caring for Elderly Loved Ones

In her book *A Bittersweet Season: Caring for Our Aging Parents—and Ourselves*, Jane Gross (a former *New York Times* journalist) writes about her experience caring for her eighty-five-year-old mother for the last several years of her mother's life. Using her personal experience as a guide, she imparts hard-earned wisdom about navigating the eldercare "system" (in quotes because, as Gross recounts, it is by no means a coordinated, well-oiled machine). Gross's book is not an easy read, but it can help us all understand the issues facing our elderly loved ones when they lose the ability to care for themselves.

ADVANCE HEALTH-CARE DIRECTIVE

In addition to a will (and possibly a trust), you and your loved ones each need an advance health care directive, which lays out in writing what each person wants to have happen if they are unable to make health decisions for themselves. It also appoints a health-care proxy, otherwise known as someone granted durable power of attorney for health care, who will follow instructions when making decisions in your stead, including possible life-and-death decisions. The health-care directive needs to be witnessed by someone other than the proxy, and the proxy and a physician should each receive a copy.

Writing an advance health-care directive requires considerable thought. Even more thought is needed to write Portable Medical Orders, often called a POLST (Physician Orders for Life-Sustaining Treatment), which is an order to physicians concerning which life-sustaining treatments you do and do not want under different circumstances.

If your loved one has a terminal illness, do they want every treatment possible to keep them alive? Do they want to be taken to a hospital where those treatments can be provided, or would they rather remain at home with palliative care and a hospice nurse and have only those medications that make them more comfortable? Under what circumstances would they like their health-care proxy to issue a DNR (do not resuscitate) order?

In thinking about these matters, it may be helpful to consult *Being Mortal: Medicine and What Matters in the End*, a book by Atul Gawande, MD. Dr. Gawande argues that for most people, the goal at the end of life is not staying alive at all costs but living meaningfully and dying peacefully.

During the past fifteen years, the percentage of people who die at home has increased, and in 2017, slightly more people died at home than in a hospital.[30] It is important for people to recognize their own end-of-life goals and communicate them to physicians, spouses, children, and friends. The job of the rest of us is to further those goals.

ASSISTED SUICIDE

While difficult to consider, assisted suicide is another option at the end of life. Ten states and the District of Columbia now permit physicians to assist in suicide under certain highly circumscribed circumstances.[31] In *A Matter of Death and Life*, a moving account of physician-assisted suicide by Marilyn Yalom and her husband, Irvin Yalom, Marilyn explains her reasons for wanting to end her life at age eighty-seven. Suffering from multiple myeloma, she found the side effects of her chemotherapy unbearable. When her doctor told her that she had about two months to live, she prepared for physician-assisted suicide. She wrote: "The idea of death does not frighten me. . . . Death at the age of 87 is no tragedy. . . . After ten months of feeling awful most of the time, it's a relief to know that my misery will come to an end."[32] Her husband and four children were all with her at her home at the time of her death.

USING THE 5Cs FRAMEWORK: INITIATING "THE TALK" (ABOUT LATE-LIFE MATTERS)

While it can be tempting to put off conversations about eldercare and end-of-life planning, it's essential to push through the discomfort and have these conversations with loved ones before the decisions are forced on you.

How can you initiate them? Tailor your approach to whatever you think will suit your loved ones best. This may mean reassuring them of your desire to support them in what they will want and need in the later stage of their lives. Humor may work better for others. However you approach these conversations, be clear that their answers will affect you and them. Also, make sure to include topics related to physical health, mental health, and financial health. Like love and money, they are all intertwined.

Step One: *Clarify*

Before initiating "the talk," start by clarifying what matters most to *you* over the long term. Do you want to maintain your independence for as long as possible? Do you want to transition into retirement gradually over time rather than stopping suddenly? Knowing where you personally stand on these topics can make it easier for you to discuss them with others. If your immediate focus is on elderly relatives, ask similar questions, but with a focus on how much time, energy, and money you're realistically willing and able to provide for their care. These are difficult questions to face, and being honest, most of all with yourself, is paramount. Vowing to do "whatever is needed" for an elderly loved one is a promise very few can keep; caregiving is costly, and it is often a nearly 24/7 undertaking that may require you, as caregiver, to quit paid work even as your expenses rise. Remember, love and self-sacrifice are not synonymous, and considering your own life—your relationships, children, career, health, and more—is a mark of responsibility, not selfishness.

As time passes, you may change your mind and your plan, but having a working hypothesis in place can be helpful. The research process can even be fun. One couple who knew they wanted to retire in a college town have continually visited various college towns on vacation, trying to get a feel for whether they'd be happy retiring there as a gay couple. It's become an ongoing project, keeping a running list of their favorite college towns and updating the list as they visit additional ones.

Step Two: *Communicate*

Once you're clearer on what you yourself want and need, communicate with your parents (and in-laws and grandparents) about these topics before it becomes an acute need—ideally by the time your parents are in their sixties. You will do your family a great service if you initiate tough dialogues proactively. Everyone is likely to be calmer, kinder, and more rational at a relaxed lunch than in a hospital emergency room. You may even discover that your loved ones are more comfortable having this conversation than you are.

In addition to talking with the senior members of your family, discuss these issues with your siblings. Sometimes these conversations can be fraught because issues that go all the way back to the sandbox suddenly raise their ugly heads, and siblings find themselves playing roles they thought they'd shed years ago. (Jane Gross writes about this extensively in *A Bittersweet Season.*) However, someday there will likely be a need for unanimity and cooperation among siblings regarding care for parents. By facing the issues before a crisis strikes, you are likely to endure the hard times more gracefully. Which siblings will manage the process? If parents need funds, which siblings will provide them? If parents need physical care or visits, which siblings will step up? In the same way that divorce can be acrimonious or civil, helping parents to negotiate aging or illness can bring the family closer together or pull it apart irrevocably.

Step Three: Consider a Broad Range of *Choices*

Make sure you have a sense of the choices available, especially for living arrangements. These options can range from aging in place with and without assistance to moving in with children to living in a life plan community (previously known as a continuing care retirement community, or CCRC).

It may make sense to use a different combination of these choices over time. After her mother's accident, Abby's parents moved to a condo in California and managed her mother's care through home health aides. Five years later, Abby's aunt came to visit and saw how much Abby's mom had declined since her last visit and how much harder it was for her dad to manage her mom's care. After her aunt encouraged her to explore additional options, Abby did some research and asked her father whether he'd considered life plan communities. Assuming they were too expensive, he hadn't looked into any. Abby encouraged him to keep an open mind and at least tour some facilities. Together, they found one nearby that accepted her mother's insurance. Her parents moved in the following year, with her father in the independent living area and her mother in the skilled nursing wing.

Step Four: *Check In*

After considering different options, reach out to friends and family who have already had to navigate eldercare decisions. What did they encounter? If you are thinking that you may want your parents to live with you at some point, talk with people who made that same decision. Discuss it with your parents as well. Intergenerational living arrangements can be beset by friction and misunderstanding, particularly if they are not preceded by extensive discussion and planning, if the arrangement goes on for longer than expected, or if the parent becomes increasingly disabled.

Keep in mind that every situation is different and try to get a few different perspectives. Since Abby had to navigate issues of eldercare earlier than many of her friends, she has become a go-to resource on the topic, which has even led to several of her friends' parents moving into the same life plan community her parents found. Her father, too, has benefited from checking in with—and ultimately hiring—various consultants with relevant expertise at different points in the process, from downsizing experts to insurance advisors. He has gotten referrals to these consultants from his caregiver support group, which has proven an important source of empathy and sustenance.

Step Five: Consider Likely *Consequences*

Research tells us that adult children may initially be enthusiastic about having their parents live with them, but as time goes on, they may feel increasingly hemmed in and angry. In the role of caregiver, they lose their freedom and the ability to adequately fund their own retirement because of the cost of caring for their aging parents. This is one potential consequence to consider, and it is an example of the result of not being brutally honest with yourself about how much you're able to give to your parents in later life. There is no shame in doing what you can for your elderly relatives—and then stopping short of self-sacrifice. After all, if your later life puts the onus on your family, you're perpetuating the cycle, asking your younger relatives to give more than they reasonably can, just as you did. Instead, address possible consequences beforehand, however challenging this may seem. When it's feasible, discuss with your loved ones how you might handle these issues before they overtake your relationship and, potentially, your life.

The coronavirus pandemic has highlighted many of the challenges related to senior living facilities. The Centers for Disease Control and Prevention reported that people over sixty-five accounted for 80 percent of all COVID-19 deaths, with nearly half of those in nursing homes or other long-term care institutions.[33] Not included in those numbers are those who died of conditions stemming from the isolation created by many months of lockdown, which can be particularly destructive for people living with Alzheimer's disease.[34]

It's too early to tell whether COVID-19 will permanently change people's attitudes toward where they want to live out their days, but one interesting trend is the increased demand for ADUs (accessory dwelling units). Also called casitas or granny flats, these are detached, self-contained living areas on the property of a single-family home. One San Francisco Bay Area realtor shared recently that she used to calculate the price of ADUs by using 50 percent of the cost per square foot of the main dwelling. However, this realtor noted that the prices people are paying for homes with ADUs are so astronomical that she's now pricing ADUs at 150 percent of the cost per square foot of the main dwelling. She shared that many of the people buying homes with ADUs are planning for their parents to move into them.

A Note on the Sandwich Generation

More and more people find themselves in the so-called sandwich generation—raising children while simultaneously caring for elderly relatives. According to the Pew Research Center, nearly half (47 percent) of adults in their forties and fifties have a parent aged sixty-five or older and are either raising a young child or financially supporting a grown child (eighteen or older). In addition, approximately one in seven middle-aged adults (15 percent) are providing financial support to both an aging parent and a child.[35] This trend will only increase; with the baby boomer generation continuing to age, the share of the population over sixty-five is projected to more than double over the next forty years.[36]

Caring for multiple generations at once can take a toll on multiple fronts. One of our survey respondents relocated to be closer to her parents, and while it gave her peace of mind to be living in the same city, the move had other consequences:

For the next four years, I went to [my dad and stepmother's] house at least once a week to check on them, attend doctor's appointments, and do what I could to help. My dad had some early signs of dementia, so talking to him was hard. I had to find ways to explain things to him that he could understand and remember. I am sure I could have read books on how to help my situation, but I barely had time to work, sleep, be in a committed relationship, take care of my son, and drive thirty minutes one way to help my parents (mostly my dad), not to mention all the hospital stays over the years. My dad passed away this year, and while I am grief-stricken, I have to say that a weight has been lifted from me, emotionally and mentally.

If you find yourself providing care for several generations, make sure that you are getting support for yourself. Individual therapy can be helpful, as can seeking out caregiver support groups and employee resource groups in which you can connect with others in similar caregiving situations. Also make sure to block out time for activities that help you manage stress, whether that's exercise, time in nature, outings with friends, or a creative pursuit. As you consider how to triage your time, you may find AARP's guidance helpful; the organization advises those caring for more than one person to "provide care by need, not 'fairness.'" In other words, don't feel that you need to give everyone you're caring for equal amounts of your time.[37]

In addition, do your best to find joy in the small moments and the silver linings. Esther Koch, who took care of her mother for several years at the end of her mother's life, has written about the joy of caring for a loved one, reminding readers to "kiss the joy as it flies by" in an article of the same title.[38] Having recognized that these years would be the last she would enjoy with her mother, she recollects the pleasures she experienced finding new, unexpected activities—drives to the beach, concerts, and picnics in the park.

Like Esther, Myra found that while caretaking for her husband was both wearing and worrying, it provided new opportunities for closeness. A Pew Research Center study reported that caregivers find it very meaningful to provide care.[39] The very act of providing care can itself result in increased intimacy.[40] Alison Gopnik, professor of philosophy and psychology at the University of California, Berkeley, postulates that we don't provide care to people because we love them; we love them because of the acts of care we do for them.

CHAPTER NINE EXERCISE:

How Can You Prepare for "the Talk" with Older Loved Ones?

This exercise focuses on the CLARIFY and COMMUNICATE steps of our 5Cs framework, since the COMMUNICATE step can be especially daunting here. First, give some thought to the kind of conversations you want to have about retirement, eldercare, and end-of-life issues.

Which relatives or older loved ones would you like to talk with?

____

What are the main topics you would like to discuss with them?

____

____

What do you hope to accomplish in the conversations?

____

____

Pick one conversation to start with. How will you begin your conversation? Why?

____

____

Then create a dress rehearsal for the conversation. Ask someone who knows your parents (or other relative or loved one) to play their part in this conversation while you play the part of yourself. Start the conversation and see where it goes.

____

____

Reflect on the dress rehearsal. What did you learn? Which topics or strategies did it suggest that you hadn't thought of before?

____

____

Did you experience hot-button issues? Do you have any thoughts on how to defuse them?

____

____

Did it suggest anything to you about timing and how long you should plan on the conversation taking?

____

____

Did it give you more confidence about holding the real conversation? If not, how can you increase your confidence?

____

____

TEN

BE THE CHANGE

Changing the Work/Family System (How You Can Play a Part)

Dawn was a successful recruiter at a well-respected consulting firm. In their five years of marriage, Dawn's wife had been open to having kids, but Dawn hadn't wanted any. Instead, they'd focused on earning the title "Best Aunts Ever" to their nephews and nieces. However, as Dawn neared her thirty-fifth birthday, she felt a maternal twinge that hadn't been there previously. One day on a hike with her wife, she raised the idea of having kids. This time, her wife admitted that she'd been longing to be a mother, too, but hadn't said anything because she thought Dawn was firmly opposed to the idea. By the end of the hike, they had agreed to pursue having kids, feeling a mixture of excitement and trepidation about the long road ahead. The next day, Dawn scoured the benefits page on her company's intranet site, learning that her employer's insurance (which both she and her wife were on) covered in vitro fertilization (IVF). She was elated until she read the fine print and saw that this benefit was available only to heterosexual couples who had experienced infertility (defined as an inability to conceive for at least a year).

Unwilling to give up, Dawn scheduled a conversation with her human resources (HR) liaison, asking why their employer, which had consistently won awards for being an LGBTQ-friendly workplace, had such a narrow definition for IVF eligibility. The response from HR was that it was their company's insurance provider's definition, not their employer's. While the HR liaison agreed with Dawn in theory, there was nothing she could do to change it. Undeterred, Dawn requested a meeting with her HR liaison's boss, and when she got the same answer from him, she continued meeting with increasingly senior HR leaders. She also shared her story in different forums, including the employee resource group for LGBTQ employees. Soon, Dawn was joined by other employees in these meetings with HR leaders. They, too, were disappointed by the disconnect between their company's reputation for being LGBTQ-friendly, which many cited as a reason they'd joined the firm, and the fine print in their insurance benefits.

In the meantime, Dawn's wife had changed jobs, and they learned that her employer—a tech company with a less established track record of being LGBTQ-friendly but a more progressive benefits package—would cover IVF for same-sex couples. They began the process of finding a sperm donor and started IVF, with Dawn as the biological mother. Even as her baby bump grew, Dawn continued to advocate internally, ultimately taking her story all the way to the chief people officer.

By this point, Dawn had gathered a strong cohort of allies, including a few of the firm's senior partners. Some were surprised that Dawn continued to spend her energy advocating for this benefit after she'd conceived. But Dawn's advocacy was never just about her own situation. She wanted her progressive employer to "walk the talk" about providing inclusive benefits, and she didn't feel that she could effectively do her job recruiting others if she didn't continue to elevate this issue.

A few weeks before Dawn was due to go on maternity leave, she logged on to her laptop and saw that her company had just released the new benefits packages for the following plan year. The accompanying email announced that it had expanded its coverage to align with its value of inclusivity; insurance plans now included IVF coverage for same-sex couples. It was a little more than two years since Dawn first learned that the IVF benefits had only applied to heterosexual couples. Feeling a surge of pride, she excitedly called to her wife from the next room. "Babe, come here!" Her wife ran in and instinctively walked over to the hospital bag they had recently packed. "No, not yet," Dawn said with a laugh, pointing to the computer screen, where information about the new benefits packages was displayed. "But hopefully my next labor will be shorter than two years!"

Dawn's story, and this chapter, are gentle reminders that we can all play a part in bringing about systemic change. Like Dawn's life and like our own lives, your life is probably full and, at times, incredibly demanding. It's hard work just getting through the day or week sometimes! However, when it comes to combining love and money, we're often asked to choose between options that are less than ideal. By using our individual voices, when and how we can, as Dawn did, we can all have an impact on our world and, in so doing, create a ripple effect of positive change over time.

AN ANTIQUATED FOUNDATION

Our institutions and government policies were created at a time when heterosexual marriage was the standard (and all other sexual preferences were taboo) and men earned income in the workforce while women raised children at home. Back then, issues such as paid parental leave and being able to find and afford quality childcare outside the family were nonissues. Although millions of women have been in the workforce for decades, many policies still reflect this single-outcome norm and therefore fall far short of meeting the needs of our evolving society. As a result, many people continue to encounter circumstances that position career and family as adversaries vying for our time, attention, and money. This makes having both career and family difficult and expensive and, at times, downright impossible.

The coronavirus pandemic highlighted just how little has changed in formal support structures for working parents in the United States, even decades after the second half of the twentieth century, when women's share of the labor force increased dramatically. (Women represented 47 percent of the civilian labor force in 2020, up from 29 percent in 1948.)[1] Prior to the pandemic, the number of dual-career families with children increased steadily, rising to 63 percent of couples in the United States in 2019, up from 44 percent in 1967.[2] Despite these shifts, policies and benefits have remained surprisingly outdated—a fact that, as we've seen, placed the burden of childcare on families, typically mothers—when schools and childcare centers abruptly closed in March 2020 as a result of lockdown.

Feeling disheartened by the picture we're painting? You're not alone! But it's only when faced with the grim reality of these headwinds that we truly grasp the extent of the need for systemic change. We've spent the previous nine chapters helping you see that it is possible to navigate your own challenges related to love and money. For conditions to improve sufficiently to meet modern families' needs, we need to examine the systems, policies, and practices that present us with suboptimal choices. Then we can band together, as Dawn did with her colleagues, and, one meeting at a time, try our best to change the system our suboptimal choices are based on.

BECOMING A CHANGE AGENT

When Dawn began to pursue getting her employer's IVF benefits changed, she'd been at her firm for a while. Having a long track record of success may have given her more access to senior decision makers. What if you don't have those credentials? Can you still be a change agent? Yes, you can! Your power comes from your experience, your ideas, and your motivation, not necessarily your status. As champions of change from within, we believe it's possible to influence change from any position within a power structure—and you don't have to go it alone. In fact, slowly but surely building coalitions of allies is likely to be critical to your long-term success. First, however, you may need to shift your mindset—especially if, like many people, you don't yet see yourself as a change agent.

TEMPERED RADICALS

Looking at our professional resumes, you might not view us as change agents, either. Myra has a PhD in economics and spent more than four decades in academia. Abby has an MBA and spent nearly a decade in a Fortune 200 company. While we don't have megaphones, we do have change-making ideas and voices we can use to broadcast them.

Soon after Myra arrived at Stanford University, when she was still a new, relatively unknown junior faculty member, she began to assemble allies among students and senior faculty. Her goal? Creating a successful proposal for what later became Stanford's Center for Research on Women. Over time, the center became a powerful resource for researching and advocating for the interests of women on campus and in the community. Eventually, it grew in prestige and funding and became the Clayman Institute for Gender Research, which now works to further the work and family interests of people on campus and around the world.

Similarly, as Abby was climbing the ranks in her corporate job, she launched and led an employee resource group for working parents. She helped secure new benefits for caregivers and created an environment where, as one of Abby's team members said after revealing she was expecting her second child, "people aren't scared to share that they are pregnant."

Debra Meyerson, author of *Tempered Radicals: How People Use Difference to Inspire Change at Work*, coined the term "tempered radicals," which describes people like us and perhaps you, as well. Meyerson describes tempered radicals as "people who want to succeed in their organizations yet want to live by their values or identities, even if they are somehow at odds with the dominant culture of their organizations."[3] "Tempered radicals," Meyerson maintains, "are more likely to think 'out of the box' because they are not fully in the box. As 'outsiders within,' they have both a critical and a creative edge. They speak new 'truths.'"[4]

Tempered radicals are often effective change agents because they know how to navigate within systems to get things done. As money and love specialists, we are often asked for advice by people who want to make major changes at their own places of work—for example, by adopting new hiring procedures, implementing less-biased methods of employee evaluation, or providing childcare benefits, paternity leave, or additional flexibility when returning to work after the birth or adoption of a child. "Where should we start?" people often ask. "How should we show the economic benefits of the changes we are seeking? Which of the changes should we ask for first?"

The answer is simple (even though the work isn't): first, do your research. How have you seen change happen in your workplace before? Who has decision rights to make this change? What data would they find compelling? And whom do they trust? Because every workplace is different, we can't advise on exactly what to do, but our framework provides a guide for how to proceed.

Being a Tempered Radical at Home

If you have children, another way to create change is by raising your children to become tempered radicals. Research shows that the sons and daughters of feminists are much more likely to favor the kinds of changes we are advocating here. As you raise your children, teach them the lessons you yourself are learning, and help them to work toward a world where the trade-offs between love and money are not as harsh as they are currently.

You can also introduce your children to the 5Cs framework, familiarizing them with the approach of gaining clarity, communicating, generating choices, checking in with others, and considering likely consequences, even about decisions that aren't related to love and money.

If you have a partner, one of the most important ways you can educate your children is to talk openly with them about how you and your partner divide up the work of breadwinning and caregiving, and why you've made the choices you've made. By showing that you have brought intentionality into the way you make decisions about love and money, you'll ensure they're aware that most decisions are really about both. And the more they're aware of that, the further along they'll be on the path toward having both—in the proportions they desire.

GATHERING DATA

As you consider ways to be a change agent, you may want to pinpoint an issue you're passionate about and look for data on it. There are typically two types of data that resonate with people most. The first is personal anecdotes. If you've heard the phrase "The plural of anecdote is not data," know that this is a misquote. The person who coined the phrase said precisely the opposite: "The plural of anecdote *is* data."[5]

The second type of data to search for is cold, hard numbers from surveys and employers' HR information systems. Especially when coupled with anecdotes, these data can play an important role in changing hearts, minds, and policies.

The inherent challenge is that while cold, hard numbers speak volumes, stories are often easier to come by. A *Harvard Business Review* article published in September 2021 about the "great resignation" pointed out that the resignation rates of employees between thirty and forty-five years of age were highest of all the age groups, with an average increase of more than 20 percent between 2020 and 2021.[6] The article exhorted employers to take a data-driven approach to improving retention, recommending that employers (1) quantify the problem, (2) identify the root causes, and (3) develop tailored retention programs.

If only it were that easy! The high resignation rates of thirty- to forty-five-year-olds makes sense, since this age group is most likely to be parents of young children and caring for elderly relatives—members of the sandwich generation—a fact that, puzzlingly, wasn't even mentioned in the article. However logical this explanation for the high resignation rate may seem, it's also hard to prove. The majority of companies (52 percent, according to one study) do not track the caregiving status of their employees. Major

HR systems also typically aren't designed to help them add these data.[7] Some progressive employers have undertaken efforts to track these data through self-identification campaigns or surveys, but they are the minority.

In the absence of official HR data, you will likely need to get creative. If your employer has an employee resource group focused on parents or caregivers, you can share a survey with members and ask them to forward it widely. If no employee resource group exists at your workplace, start one. In the meantime, you can give estimates based on studies; one from Harvard University says that about three out of four employees (73 percent) have some type of caregiving responsibility.[8]

TIMELINES (A.K.A. PLAYING THE LONG GAME)

Systemic change, even within a single organization, typically involves multiple groups who oversee numerous, sometimes conflicting, priorities. With so many cooks in the kitchen, as they say, timelines for creating change can be lengthy, especially in large, established institutions. Striking a healthy, sustainable balance between urgency and patience is difficult, especially since tempered radicals often do this work because they see norms that need attention *now*. When Abby first pitched her proposal to start an employee resource group for parents, she envisioned the group being available to all employees, not just those in headquarters locations. However, there was complexity regarding company-wide membership because labor laws differ for hourly employees. Although Abby was frustrated by this limitation, she and her cofounder decided to focus on making the change that was possible: growing membership within various headquarters locations. Fast-forward several years and the new leadership team of the parents' resource group includes two people specifically designated to help with outreach to hourly employees in stores and in distribution centers. Persistence combined with patience (eventually) paid off.

Because the timelines for making changes in most organizations are often long, be aware that you may not benefit personally from the transformations you're advocating. However, you're paying it forward to those who will come after you.

Nicole, too, unexpectedly became a change agent in her workplace. After having her first child, she was looking forward to returning to work. As a pediatrician, she felt she could better understand the parents she met in her practice now that she, too, was a parent. She was also eager to see her newly renovated work space, which had undergone a billion-dollar transformation during her maternity leave. The renovation was especially exciting because it had included an expansion of the children's hospital wing. When she showed up at the hospital on her first day back, she was shocked to discover that there was no place for her to pump breast milk for her four-month-old son, whom she had just left at day care for the first time.

"As physicians," she explained, "we repeatedly counsel parents about the health benefits of breastfeeding, encouraging them to continue nursing their babies as long as they can if that's possible for them. Given what we know as doctors, I was shocked that no one had considered the needs of female employees in the design and construction of the children's wing of our own hospital." Nicole was offered space in a lactation room in another part of the hospital. But her tight schedule made it virtually impossible for her to travel to that space, fit in the three pumping sessions she needed, and still get back in time to see her patients. Eventually, after she raised her concerns, part of a break room in the children's wing was repurposed for her to use, with a thin curtain strung up to separate her pumping space from the other part of the room. But people came in and out to use the other part of the break room while she was there, and she frequently had a hard time relaxing enough to trigger her milk letdown reflex. After several unsuccessful pumping sessions, she experienced milk leaking through her shirt. (She was grateful that her white coat hid the stains.) Only a few weeks after returning to work, her excitement had turned into frustration and resentment because no one had bothered to consider the basic needs of women doctors and staff.

One day, she opened the curtain after a pumping session and emerged into the break room only to see her department's chief physician in the break room getting coffee. "Oh, hi, Nicole," he said. "I didn't realize anyone else was in here. How are you doing being back at work after your leave?" Nicole's many years of training as a doctor had taught her to push through discomfort without complaining. She had put in grueling hours, surviving on less sleep than she'd thought was humanly possible, all in the spirit of appearing invincible. He'd had the same training, several decades before she did; she knew he likely expected her to say that she was fine. However, she felt compelled to speak up, not only because of her own experience but also because she had two pregnant colleagues who were about to go on leave. She couldn't bear for them to return to the same situation she was facing. "To tell the truth," she replied, "it's been challenging. I was in here pumping because no proper lactation rooms have been designated in the children's wing, despite all that we know about the health benefits of breastfeeding. I would love to help change that for me and for the other female employees at this hospital."

He looked up from pouring his coffee, surprised by what she'd shared. Nicole braced herself for a dismissive comment, but what he said was, "Well, we should do something about that." Later that week, he invited her to a meeting with the team of architects and space planners who had been involved in the hospital's buildout. When they got to the meeting, she looked around. She was the only woman in the room amid a group of gray-haired men. Immediately, she understood how the hospital had spent more than a billion dollars on the buildout and failed to account for the lactation needs of female employees.

The chief physician explained why he'd called the meeting and then asked Nicole to provide further details. In unison, all the gray-haired heads turned to look at her. Although initially intimidated, she took a deep breath, envisioned her pregnant colleagues, and began to explain the issue.

USING THE 5Cs FRAMEWORK: BECOMING A CHANGE AGENT

Remember, change doesn't have to happen overnight. Nor does fighting for reform have to overtake your life. However much we may want things to be different, most of us have busy, multifaceted lives that require considerable attention each and every day. By taking a methodical approach, you can prevent burnout and be a more powerful change agent over the long haul. Small changes made by many people add up. Make some small changes yourself, and then encourage others to do the same.

Step One: *Clarify*

The first step after embracing your ability to be a change agent is to clarify what changes you want to see and why you want them. The process will likely be a roller coaster with plenty of highs, lows, yea-sayers, and naysayers along the way. Being clear about why you are engaged in this work will go a long way toward helping you stay the course when you encounter obstacles.

Some find their "why" after having a negative experience that ultimately spurs them on to advocate for change, as this survey respondent did:

I had a horrendous experience coming back to work from my first parental leave to a very unaccommodating workplace and ended up leaving my job four months after I returned. Since then, I have been very motivated to do everything possible to improve working conditions for caregivers. I am currently involved in my work's employee resource group for caregivers to try to change workplace policies. And I have personally sought to model the behavior I would like to see changed (e.g., requesting a longer parental leave, using COVID caregivers' leave, putting up boundaries between work and family time).

Another survey respondent, Lori Mihalich-Levin, also had a negative, yet ultimately inspiring, experience of returning to work after having children:

*I struggled mightily with the return to work after my children (particularly my second), and I grew frustrated with the lack of resources focused on new parent professionals. All the (thoughtful) educational materials I could find were focused on the baby. I first founded a parent group at the trade association where I worked. . . . [Then] my fire and passion to make workplaces more hospitable to working parents led me to start a working parent group at the law firm where I [became] a partner. Though I was first permitted to open membership only to the lawyers who worked at the firm, I successfully mounted a nearly two-year-long campaign to open membership to *all* firm employees.*

Lori gained such clarity of purpose from this experience that she launched Mindful Return, a business focused on supporting parents returning to work. Her company started with a four-week, cohort-based online course for new parents. She has since expanded it and now offers courses for mothers, fathers, parents of special-needs children, and managers of employees taking leave. More than ninety employers currently offer the program as a parental benefit. For Lori, getting clear about the change she wanted to see in the world enabled her to help parents outside of her own workplace and to become the chief executive officer of a thriving business she's passionate about.

Another survey respondent found satisfaction by helping make flexible schedules more accepted and transparent within her Fortune 100 company. She noted that when she had her child, in the early 2000s, some women had negotiated alternative work schedules, but they had done it "under the table" with their boss, so no one really knew. This woman, whose stated personal mission is "to make the invisible visible," felt that if she could show that alternative schedules could work successfully at her level, they would become more feasible for others. So she was transparent with everyone about her schedule, which involved working from home a few afternoons a week, an arrangement that was relatively controversial in her company at the time. She was then able to offer the same schedule to the hundred or so people on her team. She reported that her own alternative schedule enabled her to continue to breastfeed her child until age one, and it "preserved a little bit of sanity." It also successfully paved the path for others in her company to adopt the same flexibility long before the days when working from home became acceptable. Even employees who didn't take advantage of the option expressed that they appreciated knowing it existed.

Step Two: *Communicate* (to Assemble Allies and Build Coalitions)

Once you're clear on your "why," it's time to begin assembling a broad range of allies. You do this by communicating about the change you're seeking. Cast your net widely; you never know who may join you. As more fathers have become involved parents, more of them have joined mothers in calling for family-related benefits such as childcare. With more people focused on the issue, more workplaces will likely provide these benefits.

Dawn's efforts to change eligibility for IVF coverage in her company worked well because of the large coalition of support she (slowly but surely) built among colleagues, including several senior partners who were in a position to influence broader company policy. Indeed, senior colleagues can be instrumental allies. One of Abby's mentors campaigned successfully to work a part-time schedule as a management consultant years before anyone else was doing it. She attributes her success to a combination of being respected for work well done, sticking to her commitment to a part-time schedule (even when pressured), and enlisting a well-respected senior male partner to "fly air cover" for her, which in this case meant convincing the other partners, who ranged from skeptical to downright dismissive, to let her test her part-time schedule on a trial basis. The senior partner helped her craft an alternative role that was client facing but not directly responsible for teams, allowing her to work three days a week. Because she'd proven herself and found a powerful ally, she was able to bring about the change she desired.

Step Three: Consider a Broad Range of *Choices*

While it may be tempting to focus on an ideal solution, systemic change sometimes requires compromise. As a result, it's important to look at different ways to solve the problem. Because you're focused on an issue that involves larger groups of people with varying wants and needs, these choices sometimes come from researching what other countries, organizations, or communities have done to solve similar problems.

One woman shared how she used the different choices she looked at to convince her new employer to change its maternity leave policy. Knowing the policy would be a problem for her down the road, she began the change-making process early:

> *When I joined my company, they provided the bare minimum leave policy federally required. That made me nervous because I knew that I wanted to have a second child eventually and that this policy would not be enough. I was just leaving an employer where I got three months paid [time off] and three months unpaid [time off], and having a full six months off with my daughter had been remarkable.*
>
> *I work with my brother-in-law, and he is the first one who brought this topic up with me. He had a team leader working for him who was about to have a baby, and when he asked her about her maternity leave in casual conversation, he realized how insufficient the leave policy was. I think our partnership (working together as a man and a woman) to advocate for increased leave policy was critical to its success. There were certainly bumps along the way—like when an older senior executive asked me, "Aren't we afraid that women might bond too much with their babies and not want to come back?" (To which I replied, "Have you ever had to care for a four-week-old baby? I'm pretty sure most women don't think it's so easy breezy that they want to sign up for it exclusively forever. And also, wouldn't we be happy for any parent who decided that caring for their child was the most important work they could do?") But, ultimately, using data (quantifying the cost, benchmarking comparable companies, explaining the upside of female retention) allowed us to prevail. While most people at the company didn't know that we played a role, the outpouring of thanks to HR for a gender-neutral, generous parental leave policy made me feel fulfilled.*

Considering choices, in this case, meant quantifying the costs of different maternity leave policies. Laying out the costs of these different choices is what ultimately convinced her employer to change the company's parental leave policy.

Step Four: *Check In*

Talking to leaders in your industry, benchmarking competitors, and connecting with tempered radicals who have relevant experience are all ways you may want to check in while you're setting out to create change. If allies fall off, check in with them as well. As always, stay open to new resources, people, and input.

Step Five: Explore Likely *Consequences*

Positive change can have some negative effects, and negative change can have some positive effects. When looking at possible outcomes, consider the good and bad, and be prepared to defend the risks and benefits of those outcomes. Most likely, as you're seeking to create change, you'll be forced to justify your decisions, actions, and reactions more than once. It's a natural part of upsetting the proverbial apple cart. The more prepared you are to respond to these inquiries, the more likely you'll be to succeed at persuading decision makers.

AREAS WHERE ACTION IS NEEDED

In addition to seeking change in the workplace, tempered radicals may seek change in the political realm—at the local, state, federal, and international levels. Given how many issues need our attention, the first challenge is determining where to put your energy.

The sections that follow describe key policy changes that, in our view, are critical to supporting working caregivers. All of these issues require thoughtful advocacy in the workplace and throughout all levels of government. Some also require cultural shifts that will help ensure these policies are deployed appropriately in the workplace.

Data Collection

The EEO-1 Component 1 report is a mandatory annual data collection that requires all private-sector employers with one hundred or more employees, as well as federal contractors with fifty or more employees that meet certain criteria, to submit demographic workforce data to the US Equal Employment Opportunity Commission, including data by race or ethnicity, sex, and job categories. There is an urgent need to expand this data collection to include employee caregiving responsibilities. Not only would such data allow companies and researchers to determine how much of the gender pay gap is due to caregiving responsibilities; it would also allow change agents within organizations to push for critical benefits that could affect employee satisfaction and retention.

Currently, several efforts are underway to establish caregiving status as a defined employee segment within federal EEO-1 reporting. One proposal was submitted to the US Department of Labor by Sarah Johal, executive director of Parents in Tech Alliance (PTA), a group formed after the leaders of parents' groups from top technology companies (Salesforce, Uber, LinkedIn, Lyft, Yelp, and others) secretly gathered in a conference room at Twitter in 2017 to "call more attention to the problems faced by working mothers."[9] Sarah's proposal reads as follows:

> *We must go beyond gender, racial, disability, and/or military identifiers related to employee data collection. Without a caregiving data profile, we miss a crucial opportunity to measure the perception of a company to be a "great place to work" compared with the actual experience of workers.*

Now a national nonprofit, PTA plans to make required caregiving status reporting one of its top advocacy priorities.

Paid Leave

The United States is the only industrialized country in the world that does not have paid maternity leave. About 40 percent of employers offer paid parental leave, six states require employers to offer some paid maternity leave, and the United States has *unpaid* family leave, which covers about 60 percent of Americans. We are woefully behind other countries in these public policies, which is partly responsible for the decrease in women's labor force participation relative to countries with more family-friendly approaches.[10]

The lack of paid paternity leave in the United States is another example of our antiquated policies. A recent UNICEF report states that among the world's forty-one richest countries, twenty-six offered paid paternity leave, but the United States did not. Sixteen of those countries provided full pay for those with average earnings. And the Organisation for Economic Co-operation and Development (OECD) found that the average length of paid leave among its member countries was 8.1 weeks.[11]

The number of weeks to be paid can be debated, but research shows that in countries where the leave is very long, there are negative effects on women's ability to return to the labor force and negative effects on their wages. Very long leaves also make it extremely difficult for employers to run their companies and reserve jobs for those on leave. As a result, especially long leaves may have a negative effect on companies' willingness to hire women of childbearing age in the first place.

Paid leave of twelve weeks for one parent followed by twelve weeks for the other would allow infants to be cared for by one of their parents during the first six months of life. Since we are so late to the paid paternity leave party, we can benefit from the experience of countries such as Sweden, which successfully figured out how to destigmatize paid paternity leave and ensure that new fathers take the time they are offered. Such a program would have multiple benefits, including the opportunity for fathers to bond with their infants, which child development professionals regard as a major bonus for the entire family.[12] In cases where the father is not a part of the children's lives, the second twelve weeks could be taken by another family member, such as a grandparent or one of the mother's siblings.

Federally Subsidized Childcare

The third policy change we recommend is federally subsidized childcare for families whose childcare costs exceed a certain percentage (currently 7 percent) of their income, meaning the government would cover some or all of the cost associated with childcare for families who can't afford it.

Although important, subsidizing care for those who need it is only part of the childcare solution. The quality of childcare also needs to be elevated. Subsidies are also needed for community colleges, which can then train childcare workers and aides. As part of an effort to raise the quality of childcare centers nationwide, it may also be necessary to mandate minimum pay for childcare workers.

The economic rationale for high-quality childcare is exactly the same as the economic rationale for public education. The more we learn from brain research about young children's extraordinary capacity for learning, the more we need to ensure that education begins long before kindergarten. By subsidizing childcare and improving its quality, as a nation, we make it possible for parents to work and for children to begin developing earlier.

One benefit of improved childcare is an increased birth rate (the birth rate in the United States is currently on the decline).[13] Overall, countries that spend more on supporting families have higher birth rates. For example, Germany and Estonia have seen increases in their birth rates as they rolled out better childcare options and better-paid parental leave.[14]

In the absence of federally subsidized childcare, some ask about corporate childcare. While corporate care is often of good quality, reliable, and partially subsidized, very few employers are large enough to profitably run their own childcare centers. Moreover, it's typically children of white-collar workers—the very people who have other options for high-quality care—who benefit from these corporate childcare centers. Also, as we move toward remote and hybrid work environments, it's unclear whether colocating childcare centers in office buildings will be sufficiently useful.

Paid Sick Leave

The world has 193 countries. Among them, 179 have paid sick leave, but the United States is not one of these.[15] If the coronavirus pandemic has taught us anything, it is that people should not go to work while sick, but many are still forced to do so because they can't afford to stay home without pay. Again, it's great for forward-looking companies to provide sick leave for their workers, but the government needs to go further. Paid sick leave needs to be required by law, or the government itself must provide sick leave benefits.

Congress did pass the first-ever federal sick leave provision in March 2020, which provided up to two weeks of paid sick and family leave for reasons related to COVID-19 (although only employees in companies with fewer than five hundred employees were eligible). Researchers studied the use of this historic provision, which was ultimately extended through March 2021 (an additional provision provided another ten days through September 2021). They concluded that despite the fact that eight million employees used emergency sick leave during the first six to eight months, "the share of employees who needed but could not take paid sick leave tripled in the pandemic; unaddressed sick leave needs total 15 million employees per month and are 69%

higher among women." In other words, the policies were a starting point but did not go far enough. Ultimately, the researchers noted the health-improving benefits of a permanent policy, stating, "Government-provided or -facilitated access to paid sick leave has the potential to significantly reduce unaddressed sick leave needs, reduce infection rates, and improve population health."[16]

Flexible Work Options and Stable Schedules

Flexible options for when, where, and how work is done, as well as stable, predictable schedules for employees, are also high-priority issues for employees juggling work and caregiving. It's impossible to plan for childcare when you don't know until the day before or the morning of your workday what your work schedule will be. Far too many workers have stories about lining up childcare only to show up at work and learn their shift has been canceled. Unable to recoup the money they spent on childcare for the day, they've also lost out on income for that day's shift. Companies might be able to optimize profitability by maintaining a flexible workforce, but such unstable schedules are incompatible with raising children.

The Center for WorkLife Law has conducted research on the effects of introducing more stable schedules for frontline employees at Gap stores. The team defined stability using four dimensions: "consistency (increasing the consistency of schedules from week to week), predictability (improving the ability of employees to anticipate when they will work), adequacy (giving more hours to employees who want them), and input (enhancing employees' say as to when they work and when they don't)."[17] An interdisciplinary team, led by Joan C. Williams, found that interventions including eliminating on-call shifts, publishing schedules two weeks in advance, and increasing the consistency of shift start and end times across days of the week led to an increase in business outcomes for the participating stores (through higher sales and productivity) as well as positive health outcomes for the employees in those stores (through better sleep quality and reduced stress).[18] Notably, parents experienced a 15 percent reduction in stress as a result of the increased schedule stability.[19]

While predictable schedules are an especially acute need for workers at the lowest end of the wage scale, they're also necessary at the highest end, in client-facing industries such as finance, law, and consulting. Social scientists call these the "greedy professions" because they reward workers, most of whom are men, for giving nearly every waking hour to their jobs. Giving all workers flexibility about when and where work gets done, as well as predictable hours, will reduce the gender pay gap and help diversify companies that struggle to retain women.[20] Eliminating the stigma and inequity associated with taking advantage of flexible work policies will help as well.

Incentives for Retirement Plan Contributions

Too many workers in their sixties have insufficient income to retire. To address this challenge, employers can provide additional incentives, such as matching programs, for employees to contribute to retirement programs. The federal government, too, should provide more of those incentives. A simple change, such as making retirement contributions something that people must opt out of instead of something they need to opt in to, has been shown to be effective in helping boost contributions.

Saving for retirement will become increasingly important as healthier lifestyles, combined with advances in longevity science, help people live longer and enjoy an increased number of vibrant, active years. Demographers estimate that children who are born today are likely to have a life expectancy of one hundred years. If that is the case, retirement at sixty-two will be out of reach for the majority, since few workers will be able to fund four decades of retirement. Most likely, the future retirement age will likely be closer to eighty. Even with an older retirement age, however, funding a twenty-year retirement will take more savings than the average retiree has.

Long-Term Care Insurance

As life expectancy increases, long-term care needs will also likely increase. That will necessitate additional workplace and government incentives for people to purchase long-term care insurance. Again, this can be a work-related benefit, but governments also need to provide incentives for people to buy it.

Washington State was the first state in the United States to introduce a long-term care program, funded by a mandatory payroll tax. The program, which was signed into law in 2019, works by deducting about 50 cents per every $100 paycheck; beginning in 2025, it will pay up to $36,500 for individuals who meet eligibility criteria, funding home health care and other services older residents need to age in their own homes.[21] While the plan has been criticized, including for allowing residents with private coverage to opt out (which changes the economics), it will undoubtedly serve as a useful case study for other states as their populations continue to age.[22]

Cultural Norms

Last but not least are the cultural changes necessary to support even the best-laid policy. If the prevailing culture—"the way things get done around here," as organizational consultants Terrence Deal and Allan Kennedy famously put it—doesn't support the adoption of updated policies, those policies will have little effect.[23] It's incumbent on leaders to create a culture that makes it acceptable to take advantage of policies that exist. One survey respondent described the difference in her own leadership style before and after she had her own children, which dramatically altered the culture of her entire organization:

> *My first stint as a CEO was before I was a mom, and I'm very conscious now of the ways I led that sent anti-family and even just anti-human messages, resulting in an unsustainable experience. I didn't expect to return to a CEO role, but when I did, I was so much clearer on WHY it mattered to build an organization where people can be their full selves, particularly from a lens that focuses on diversity, equity, and inclusion. We've of course changed things like benefits and policies, but the real change this has required is deep, personal, and authentic at every level of the organization and in me as its leader. When the pandemic hit, we supported parents who had to step back AND created a financial benefit for employees with unexpected dependent care costs.*
>
> *Just last month, I got to offer a major promotion to someone who'd had to step back to less than full time because of parenting responsibilities and the pandemic. We were both really, really proud of that as a mile-marker of where the organization has come over four years. I see pieces of this in very large companies, but doing it in a place with about twenty-five [full-time employees] means EVERYONE in the org has to be on board, as ebbs and flows from their colleagues are felt more immediately.*

Another survey respondent, also in a chief executive role, shared how she now works to create an environment that is more family friendly than the one she encountered earlier in her tenure with that same organization:

> *When I was pregnant with our first, I was the only woman on the management team, and we didn't have a family leave policy (this was before it was California and San Francisco law). It was terrifying approaching the COO and CEO with the idea. I got it through, and since*

I've been CEO, I've tried to make our workplace incredibly welcoming and flexible for new parents and especially new (breastfeeding and pumping) moms.

While not everyone will be in a CEO position, even employees without management responsibility can set an example for others. The simple act of taking the full parental leave available, especially for fathers, who are more likely to take less time than they can or to forgo taking time at all, can be a powerful way to influence others to do the same. Talking openly about how different people, especially single parents, make childcare work can also be enormously helpful and informative. The more we push back against the ideal worker myth that assumes a lack of any real priorities outside of work, the more we all benefit—including those of us who never plan to have children but may someday care for a sick mate or elderly parent.

In their report titled "Supporting Dual Career Couples," Genevieve Smith and Ishita Rustagi of Berkeley Haas's Center for Equity, Gender, and Leadership (EGAL) outline several changes that can help shift workplace culture and ensure that benefits that do exist get used. Training managers on how to support parents and caregivers (especially in taking parental and caregiving leave) can help employees feel supported, not penalized, when they take leave or request schedule accommodations. Developing employee resource groups can offer a supportive environment for caregivers, help them see they're not alone, and provide a forum for voicing their needs to leadership. And reevaluating what successful career paths look like and developing flexible career tracks provide alternatives to asking employees to relocate every few years to advance within the organization. We encourage change agents to read this playbook to learn more about how to influence and implement these important shifts.[24]

CHAPTER TEN EXERCISE:

How Will You Change the Work/Family System?

This exercise helps you CLARIFY where you want to make change and asks you to consider where the CHECK-IN step might be helpful. Think about your workplace or an organization you're connected to (whether in a volunteer capacity, as an alumnus, or through another affiliation). Consider the following questions as you determine how the organization could evolve to better support employees in combining work and family.[25] While there are shades of gray, for now we encourage yes/no answers for simplicity.

Does your organization capture data on caregiving responsibilities, either formally as part of an HR information system or informally through a survey?

____

Does the organization currently have a policy and benefits for the following?

Flexible work options, predictable schedules, or both

____

Paid parental leave (including for adoption) and caregiving leave

____

Access to quality childcare and eldercare

____

Paid sick leave

____

Retirement programs and long-term care insurance

____

Do the foregoing policies and benefits apply to—and are they used by—employees of all genders and sexual orientations?

___

Does your organization offer training or resources for managers in helping new parents return to work and supporting the use of flexible schedules?

___

Does your organization offer an employee resource group (ERG) or an affinity group for parents, caregivers, or both?

___

Does your organization offer career development tracks that are flexible (instead of heavily encouraging travel or relocation to advance within the company)?

___

Look at the questions to which you answered no.

Which one of these "no" answers gets you most fired up?

___

How might you collect data on how many others within the organization this issue affects?

___

Who has decision rights to change the answer from no to yes?

___

Who else might care about this issue? (These are your potential allies.)

___

What's the first step you might take to reach out to your allies about partnering with them?

____

When will you take this first step?

____

If you're more drawn to creating change at the policy level than within a specific organization, reflect on the following questions:

Which issue are you most interested in working on at the local, state, or national level?

____

Are there organizations already working on this policy issue? If so, which ones are they, and how might you get involved?

____

If there are none, would you consider starting one (with potential allies)?

____

CONCLUSION

When we sat down in early 2020 to begin writing this book, we had only an inkling of the love and money challenges that we, and billions of people around the world, would face during the two years we spent crafting these pages. As our chapters took shape, COVID-19 struck again and again, continually upending everyone's lives in countless ways. Sometimes the results were merely frustrating (will the kids *ever* keep their headphones on while in online class?); at other times they were heart-wrenching as loved ones fell sick, millions around the globe died, and many millions more lay awake most nights, trying to figure out how to cope with never-ending fear, worry, and a deep sense of loss. Throughout the pandemic, people were obliged to make exhaustingly complex decisions about money and love, and we did as well. As we managed the required procession of choices that cropped up, we realized we were using our decision-making framework pretty much nonstop. We consistently found the framework valuable, but we also noticed how difficult it could be to take our own advice. When we were exhausted and overwhelmed, we experienced firsthand the challenge of slowing down and engaging in System 2 rational thinking, as described in chapter one.

Just as we began pitching this book to publishers, Abby's mother entered hospice care and died, and Abby and her relatives joined the millions around the world mourning their loved ones on Zoom, hundreds or thousands of miles away from one another. It was the safest way to honor her mother's life, but it made grieving feel heavier and lonelier; sharing tearful hugs with relatives and close friends was simply out of the question.

At the same time, Myra's husband, Jay, was suffering from Parkinson's disease, his symptoms worsening each week. During the long months before coronavirus vaccines were available, Myra was not able to hire in-home help without risking infection. Like millions around the world, she became Jay's full-time caregiver practically overnight. It was round-the-clock work born of deep love and devotion.

As the months rolled on, Abby and Ross began to question the feasibility of continuing to function in their small-footprint home that, like so many family homes, was also serving as a makeshift schoolhouse and office. Months into the pandemic, their two young children were still learning remotely while Abby and Ross (attempted to) perform demanding, high-visibility jobs. Soon, they began searching for a house in the suburbs, despite Abby's long-standing preference for the city. Debating the pros and cons of a bigger space (and a larger mortgage), wondering alongside millions when in-person school would resume, they decided, in the end, to stay in the city. The decision brought them a sense of resolve, even relief, but not without consternation, given that several additional months of remote school rolled out before them. In the fall of 2021, at long last, in-person school began again. But just when young children were eligible for vaccination, a vaccine-resistant variant began brewing, and soon it was circulating at lightning speed.

The worst wasn't yet over. Nonetheless, we forged ahead, outlining, writing, and reviewing one chapter after another. As uncertainty and chaos swirled around us, a book was steadily taking shape, one word, one sentence at a time. As we used our framework over and over to make exceedingly difficult decisions, our conviction about its usefulness grew.

* * *

After acting as Jay's 24/7 caregiver for months, Myra suffered two serious falls that resulted in four broken ribs, one broken wrist, a badly gashed forehead, and a newly installed pacemaker. All of this occurred as she sold her and Jay's house (his disease had progressed to the point that stairs presented a danger). She then oversaw the renovation of their new ground floor condominium before finally moving them in. With a dizzying number of transactions, contractors, and small and large decisions demanding attention each day, her health seemed increasingly impacted; caring for Jay, whose condition was declining even faster, while managing the details of their shared life proved an unsustainable balancing act. Eventually, Jay moved into a care facility. The decision was heartbreaking. Initially, it was also unpopular; Jay's three children all reacted to the news with complete silence. Eager to reach a consensus, or at least some measure of understanding, they all gathered for a family therapy session that, thankfully, gave them each the opportunity to air their thoughts and feelings. They have been communicating effectively ever since.

Visiting Jay in his new residence every day, Myra continuously mourned his absence in their home, even as she adopted new routines, trying to find a new rhythm to daily life without Jay's physical presence. Months later, Jay passed away. Less than four weeks afterward, Myra's first husband, Sam, also passed away. The grief and sense of loss in her family was overwhelming, yet almost two years into the pandemic, funerals still had to be carefully planned to minimize the risk of exposure. The endless decisions involved in putting a person's will and estate to rest, too, demanded focus and energy that felt difficult to muster.

Two grueling years had rocked our individual and shared foundations. We'd grown more resilient but more weary and wary, too.

Meanwhile, chapter edits were due. A book was coming together, and pages needed to be finalized.

The Okinawans believe in living life with *ikigai*, which is similar to what Costa Ricans call *plan de vida*. Both principles underscore what longevity research has consistently found—that as humans, we are wired to live with purpose and meaning. Doing so, science indicates, can extend our life span.[1] Purpose and meaning appear to be integral to our health and wellness—mentally, emotionally, and at the cellular level, too.

It's an effect we experienced while writing this book. Having an opportunity to bring this life-enhancing work to a wider audience has steeped our own daily lives in purpose and meaning, invigorating us on brighter days and making darker days feel a little less daunting.

For years, the 5Cs framework has allowed us and so many others to make more thoughtful, fruitful decisions while simultaneously helping to manifest silver linings when circumstances don't initially seem favorable. Using this framework, we can all feel better equipped to make decisions that move us forward, toward our hopes and dreams. We then have more space and freedom to focus on the people and pursuits that add joy and ease—as well as essential purpose and meaning—to daily life.

What is more intrinsic to living with purpose and meaning than love and money? While love fills our heart and soul, money provides the freedom to make choices that support us in living a life of meaning and purpose. The idea that it's love *versus* money, that it's a zero-sum game—as in, you can have a great relationship *or* a successful career; be an attentive parent *or* a high-achieving professional—is unhealthy and unjust. While writing this book, we have been struck repeatedly by the stark reality that, despite the nearly forty-year age gap between us, the money/love trade-offs we've navigated are remarkably similar at their core. As a society, we still view caring for the young and old as a problem for individuals to solve as opposed to a collective responsibility that requires consideration at a systemic level. Our societal orientation toward compartmentalization—love *or* money instead of love *and* money—persists, creating impossible choices that endure across generations. The origins of this compartmentalization are obscure and in contention, but one interesting observation was put forth by the late anthropologist David Graeber. He pointed out that many of the major religions of the world, with their concerns about love for humanity, arose during the same time period (800 BC to AD 600) and in the same places as the invention of coinage. In his book on the history of money, Kabir Sehgal references Graeber and notes: "It's plausible that some organized religions spread as a response to the rising importance of the marketplace."[2]

Regardless of why we started to compartmentalize money and love, it is time to recognize that the two are profoundly intertwined, and both are fundamental to living a life of purpose, health, and well-being. No one should have to choose between a good job and safe, nurturing childcare or eldercare. Yet every day, millions of people are forced to make decisions exactly like these. The pandemic has only made those decisions even more fraught and less clear-cut.

Throughout our lives, we have had more opportunities than most. But even with access to health care, caregivers, and other forms of essential support, we have struggled mightily during this time. As we put the finishing touches on these pages, we continue to acknowledge the significant challenges faced by those with less privilege. How can we, as a civilized society, continue to expect people to choose love over money, or money before love? Asking that is like asking to choose between your heart and your lungs. Which do you need more—blood running through your veins or the ability to breathe? Love and money are both essential components of health and wellness, not an either/or equation.

While writing this book and co-teaching a course based on it, our collaboration has been an ongoing anchor, tethering us to something consequential and underscoring our determination to bring this long-overdue conversation to the forefront of more hearts and minds. However, this book is only a first step. Change is desperately required in our society, and we hope you will join us in helping to bring this long-overlooked topic to the fore.

Everyone deserves the resources and skills to enjoy both love *and* money. By the time you read this book, we sincerely hope the pandemic's peaks will have diminished and life will feel more manageable. Whether or not the coronavirus recedes soon, the past few years will remain a societal marker. Some of the changes initiated during the COVID-19 years will likely become permanent, such as, perhaps, a massive global increase in the remote workforce, which will solve some old work/family conflicts and create new ones. Much as with the Great Depression or World War II, those who lived through the onset of the pandemic will forever remember and be shaped by their experiences during this time.

As we go to press, the Supreme Court has just issued its abortion ruling in *Dobbs v. Jackson*. In addition to the COVID-19 pandemic, this period in our history will be marked by this ruling, which will significantly affect money and love decisions for numerous Americans, particularly for those with limited financial resources.

However the future unfolds, hard choices will remain part of our lives. We hope this book will help you—and everyone—gain access to the kinds of money and love decisions that grant you more freedom to pursue the joy, purpose, and meaning that give everyday life greater value and significance. We wish you a splendid life journey filled with experiences that are fulfilling and rewarding in every way.

ACKNOWLEDGMENTS

Myra and Abby owe a great deal of gratitude to the extraordinary team who helped this book take shape. We thank Tara Mohr and Eric Ries for being early believers in this book and for introducing us to Christy Fletcher at Fletcher & Co., who connected us with our wonderful agent, Gráinne Fox. Gráinne's good cheer, good sense, and Irish expressions kept us going throughout all the twists and turns of this process. We also thank Daniella Wexler for her vision and insight, Ghjulia Romiti, and the entire team at HarperOne, including Shannon Welch, who started us off at HarperOne. Mandy Mooney helped strengthen our proposal and Ana Homayoun served as our book whisperer, introducing us to a team—including the magnificent Wyndham Wood—who helped make this book better in numerous ways. We also thank our many survey respondents, interviewees, early readers (including Barbara Kiviat, Charles Moore, Sareena Singh, and Katie Soroye), and staff of the Career Management Center at Stanford Graduate School of Business (especially Laura Bunch, Jordanne Dickson, and Carly Janson) for helping us road test the concepts of the book with alumni through an online course. Thanks also to our GSB alumni course participants, who were a joy to teach and whose positive feedback was so affirming.

Friends and colleagues are critical when writing a book, and even more so when an author is facing a spouse's illness and death. Myra offers heartfelt thanks to Cecile and Paul Andrews, Merry and Michael Asimow, Miriam Ben Natan, Jasmina Bojic, Richard Caputo, Martin Carnoy, Agnes Chan, David Gaskill, Mark

Graham, Al Henning, Cindy Jones, Peg Krome, Carol Muller, James and Wenda O'Reilly, Lisa Petrides, and Allen and Janet Podell, and to the members of her walking group, Miriam Bodin, Sandy Citrin, Ellen Fox, Leora Gaster, Linda Greenberg, Lori Holzberg, Paula Kushlan, Rinah Mullins, and Shari Ornstein.

Myra is indebted for friendship for almost thirty years to her book group: Diane Feldman, Mary Felstiner, Leah Friedman, Edith Gelles, Suzanne Greenberg, Shoshana Levy, Elyce Melmon, Joyce Moser, and Ellen Turbow. Fellow Cornellians also provided long, supportive friendships: Janice Agatson, Amelia Bryant, Evelyn Eskin, Rita Gershengorn and Kent Gershengorn, Nina Gershon, Jane Giddan, Nancy Simon Hodin, Linda Klineman, Dania Moss, Helen Neuborne and Burt Neuborne, Linda Roberts, Caroline Simon, Liz Stiel, and Barbara Wecker and Lane Brandenberg. Finally, special thanks to Joanne Brody, Diane Feldman, Mary Felstiner, Leah Friedman, Suzanne Greenberg, Diane Pincus, and Deedee Schurman, who have had open phone lines and open hearts over too many decades to count.

Myra thanks her family for their love, support, and inexhaustible willingness to discuss new questions and ideas: her children, Jason Strober and Elizabeth Strober, and their spouses, Joanna Strober and Bryan Cohen; her stepchildren, Tenaya Jackman, Rashi Jackman and Rashi's wife, Maike Ahrends, and Jason Scott; her sister-in-law, Evelyn Topper; and her cousins, Natalie Hieger, Marty Latman, Ted Latman, Janice Latman, and Marilyn Latman. And a special shout-out to her grandchildren for delightfully illuminating conversations about their sense of the connections between love and money: Sarah Strober, Jared Strober, Jasper Ahrends, Lyn Strober-Cohen, Ari Strober, and Leander Scott (who mostly supplied excellent hugs and big smiles).

Myra is especially grateful to her late husband, Jay Jackman, for thirty years of a loving, joyful, and exciting partnership. Many of the concepts in this book were born during conversations with Jay, who used the lens of a wise psychiatrist to enrich Myra's thinking, and despite a seven-year bout with Parkinson's disease, his enthusiasm and support for her work never flagged.

Abby thanks the many supportive friends, family members, and colleagues who cheered her on during this process. This includes her Morse roommates Susan Asam, Cherie Fu, Gayle Horn, Kapila Juthani, Saira Mohamed, and Julie Stoltey; the OG SF crew (especially Alexa Frankenberg, Emily Himes, and Kristy Wang); the GSBAC members Ellen Kim, Kate Agresta Price, Abby Schlatter, and especially Emily Rummo, whose Nest provided a blissfully quiet and cozy place to write some of these chapters; her GSB Women's Circle (Catherine Chien, Philippa Duffy, Diana Rothschild, Medhavi Sahai, and Mandira Singh); the Cult Buddies (Jessica Albertson, Jessie Turnbaugh, and Jenny Yelin); Grattan friends Vivian Chang and Ibone Santiago Trojaola; and too many Gap Inc. friends and colleagues to name (but she'll name a few anyway, including Gail Gershon, who hired her at thirty-eight weeks pregnant, Abby Frost and the Gap Foundation and Opportunity Teams, Will Riffelmacher, and the world's best officemate and work wife, Christina Nicholson). Abby also thanks the paid caregivers who provided care for her children over the years. As every parent knows, it takes a village; in particular, Katherine Karimi, Gemma Lee, and Sarah O'Toole have been instrumental members of hers.

Abby is grateful to her mentors, including Seth Barad, Susan Colby, Bobbi Silten, and, of course, her mentor turned coauthor Myra Strober, for believing in her and serving as money and love sounding boards at pivotal junctures. Before Abby was a writer, she was a reader. She remains forever indebted to her parents, Ellen and Allen Rubin, for fostering a love of books (and pretending not to notice when she read them under the covers with a flashlight).

She also thanks her brother, Steven Rubin, for not telling on her when she was reading books under the covers; Sherry and Norm Malmon for being a wonderful aunt and uncle; and her cousin Patricia Sloane-White for serving as an early (and ongoing) role model. She's grateful to Marji and Roger Davisson and the Liegls, who sustained her in big and small ways throughout this process—not least of which by supporting Ross, who did substantially more than his share of parenting and household work while this book was being birthed.

Abby reserves her most heartfelt thank-you for Ross, Sam, and Max, who continue to serve as her personal money and love learning laboratory. Ross's unwavering support and generosity, "extra bitter" sense of humor, and good cooking have nourished her (figuratively and literally) over all these years. Thanks also to Sam and Max for giving the best hugs on the planet, for enthusiastically joining in thirty-second dance parties, and for being her constant teachers.

FURTHER READING

Dowling, Daisy. *Workparent: The Complete Guide to Succeeding on the Job, Staying True to Yourself, and Raising Happy Kids*. Boston, MA: Harvard Business Review Press, 2021.

Florida, Richard L. *Who's Your City? How the Creative Economy Is Making Where to Live the Most Important Decision of Your Life*. New York: Basic Books, 2008.

Gottlieb, Lori. *Mr. Good Enough: The Case for Choosing a Real Man over Holding Out for Mr. Perfect*. New York: Dutton, 2010.

Gottman, John. *Why Marriages Succeed or Fail: And How You Can Make Yours Last*. New York: Simon & Schuster, 2012.

Gratton, Lynda, and Andrew J. Scott. *The 100-Year Life: Living and Working in an Age of Longevity*. London: Bloomsbury Information, 2016.

Gross, Jane. *A Bittersweet Season: Caring for Our Aging Parents—and Ourselves*. New York: Alfred A. Knopf, 2011.

Kahneman, Daniel. *Thinking, Fast and Slow*. New York: Farrar, Straus and Giroux, 2011.

Meers, Sharon, and Joanna Strober. *Getting to 50/50: How Working Parents Can Have It All*. Berkeley, CA: Viva Editions, 2013. Original hardback edition published by Bantam Dell, 2009.

Nooyi, Indra. *My Life in Full: Work, Family, and Our Future*. New York: Penguin Random House, 2021.

Petriglieri, Jennifer. *Couples That Work: How Dual-Career Couples Can Thrive in Love and Work*. Boston, MA: Harvard Business Review Press, 2019.

Rodsky, Eve. *Fair Play: A Game-Changing Solution for When You Have Too Much to Do (and More Life to Live)*. New York: G. P. Putnam's Sons, 2019.

Strober, Myra. *Sharing the Work: What My Family and Career Taught Me About Breaking Through (and Holding the Door Open for Others)*. Cambridge, MA: MIT Press, 2016.

Susanka, Sarah. *The Not So Big House: A Blueprint for the Way We Really Live*. Newtown, CT: Taunton Press, 2008.

NOTES

One: Introducing the 5Cs Framework

1. Ruth Chang, interview by Meghan Keane, "Faced with a Tough Decision? The Key to Choosing May Be Your Mindset," NPR (KQED), January 4, 2021.
2. Daniel Kahneman, *Thinking, Fast and Slow* (New York: Farrar, Straus and Giroux, 2011).
3. Adam Grant (@AdamMGrant), Twitter, August 30, 2018, https://twitter.com/adammgrant/status/1035150432295940102?lang=en.
4. Peter Suciu, "History of Influencer Marketing Predates Social Media by Centuries—but Is There Enough Transparency in the 21st Century?," *Forbes*, December 7, 2020, https://www.forbes.com/sites/petersuciu/2020/12/07/history-of-influencer-marketing-predates-social-media-by-centuries-but-is-there-enough-transparency-in-the-21st-century/.
5. Plato, *Plato's Phaedrus*, Translated by R. Hackforth (Cambridge: University Press, 1952); Réne Descartes, *The Passions of the Soul* (Paris: H. Legras, 1649).
6. Ellie Lisitsa, "The Four Horsemen: Criticism, Contempt, Defensiveness, and Stonewalling," *Gottman Relationship Blog*, Gottman Institute, accessed October 11, 2021, https://www.gottman.com/blog/the-four-horsemen-recognizing-criticism-contempt-defensiveness-and-stonewalling.
7. Lisitsa, "Four Horsemen."
8. Lonnie Golden, "Part-Time Workers Pay a Big-Time Penalty," Economic Policy Institute, February 27, 2020, https://www.epi.org/publication/part-time-pay-penalty/.
9. Centers for Disease Control and Prevention, "CDC: 1 in 4 US Adults Live with a Disability," press release, August 16, 2018, https://www.cdc.gov/media/releases/2018/p0816-disability.html.
10. Gary Klein, "Performing a Project Premortem," *Harvard Business Review*, September 2007, https://hbr.org/2007/09/performing-a-project-premortem.

Two: Finding Your Person

1. Gaby Galvin, "U.S. Marriage Rate Hits Historic Low," *U.S. News & World Report*, April 29, 2020, https://www.usnews.com/news/healthiest-communities/articles/2020-04-29/us-marriage-rate-drops-to-record-low.
2. Patrick T. Brown and Rachel Sheffield, "U.S. Marriage Rates Hit New Recorded Low," US Congress Joint Economic Committee, April 29, 2020, https://www.jec.senate.gov/public/index.cfm/republicans/2020/4/marriage-rate-blog-test.

3. Kaitlyn Greenidge, "What Does Marriage Ask Us to Give Up?," *New York Times*, January 4, 2022, https://www.nytimes.com/2022/01/04/opinion/marriage-divorce.html.
4. Joe Pinsker, "The Hidden Costs of Living Alone," *Atlantic*, October 20, 2021, https://www.theatlantic.com/family/archive/2021/10/living-alone-couple-partner-single/620434/.
5. Ellen Byron, "More Americans Are Living Solo, and Companies Want Their Business," *Wall Street Journal*, June 2, 2019, https://www.wsj.com/articles/more-americans-are-living-solo-and-companies-want-their-business-11559497606.
6. Alexandra Sifferlin, "Do Married People Really Live Longer?," *Time*, February 12, 2015, https://time.com/3706692/do-married-people-really-live-longer/.
7. Bella DePaulo, "Research Shows Life-Threatening Bias Against Single People," *Psychology Today*, July 7, 2019, https://www.psychologytoday.com/us/blog/living-single/201907/research-shows-life-threatening-bias-against-single-people.
8. Alexander H. Jordan and Emily M. Zitek, "Marital Status Bias in Perceptions of Employees," *Basic and Applied Social Psychology* 34, no. 5 (2012): 474–481, https://doi.org/10.1080/01973533.2012.711687.
9. Juliana Menasce Horowitz, Nikki Graf, and Gretchen Livingston, "Marriage and Cohabitation in the U.S.," Pew Research Center, November 6, 2019, https://www.pewresearch.org/social-trends/2019/11/06/marriage-and-cohabitation-in-the-u-s/.
10. Bella DePaulo, "The Social Lives of Single People," *Psychology Today*, May 17, 2019, https://www.psychologytoday.com/us/blog/living-single/201905/the-social-lives-single-people.
11. Josie Santi, "What 'Finding the One' Really Means in 2020," Everygirl, February 16, 2020, https://theeverygirl.com/finding-the-one/.
12. Myra Strober, *Sharing the Work: What My Family and Career Taught Me About Breaking Through (and Holding the Door Open for Others)* (Cambridge, MA: MIT Press, 2016).
13. Community Research and Development Information Service, "New Evidence That Humans Choose Their Partners Through Assortative Mating," January 13, 2017, https://phys.org/news/2017-01-evidence-humans-partners-assortative.html.
14. Rhymer Rigby, "The Wealthy Marrying Their Own. Does It Even Matter?," *Financial Times*, September 1, 2018, https://www.ft.com/content/2f0b77da-89d2-11e8-affd-da9960227309.
15. Gina Potarca, "Does the Internet Affect Assortative Mating? Evidence from the U.S. and Germany," *Social Science Research* 61 (January 2017): 278–297, https://doi.org/10.1016/j.ssresearch.2016.06.019.

16. Paul Oyer, *Everything I Ever Needed to Know About Economics I Learned from Online Dating* (Boston, MA: Harvard Business Review Press, 2014), 151.
17. Lasse Eika, Magne Mogstad, and Basit Zafar, "Educational Assortative Mating and Household Income Inequality," Federal Reserve Bank of New York, Staff Report no. 682, August 2014, revised March 2017, https://www.newyorkfed.org/medialibrary/media/research/staff_reports/sr682.pdf?la=en.
18. Minda Zetlin, "Want a Happy Marriage? Science Says Look for These Personality Traits in Your Spouse," *Inc.*, September 29, 2019, https://www.inc.com/minda-zetlin/marriage-partner-personality-traits-what-to-look-for.html.
19. Marina Krakovsky, "The Trouble with One at a Time," Stanford Graduate School of Business, Insights by Stanford Business, September 14, 2012, https://www.gsb.stanford.edu/insights/trouble-one-time.
20. Alyson Krueger, "What It's Like to Work with a Matchmaker," *New York Times*, February 27, 2021, updated March 4, 2021, https://www.nytimes.com/2021/02/27/style/what-its-like-to-work-with-a-matchmaker.html.
21. Krakovsky, "Trouble with One at a Time."
22. Lori Gottlieb, "Marry Him! The Case for Settling for Mr. Good Enough," *Atlantic*, March 2008, https://www.theatlantic.com/magazine/archive/2008/03/marry-him/306651/.
23. The authors are grateful to Myra's former student Sophie Pinkard, who contributed to this section with research on how dual-career couples should approach their finances in her 2009 final paper submitted to Myra's Work & Family Class "Combining Finances in Dual-Income Relationships: Approaches, Research, and Best Practices."
24. Pinkard, "Combining Finances," 5.
25. Such as this one: "Values Exercise," Carnegie Mellon University, Career & Professional Development Center, accessed July 6, 2021, https://www.cmu.edu/career/documents/my-career-path/values-exercise.pdf
26. Krakovsky, "Trouble with One at a Time."
27. Joel Peterson, remarks made at the GSB Class of 2008 Last Lecture, Stanford, California, May 2008.
28. Some questions were inspired by Eleanor Stanford, "13 Questions to Ask Before Getting Married," *New York Times*, March 24, 2016, https://www.nytimes.com/interactive/2016/03/23/fashion/weddings/marriage-questions.html.

Three: Pop the Question (or Skip It Altogether?)

1. Amanda Barroso, "More than Half of Americans Say Marriage Is Important but Not Essential to Leading a Fulfilling Life," Pew Research Center, February 14, 2020, https://www.pewresearch.org/fact-tank/2020/02/14/more-than-half-of-americans-say-marriage-is-important-but-not-essential-to-leading-a-fulfilling-life/.
2. "Marriage license," Wikipedia, accessed January 17, 2022, https://en.wikipedia.org/wiki/Marriage_license.

3. Stephanie Coontz, *Marriage, a History: How Love Conquered Marriage* (New York: Penguin Books, 2006).
4. Julia Carpenter, "The Unpaid Work That Always Falls to Women," CNN Money, February 21, 2018, https://money.cnn.com/2018/02/21/pf/women-unpaid-work/index.html.
5. Lori Gottlieb, "Marry Him! The Case for Settling for Mr. Good Enough," *Atlantic*, March 2008, https://www.theatlantic.com/magazine/archive/2008/03/marry-him/306651/.
6. Juliana Menasce Horowitz, Nikki Graf, and Gretchen Livingston, "Marriage and Cohabitation in the U.S.," Pew Research Center, November 6, 2019, https://www.pewresearch.org/social-trends/2019/11/06/marriage-and-cohabitation-in-the-u-s/.
7. Julie Sullivan, "Comparing Characteristics and Selected Expenditures of Dual- and Single-Income Households with Children," US Department of Labor, Bureau of Labor Statistics, *Monthly Labor Review*, September 2020, https://doi.org/10.21916/mlr.2020.19.
8. TD Ameritrade, "Breadwinners Survey," March 2020, https://s2.q4cdn.com/437609071/files/doc_news/research/2020/breadwinners-survey.pdf.
9. Richard V. Reeves and Christopher Pulliam, "Middle Class Marriage Is Declining, and Likely Deepening Inequality," Brookings Institution, March 11, 2020, https://www.brookings.edu/research/middle-class-marriage-is-declining-and-likely-deepening-inequality/.
10. USAFacts, "The State of American Households: Smaller, More Diverse and Unmarried," *U.S. News & World Report*, February 14, 2020, https://www.usnews.com/news/elections/articles/2020-02-14/the-state-of-american-households-smaller-more-diverse-and-unmarried.
11. Richard V. Reeves, Christopher Pulliam, and Ashley Schobert, "Are Wages Rising, Falling, or Stagnating?," Brookings Institution, September 10, 2019, https://www.brookings.edu/blog/up-front/20191/09/10/are-wages-rising-falling-or-stagnating/.
12. US Census Bureau, "2016 ACS 1-Year Estimates," updated October 8, 2021, https://www.census.gov/programs-surveys/acs/technical-documentation/table-and-geography-changes/2016/1-year.html.
13. The reasons why Black women do not marry out (marry a non-Black partner) at the same rate as Black men are complex and most likely have more to do with differences in their sense of community than with their economic interests. See Ralph Richard Banks, *Is Marriage for White People? How the African American Marriage Decline Affects Everyone* (New York: Penguin Group, 2012).
14. US Department of Labor, Bureau of Labor Statistics, "Usual Weekly Earnings of Wage and Salary Workers, Fourth Quarter 2021," News Release no. USDL-22-0078, January 19, 2021, https://www.bls.gov/news.release/pdf/wkyeng.pdf.

15. Black Demographics, "Black Marriage in America," accessed March 3, 2021, https://blackdemographics.com/households/marriage-in-black-america/. See also the Pew Research Center report finding that in 2015, 24 percent of Black male newlyweds married non-Black women compared with 12 percent of Black women who "married out." Kristen Bialik, "Key Facts About Race and Marriage, 50 Years After *Loving v. Virginia*," Pew Research Center, June 12, 2017, http://pewrsr.ch/2tcaRtz.
16. USAFacts, "State of American Households."
17. The 2020 Census should provide even more recent estimates, including the number of same-sex couples living together but not married. See USAFacts, "State of American Households."
18. Alicia Tuovila, "What You Should Know About Same-Sex Marriage Tax Benefits," Investopedia, updated January 21, 2022, https://www.investopedia.com/articles/personal-finance/080415/gay-marriage-and-taxes-everything-you-should-know.asp.
19. Horowitz, Graf, and Livingston, "Marriage and Cohabitation in the U.S."
20. Such as Elizabeth Thomson and Ugo Colella, "Cohabitation and Marital Stability: Quality or Commitment?," *Journal of Marriage and Family* 54, no. 2 (May 1992): 259–267, https://doi.org/10.2307/353057.
21. Ashley Fetters, "So Is Living Together Before Marriage Linked to Divorce or What?," *Atlantic*, October 24, 2018, https://www.theatlantic.com/family/archive/2018/10/premarital-cohabitation-divorce/573817/.
22. Kelli B. Grant, "Why Do So Many Parents Lack Life Insurance and Wills?," CNBC, July 8, 2015, https://www.cnbc.com/2015/07/07/why-do-so-many-parents-lack-life-insurance-and-wills.html.
23. Susan Shain, "The Rise of the Millennial Prenup," *New York Times*, July 6, 2018, https://www.nytimes.com/2018/07/06/smarter-living/millennial-prenup-weddings-money.html.
24. Juliana Menasce Horowitz, Nikki Graf, and Gretchen Livingston, "Why People Get Married or Move In with a Partner," Pew Research Center, November 6, 2019, https://www.pewresearch.org/social-trends/2019/11/06/why-people-get-married-or-move-in-with-a-partner/
25. Horowitz, Graf, and Livingston, "Why People Get Married or Move In."
26. Some questions were inspired by Eleanor Stanford, "13 Questions to Ask Before Getting Married," *New York Times*, March 24, 2016, https://www.nytimes.com/interactive/2016/03/23/fashion/weddings/marriage-questions.html."

Four: Baby Talk

1. US Census Bureau, "Historical Table 2. Distribution of Women Age 40 to 50 by Number of Children Ever Born and Marital Status: Selected Years, 1970 to 2018," Updated October 8, 2021, https://www.census.gov/data/tables/time-series/demo/fertility/his-cps.html#par_list

2. It is estimated that about 7 percent of children under eighteen are living with an adoptive parent or a stepparent. See Gretchen Livingston, "Childlessness Falls, Family Size Grows Among Highly Educated Women," Pew Research Center, May 7, 2015, https://www.pewresearch.org/social-trends/2015/05/07/childlessness-falls-family-size-grows-among-highly-educated-women/.
3. Gladys M. Martinez, Kimberly Daniels, and Isaedmarie Febo-Vazquez, "Fertility of Men and Women Aged 15–44 in the United States: National Survey of Family Growth, 2011–2015," *National Health Statistics Reports* 113 (July 11, 2018): 3, PMID: 30248009.
4. US Census Bureau, "Table FM-3. Average Number of Own Children Under 18 by Type of Family, 1955 to Present," Updated November 22, 2021, https://www.census.gov/data/tables/time-series/demo/families/families.html.
5. "Birth Rate in the United States in 2019, by Ethnic Group of Mother," Statista, January 27, 2022, https://www.statista.com/statistics/241514/birth-rate-by-ethnic-group-of-mother-in-the-us/.
6. Quoctrung Bui and Claire Cain Miller, "The Age That Women Have Babies: How a Gap Divides America," *New York Times*, August 4, 2018, https://www.nytimes.com/interactive/2018/08/04/upshot/up-birth-age-gap.html.
7. US Bureau of Labor Statistics, "Average Hours per Day Spent in Selected Activities on Days Worked by Employment Status and Sex," accessed November 14, 2021, https://www.bls.gov/charts/american-time-use/activity-by-work.htm.
8. Whitney Leach, "This Is Where People Work the Longest Hours," World Economic Forum, January 16, 2018, https://www.weforum.org/agenda/2018/01/the-countries-where-people-work-the-longest-hours/.
9. Joseph Chamie, "Out-of-Wedlock Births Rise Worldwide," YaleGlobal Online, March 16, 2017, https://archive-yaleglobal.yale.edu/content/out-wedlock-births-rise-worldwide.
10. Rham Dhel, "10 Reasons Why People Want Kids (and 10 Reasons They Don't)," March 2, 2022, https://wehavekids.com/having-baby/Most-Common-Reasons-Why-People-Want-Children.
11. Alex Williams, "To Breed or Not to Breed?," *New York Times*, November 20, 2021, updated December 2, 2021, https://www.nytimes.com/2021/11/20/style/breed-children-climate-change.html.
12. Leslie W. Price, "11 Reasons Some People Are Childless by Choice (and Why You Need to Stay Out of It)," Fairygodboss, accessed April 3, 2021, https://fairygodboss.com/career-topics/childless-by-choice.
13. Alyson Fearnley Shapiro, John M. Gottman, and Sybil Carrère, "The Baby and the Marriage: Identifying Factors That Buffer Against Decline in Marital Satisfaction After First Baby Arrives," *Journal of Family Psychology* 14, no. 1 (2000), 59–70, https://doi.org/10.1037//0893-3200.14.1.59.
14. Alyson F. Shapiro and John M. Gottman, "Effects on Marriage of a Psycho-Communicative-Educational Intervention with Couples Undergoing the

Transition to Parenthood, Evaluation at 1-Year Post Intervention," *Journal of Family Communication* 5, no. 1 (2005): 1–24, https://doi.org/10.1207/s15327698jfc0501_1.

15. "Child Labor," History.com, October 27, 2009, updated April 17, 2020, https://www.history.com/topics/industrial-revolution/child-labor.
16. Tim Parker, "The Cost of Raising a Child in the United States," Investopedia, updated January 9, 2022, https://www.investopedia.com/articles/personal-finance/090415/cost-raising-child-america.asp; Maryalene LaPonsie, "How Much Does It Cost to Raise a Child?," *U.S. News & World Report*, September 7, 2021, https://money.usnews.com/money/personal-finance/articles/how-much-does-it-cost-to-raise-a-child.
17. Parker, "Cost of Raising a Child in the United States."
18. "What Is Room and Board & What Will It Cost You?," Scholarship System, updated October 12, 2021, https://thescholarshipsystem.com/blog-for-students-families/what-is-room-and-board-what-will-it-cost-you/.
19. Melanie Hanson, "Average Cost of College & Tuition," Education Data Initiative, updated March 29, 2022, https://educationdata.org/average-cost-of-college.
20. "Parents Now Spend Twice as Much Time with Their Children as 50 Years Ago," *Economist*, November 27, 2017, https://www.economist.com/graphic-detail/2017/11/27/parents-now-spend-twice-as-much-time-with-their-children-as-50-years-ago; Joe Pinsker, "'Intensive' Parenting Is Now the Norm in America," *Atlantic*, January 16, 2019, https://www.theatlantic.com/family/archive/2019/01/intensive-helicopter-parenting-inequality/580528/.
21. Suzanne M. Bianchi, John P. Robinson, and Melissa A. Milkie, *Changing Rhythms of American Family Life* (New York: Russell Sage, 2006); online abstract at https://www.russellsage.org/publications/changing-rhythms-american-family-life-1.
22. Veronica Graham, "Parents Put 'Intensive Parenting' on a Pedestal; Experts Say There's a Better Approach," *Washington Post*, February 15, 2019, https://www.washingtonpost.com/lifestyle/2019/02/15/parents-put-intensive-parenting-pedestal-experts-say-theres-better-approach/.
23. Patrick Ishizuka, "Social Class, Gender, and Contemporary Parenting Standards in the United States: Evidence from a National Survey Experiment," *Social Forces* 98, no. 1 (September 2019): 31–58, https://doi.org/10.1093/sf/soy107.
24. Barbara Bronson Gray, "Over-Scheduling Kids May Be Detrimental to Their Development," CBS News, July 8, 2014, https://www.cbsnews.com/news/over-scheduling-kids-may-be-detrimental-to-their-development/.
25. "How Will the Wait Until 8th Pledge Work?," Wait Until 8th, accessed January 31, 2022, https://www.waituntil8th.org/faqs.
26. We are not suggesting that congenital abnormalities are something to be avoided at all costs, just that people may want to consider this in deciding when to have a child.

27. Carla Dugas and Valori H. Slane, *Miscarriage* (Treasure Island, FL: StatPearls, 2022), online edition last updated June 29, 2021, https://www.ncbi.nlm.nih.gov/books/NBK532992/.
28. "Risk of Miscarriage Linked Strongly to Mother's Age and Pregnancy History," BMJ, March 20, 2019, https://www.bmj.com/company/newsroom/risk-of-miscarriage-linked-strongly-to-mothers-age-and-pregnancy-history/.
29. American College of Obstetricians and Gynecologists, "FAQs: Having a Baby After Age 35: How Aging Affects Fertility and Pregnancy," accessed April 3, 2021, https://www.acog.org/womens-health/faqs/having-a-baby-after-age-35-how-aging-affects-fertility-and-pregnancy.
30. Sarah DeWeerdt, "The Link Between Parental Age and Autism, Explained," Spectrum, January 28, 2020, https://www.spectrumnews.org/news/link-parental-age-autism-explained/.
31. "Infertility and In Vitro Fertilization," WebMD, August 1, 2021, https://www.webmd.com/infertility-and-reproduction/guide/in-vitro-fertilization.
32. Abby Budiman and Mark Hugo Lopez, "Amid Decline in International Adoptions to U.S., Boys Outnumber Girls for the First Time," Pew Research Center, October 17, 2017, https://www.pewresearch.org/fact-tank/2017/10/17/amid-decline-in-international-adoptions-to-u-s-boys-outnumber-girls-for-the-first-time/.
33. Joyce A. Martin, Brady E. Hamilton, and Michelle J. K. Osterman, "Births in the United States, 2015," NCHS Data Brief no. 258 (September 2016): 1–8, http://www.cdc.gov/nchs/data/databriefs/db258.pdf.
34. Mary Boo, "Foster Care Population Rises Again in 2015," North American Council on Adoptable Children, February 7, 2016, https://nacac.org/resource/foster-care-population-risen-2015.
35. "US Adoption Statistics," Adoption Network, accessed April 3, 2021, https://adoptionnetwork.com/adoption-myths-facts/domestic-us-statistics/.
36. Budiman and Lopez, "Amid Decline in International Adoptions."
37. "Annual Report on Intercountry Adoption," Travel.State.Gov, accessed April 3, 2021, https://travel.state.gov/content/dam/NEWadoptionassets/pdfs/FY%202019%20Annual%20Report%20.pdf.
38. "What Is the Cost of Adoption from Foster Care?," AdoptUSKids, accessed November 26, 2021, https://www.adoptuskids.org/adoption-and-foster-care/overview/what-does-it-cost; David Dodge, "What I Spent to Adopt My Child," *New York Times*, February 11, 2020, updated February 18, 2020, https://www.nytimes.com/2020/02/11/parenting/adoption-costs.html.
39. Nancy Rosenhaus, "How Long Does It Take to Adopt a Baby?," Adoptions with Love, November 25, 2021, https://adoptionswithlove.org/adoptive-parents/how-long-does-it-take-to-adopt.

40. Caitlin Snyder, "What Is the Timeline for an International Adoption?," RainbowKids, July 7, 2016, https://www.rainbowkids.com/adoption-stories/what-is-the-timeline-for-an-international-adoption-1684.
41. David Dodge, "What to Know Before Adopting a Child," *New York Times*, April 18, 2020, updated March 25, 2022, https://www.nytimes.com/2020/04/18/parenting/guides/adopting-a-child.html. This article provides the names of numerous agencies and organizations that can help you make adoption decisions.
42. Dodge, "What to Know Before Adopting a Child."
43. Abby wrote about celebrating "Airplane Day," or the day her brother arrived, in a short piece in an anthology of stories of adoption edited by Sarah Holloway called *Family Wanted: True Stories of Adoption* (New York: Random House, 2006).
44. JaeRan Kim, "Advice to Parents Adopting a Child of Another Race," Adopt USKids, July 12, 2021, https://blog.adoptuskids.org/advice-to-parents-adopting-a-child-of-another-race/.
45. Claire Cain Miller, "Americans Are Having Fewer Babies. They Told Us Why," *New York Times*, July 5, 2018, https://www.nytimes.com/2018/07/05/upshot/americans-are-having-fewer-babies-they-told-us-why.html.
46. Virginia Sole-Smith and Nicole Harris, "Are You at Risk of Having a Baby with Down Syndrome?," *Parents*, updated September 9, 2020, https://www.parents.com/health/down-syndrome/are-you-at-risk-of-having-a-baby-with-down-syndrome/.
47. For more on this, see Indra Nooyi's memoir, *My Life in Full: Work, Family, and Our Future* (New York: Penguin Random House, 2021).
48. Larry Light, "Why You Shouldn't Buy Insurance (OK, Some May Need It)," *Forbes*, March 20, 2018, https://www.forbes.com/sites/lawrencelight/2018/03/20/why-you-shouldnt-buy-life-insurance-ok-some-may-need-it/.
49. Maxime Croll, "The Pros and Cons of Permanent Life Insurance," ValuePenguin, updated September 15, 2021, https://www.valuepenguin.com/life-insurance/permanent-life-insurance.
50. Daisy Dowling, chap. 6 in *Workparent: The Complete Guide to Succeeding on the Job, Staying True to Yourself, and Raising Happy Kids* (Boston, MA: Harvard Business Review Press, 2021), 174–185.
51. Thomas Gilovich and Victoria Husted Medvec, "The Temporal Pattern to the Experience of Regret," *Journal of Personality and Social Psychology* 67, no. 3 (September 1994): 357–365, https://content.apa.org/doi/10.1037/0022-3514.67.3.357.

Five: Let's Make a Deal

1. Sarah Jane Glynn, "An Unequal Division of Labor," Center for American Progress, May 18, 2018, https://www.americanprogress.org/article/unequal-division-labor/.

2. Glynn, "Unequal Division of Labor," 7–9.
3. Glynn, "Unequal Division of Labor," 8. See Katherine Guyot and Isabel V. Sawhill, "Telecommuting Will Likely Continue Long After the Pandemic," Brookings Institution blog, April 6, 2020, https://www.brookings.edu/blog/up-front/2020/04/06/telecommuting-will-likely-continue-long-after-the-pandemic/.
4. Kristin W. Vogan, "This Is Your Kid's School and Even Though the Emergency Contact Form Lists Your Husband, We Need You, the Mom," McSweeney's Internet Tendency, December 28, 2021, https://www.mcsweeneys.net/articles/this-is-your-kids-school-and-even-though-the-emergency-contact-form-lists-your-husband-we-need-you-the-mom.
5. Arlie Russell Hochschild and Anne Machung, *The Second Shift: Working Parents and the Revolution at Home* (New York: Avon Books, 1989).
6. Hochschild and Machung, *The Second Shift*.
7. Aliya Hamid Rao, "Even Breadwinning Wives Don't Get Equality at Home," *Atlantic*, May 12, 2019, https://www.theatlantic.com/family/archive/2019/05/breadwinning-wives-gender-inequality/589237/. See also Aliya Hamid Rao, *Crunch Time: How Married Couples Confront Unemployment* (Berkeley: University of California Press, 2020).
8. Wendy Klein and Marjorie Harness Goodwin, "Chores," in *Fast-Forward Family: Home, Work, and Relationships in Middle-Class America*, ed. Elinor Ochs and Tamar Kremer-Sadlik (Berkeley: University of California Press, 2013), 111–129.
9. Eve Rodsky, "I Created a System to Make Sure My Husband and I Divide Household Duties Fairly. Here's How It Works," *Time*, October 1, 2019, https://time.com/5690007/divide-household-chores-fairly/.
10. Maaike van der Vleuten, Eva Jaspers, and Tanja van der Lippe, "Same-Sex Couples' Division of Labor from a Cross-National Perspective," *Journal of GLBT Family Studies* 17, no. 2 (2021): 150–167, https://doi.org/10.1080/1550428X.2020.1862012.
11. US Bureau of Labor Statistics, "American Time Use Survey," accessed October 23, 2021, https://www.bls.gov/charts/american-time-use/activity-by-hldh.htm>>
12. Lauren Bauer et al., "Ten Economic Facts on How Mothers Spend Their Time," The Hamilton Project at Brookings Institution, March 2021, 6, https://www.brookings.edu/wp-content/uploads/2021/03/Maternal_Time_Use_Facts_final-1.pdf.
13. Eve Rodsky, chaps. 7 and 8 in *Fair Play: A Game-Changing Solution for When You Have Too Much to Do (and More Life to Live)* (New York: G. P. Putnam's Sons, 2019), 163–243.
14. Sharon Meers and Joanna Strober, *Getting to 50/50: How Working Parents Can Have It All* (Berkeley, CA: Viva Editions, 2013; original hardback edition published by Bantam Dell, 2009), 190.

15. Steven Rowe, "How to Split Chores When the Honey-Do List Gets Heated," PsychCentral, updated July 30, 2021, https://psychcentral.com/lib/chore-war-household-tasks-and-the-two-paycheck-couple#6.
16. Eric Rosenberg, "Is a Maid Worth the Money or Should I Clean Myself?," Investopedia, updated March 8, 2022, https://www.investopedia.com/articles/personal-finance/120815/maid-worth-money-or-should-i-clean-myself.asp.
17. Klein and Goodwin, "Chores."
18. Chef Chang, "Eating Out vs. Cooking at Home: The 12 Statistics You Must See," Slice of Kitchen, May 17, 2019, https://sliceofkitchen.com/eating-out-vs-cooking-at-home-statistics/.
19. Roberto A. Ferdman, "The Slow Death of the Home-Cooked Meal," *Washington Post*, March 5, 2015, https://www.washingtonpost.com/news/wonk/wp/2015/03/05/the-slow-death-of-the-home-cooked-meal/.
20. Nir Halevy and Matt Abrahams, "Dissolve Disagreements: How Communication Impacts Conflict," Stanford Graduate School of Business, Insights by Stanford Business, April 1, 2021, https://www.gsb.stanford.edu/insights/dissolve-disagreements-how-communication-impacts-conflict.
21. Raven Ishak, "The Relationship-Saving Way to Split Chores with Your Partner," Everygirl, July 30, 2019, https://theeverygirl.com/split-chores-with-your-partner/.
22. Jennifer Miller, "Family Life Is Chaotic. Could Office Software Help?," *New York Times*, May 27, 2020, https://www.nytimes.com/2020/05/27/style/family-calendar.html?searchResultPosition=1.

Six: There's No Place Like Home

1. D'Vera Cohn and Rich Morin, "Who Moves? Who Stays Put? Where's Home?," Pew Research Center, December 17, 2008, updated December 29, 2008, https://www.pewresearch.org/social-trends/2008/12/17/who-moves-who-stays-put-wheres-home/.
2. Quoctrung Bui and Claire Cain Miller, "The Typical American Lives Only 18 Miles from Mom," *New York Times*, December 23, 2015, https://www.nytimes.com/interactive/2015/12/24/upshot/24up-family.html.
3. Elissa Strauss, "How 'Alloparenting' Can Be a Less Isolating Way to Raise Kids," CNN, updated June 15, 2021, https://www.cnnphilippines.com/lifestyle/2021/6/16/Alloparenting-raising-kids.html.
4. D'Vera Cohn, "As the Pandemic Persisted, Financial Pressures Became a Bigger Factor in Why Americans Decided to Move," Pew Research Center, February 4, 2021, https://www.pewresearch.org/fact-tank/2021/02/04/as-the-pandemic-persisted-financial-pressures-became-a-bigger-factor-in-why-americans-decided-to-move/.
5. Cohn, "As the Pandemic Persisted."
6. Richard L. Florida, *Who's Your City? How the Creative Economy Is Making*

Where to Live the Most Important Decision of Your Life (New York: Basic Books, 2008), 196.

7. Florida, *Who's Your City?*, 200.
8. "What the Future: Housing," Ipsos, November 16, 2021, https://www.ipsos.com/sites/default/files/What-The-Future-Housing.pdf.
9. "What the Future: Housing," 19.
10. Ron Lieber, "Make Your First Home Your Last: The Case for Not Moving Up," *New York Times*, October 17, 2020, https://www.nytimes.com/2020/10/17/your-money/real-estate-coronavirus-mortgage.html.
11. Carly M. Thornock et al., "There's No Place Like Home: The Associations Between Residential Attributes and Family Functioning," *Journal of Environmental Psychology* 64 (August 2019): 39–47, https://doi.org/10.1016/j.jenvp.2019.04.011.
12. "What the Future: Housing," 5.
13. "What Is MUJI?," Ryohin Keikaku Co., accessed November 7, 2021, https://ryohin-keikaku.jp/eng/about-muji/whatismuji/.
14. Drew DeSilver, "As National Eviction Ban Expires, a Look at Who Rents and Who Owns in the U.S.," Pew Research Center, August 2, 2021, https://www.pewresearch.org/fact-tank/2021/08/02/as-national-eviction-ban-expires-a-look-at-who-rents-and-who-owns-in-the-u-s/.
15. DeSilver, "As National Eviction Ban Expires."
16. Debra Kamin, "The Market for Single-Family Rentals Grows as Homeownership Wanes," *New York Times*, October 22, 2021, https://www.nytimes.com/2021/10/22/realestate/single-family-rentals.html.
17. Florida, *Who's Your City?*, 154.
18. "What the Future: Housing."
19. "Renovate or Move: Our Flowchart Will Help You Decide," Zebra, updated August 9, 2021, https://www.thezebra.com/resources/home/renovate-or-move/.
20. Barry Schwartz et al., "Maximizing Versus Satisficing: Happiness Is a Matter of Choice," *Journal of Personality and Social Psychology* 83, no. 5 (2002): 1178–1197, https://doi.org/10.1037/0022-3514.83.5.1178.
21. P. Brickman, D. Coates, and R. Janoff-Bulman, "Lottery Winners and Accident Victims: Is Happiness Relative?," *Journal of Personality and Social Psychology* 36, no. 8 (August 1978): 917–927, https://doi.org/10.1037//0022-3514.36.8.917.
22. Kennon M. Sheldon and Sonja Lyubomirsky, "The Challenge of Staying Happier: Testing the Hedonic Adaptation Prevention Model," *Personality and Social Psychology Bulletin* 38, no. 5 (2012): 670–680, https://doi.org/10.1177%2F0146167212436400.
23. Ron Lieber, "43 Questions to Ask Before Picking a New Town," *New York Times*, May 2, 2014, https://www.nytimes.com/2014/05/03/your-money/43-questions-to-ask-before-picking-a-new-town.html.

24. Alexis Grant, "How We Decided Where to Live, and Chose an Unexpected Place," January 6, 2020, https://alexisgrant.com/2020/01/06/how-to-decide-where-to-live/.

Seven: Making It Work

1. "PayScale Research Shows Women Who Leave the Workforce Incur Up to a 7 Percent Pay Penalty upon Their Return," PayScale, April 5, 2018, https://www.payscale.com/compensation-trends/gender-pay-gap-research/.
2. Courtney Connley, "More Dads Are Choosing to Stay at Home with Their Kids. Will Covid-19 Accelerate This Trend?," CNBC, May 7, 2021, https://www.cnbc.com/2021/05/07/stay-at-home-dads-were-on-the-rise-pre-pandemic-will-covid-accelerate-the-trend.html.
3. Kim Eckart, "Why 9 to 5 Isn't the Only Shift That Can Work for Busy Families," UW News, University of Washington, June 20, 2018, https://www.washington.edu/news/2018/06/20/why-9-to-5-isnt-the-only-shift-that-can-work-for-busy-families/.
4. Jianghong Li et al., "Parents' Nonstandard Work Schedules and Child Well-Being: A Critical Review of the Literature," *Journal of Primary Prevention* 35 (2014): 53–73, https://doi.org/10.1007/s10935-013-0318-z.
5. Eckart, "Why 9 to 5 Isn't the Only Shift."
6. US Census Bureau, "Table F-22. Married-Couple Families with Wives' Earnings Greater than Husbands' Earnings," accessed October 12, 2021, https://www.census.gov/data/tables/time-series/demo/income-poverty/historical-income-families.html.
7. US Census Bureau, "Table F-14. Work Experience of Husband and Wife—Married-Couple Families, by Presence of Children Under 18 Years Old and by Median and Mean Income," accessed August 30, 2021, http://www.census.gov/data/tables/time-series/demo/income-poverty/historical-income-families.html. See also "PayScale Research Shows Women Who Leave the Workforce."
8. Brian Knop, "Among Recent Moms, More Educated Most Likely to Work," US Census Bureau, August 19, 2019, https://www.census.gov/library/stories/2019/08/are-women-really-opting-out-of-work-after-they-have-babies.html.
9. Dina Gerdeman, "Kids of Working Moms Grow into Happy Adults," *Harvard Business School Working Knowledge*, July 16, 2018, https://hbswk.hbs.edu/item/kids-of-working-moms-grow-into-happy-adults. The article is based on research by Harvard Business School professor Kathleen McGinn.
10. Cathy Benko, "How the Corporate Ladder Became the Corporate Lattice," *Harvard Business Review*, November 4, 2010, https://hbr.org/2010/11/how-the-corporate-ladder-becam.
11. Mark J. Perry, "Women Earned Majority of Doctoral Degrees in 2019 for 11th Straight Year and Outnumber Men in Grad School 141 to 100," American Enterprise Institute, October 15, 2020, https://www.aei.org/carpe-diem

/women-earned-majority-of-doctoral-degrees-in-2019-for-11th-straight-year-and-outnumber-men-in-grad-school-141-to-100/.

12. "The Majority of U.S. Medical Students Are Women, New Data Show," Association of American Medical Colleges, December 9, 2019, https://www.aamc.org/news-insights/press-releases/majority-us-medical-students-are-women-new-data-show.
13. Enjuris, "Report: Where Do Women Go to Law School in the U.S.?," GlobeNewswire, March 1, 2021, https://www.globenewswire.com/news-release/2021/03/01/2183996/0/en/Report-Where-Do-Women-Go-to-Law-School-in-the-U-S.html.
14. Enjuris, "Where Do Women Go to Law School?"
15. Amy Paturel, "Why Women Leave Medicine," Association of American Medical Colleges, October 1, 2019, https://www.aamc.org/news-insights/why-women-leave-medicine.
16. Paturel, "Why Women Leave Medicine."
17. James Allen, "The Total Cost to Train a Physician," *The Hospital Medical Director* (blog), July 11, 2019, https://hospitalmedicaldirector.com/the-total-cost-to-train-a-physician/.
18. Paturel, "Why Women Leave Medicine."
19. Emma Goldberg, "When the Surgeon Is a Mom," *New York Times*, December 20, 2019, https://www.nytimes.com/2019/12/20/science/doctors-surgery-motherhood-medical-school.html.
20. Roberta D. Liebenberg and Stephanie A. Scharf, "Walking Out the Door: The Facts, Figures, and Future of Experienced Women Lawyers in Private Practice," American Bar Association and ALM Intelligence Legal Compass, 2019, https://www.americanbar.org/content/dam/aba/administrative/women/walking-out-the-door-4920053.pdf.
21. Liebenberg and Scharf, "Walking Out the Door."
22. "Data Snapshot: Full-Time Women Faculty and Faculty of Color," American Association of University Professors, December 9, 2020, https://www.aaup.org/news/data-snapshot-full-time-women-faculty-and-faculty-color#.YWOLfRDMI7Y.
23. Wendy Wang, "Mothers and Work: What's 'Ideal'?," Pew Research Center, August 19, 2013, https://www.pewresearch.org/fact-tank/2013/08/19/mothers-and-work-whats-ideal/.
24. Lonnie Golden, "Part-Time Workers Pay a Big-Time Penalty," Economic Policy Institute, February 27, 2020, https://www.epi.org/publication/part-time-pay-penalty/.
25. Monica Torres, "Going Part Time Can Be a Cruel Trap for Women, but There's a Way to Do It Right," HuffPost, June 21, 2019, updated July 15, 2019, https://www.huffpost.com/entry/part-time-work-trap-tips-women_l_5d091ea2e4b06ad4d256f856.

26. Megan Dunn, "Who Chooses Part-Time Work and Why?," *Monthly Labor Review*, US Bureau of Labor Statistics, March 2018, https://www.bls.gov/opub/mlr/2018/article/pdf/who-chooses-part-time-work-and-why.pdf.
27. Boris Groysberg, Paul Healy, and Eric Lin, "Job-Hopping Toward Equity," *MIT Sloan Management Review*, July 14, 2021, https://sloanreview.mit.edu/article/job-hopping-toward-equity/.
28. The percentages of care arrangements exceed 100 percent because slightly more than 25 percent of children are cared for in multiple arrangements, including by their fathers, who work different shifts from their mothers.
29. "51 Percent of People in the United States Live in a Child Care Desert," Center for American Progress, 2020, accessed October 15, 2021, https://childcaredeserts.org/2018/.
30. Sylvia Ann Hewlett and Carolyn Buck Luce, "Off-Ramps and On-Ramps: Keeping Talented Women on the Road to Success," *Harvard Business Review*, March 1, 2005, https://hbr.org/2005/03/off-ramps-and-on-ramps-keeping-talented-women-on-the-road-to-success; Sylvia Ann Hewlett et al., *Off-Ramps and On-Ramps Revisited* (New York: Center for Work-Life Policy, 2010).
31. Elaine Pofeldt, "Survey: Nearly 30% of Americans Are Self-Employed," *Forbes*, May 30, 2020, https://www.forbes.com/sites/elainepofeldt/2020/05/30/survey-nearly-30-of-americans-are-self-employed/?sh=35c3265e2d21.
32. Pamela Stone and Meg Lovejoy, *Opting Back In: What Really Happens When Mothers Go Back to Work* (Oakland: University of California Press, 2019).
33. Sylvia Ann Hewlett, Laura Sherbin, and Diana Forster, "Off-Ramps and On-Ramps Revisited," *Harvard Business Review*, June 2010, https://hbr.org/2010/06/off-ramps-and-on-ramps-revisited.
34. "Why Lack of Sleep Is Bad for Your Health," UK National Health Service, accessed October 13, 2021, https://www.nhs.uk/live-well/sleep-and-tiredness/why-lack-of-sleep-is-bad-for-your-health/ (page discontinued).

Eight: Choppy Waters

1. John Gottman, *Why Marriages Succeed or Fail: And How You Can Make Yours Last* (New York: Simon & Schuster, 2012).
2. Chrisanna Northrup, Pepper Schwartz, and James Witte, "Sex at 50-Plus: What's Normal?," AARP, accessed April 19, 2021, https://www.aarp.org/home-family/sex-intimacy/info-01-2013/seniors-having-sex-older-couples.html.
3. Belinda Luscombe, "Yes, Couples Who Share Chores Have More Sex," *Time*, June 22, 2016, https://time.com/4378502/yes-couples-who-share-chores-have-more-sex/.
4. Susan Dominus, "The Sexual Healer," *New York Times*, January 24, 2014, https://www.nytimes.com/2014/01/26/fashion/Sex-Esther-Perel-Couples-Therapy.html.

5. Wendy Wang, "Who Cheats More? The Demographics of Infidelity in America," Institute for Family Studies, January 10, 2018, https://ifstudies.org/blog/who-cheats-more-the-demographics-of-cheating-in-america.
6. Rebeca A. Marín, Andrew Christensen, and David C. Atkins, "Infidelity and Behavioral Couple Therapy: Relationship Outcomes over 5 Years Following Therapy," *Couple and Family Psychology: Research and Practice* 3, no. 1 (2014): 1–12, https://psycnet.apa.org/doi/10.1037/cfp0000012.
7. Marín, Christensen, and Atkins, "Infidelity and Behavioral Couple Therapy."
8. Bank of America, "2018 Better Money Habits Millennial Report," Winter 2018, https://bettermoneyhabits.bankofamerica.com/content/dam/bmh/pdf/ar6vnln9-boa-bmh-millennial-report-winter-2018-final2.pdf.
9. Jennifer Petriglieri, *Couples That Work: How Dual-Career Couples Can Thrive in Love and Work* (Boston, MA: Harvard Business Review Press, 2019).
10. Brianna Holt, "Counseling Is Not Only for Couples in Crisis," *New York Times*, April 13, 2021, https://www.nytimes.com/2021/04/13/style/couples-therapy.html.
11. The rate is lower for couples who marry after age twenty-five, for couples whose first baby is born more than seven months after marriage, for couples with some college education, and for couples with incomes above the median. The rate for second or third marriages is higher than the rate for first marriages (60–67 percent for second marriages and 73–74 percent for third marriages). The higher rate for additional marriages is partly what pundits have in mind when they say that remarriage is the triumph of hope over experience.
12. Hal Arkowitz and Scott O. Lilienfeld, "Is Divorce Bad for Children?," *Scientific American* (March 1, 2013): 68–69, https://www.scientificamerican.com/article/is-divorce-bad-for-children/.
13. Arkowitz and Lilienfeld, "Is Divorce Bad for Children?," 68–69.
14. Bruce Fredenburg, "How to Lessen the Stress Divorce Has on Your College-Aged Child," Divorced Moms, September 8, 2020, https://divorcedmoms.com/how-to-lessen-the-stress-divorce-has-on-your-college-aged-child.
15. Aaron Thomas, "What Types of Divorces Typically Go to Trial?," Lawyers.com, March 31, 2016, https://www.lawyers.com/legal-info/family-law/divorce/what-types-of-divorces-typically-go-to-trial.html.
16. Myra H. Strober, "What's a Wife Worth?," in *Inside the American Couple: New Thinking, New Challenges*, ed. Marilyn Yalom and Laura L. Carstensen (Berkeley: University of California Press, 2002), 174–188.
17. Edward Tsui, "Divorce and Child Custody: Everything You Need to Know," Expertise.com, updated February 24, 2022, https://www.expertise.com/divorce-attorney/divorce-and-child-custody-everything-you-need-to-know.
18. "Who Gets Custody of the Child(ren)?," LawFirms, accessed April 26, 2021, https://www.lawfirms.com/resources/child-custody/custody-during-divorce/who-gets-custody.htm.

19. "Child Support Requirements for Post-Secondary Education by State," DivorceNet, accessed April 28, 2021, https://www.divorcenet.com/states/washington/wa_art02.
20. "How Is California Child Support Calculated When There Is Joint Physical Custody?," Law Offices of Paul H. Nathan, accessed February 9, 2022, https://www.nathanlawoffices.com/faqs/how-is-california-child-support-calculated-when-there-is-joint-physical-custody-.cfm.
21. US Census Bureau, "44 Percent of Custodial Parents Receive the Full Amount of Child Support," press release, January 30, 2018, https://www.census.gov/newsroom/press-releases/2018/cb18-tps03.html.
22. Law Office of Jody L. Fisher, "How Does a Judge Determine Alimony?," Jody Fisher Law, April 20, 2020, https://www.attorney-fisher.com/blog/2020/april/how-does-a-judge-determine-alimony-/.
23. Lynda Gratton and Andrew J. Scott, *The 100-Year Life: Living and Working in an Age of Longevity* (London: Bloomsbury Information, 2016), 207.
24. Ann Gold Buscho, "Do Trial Separations Ever Work?," *Psychology Today*, November 23, 2021, https://www.psychologytoday.com/us/blog/better-divorce/202111/do-trial-separations-ever-work.
25. Robert Taibbi, "Why Separations Usually Lead to Divorce," *Psychology Today*, August 8, 2020, https://www.psychologytoday.com/us/blog/fixing-families/202008/why-separations-usually-lead-divorce.

Nine: The Senior Years

1. Lauren Medina, Shannon Sabo, and Jonathan Vespa, "Living Longer: Historical and Projected Life Expectancy in the United States, 1960 to 2060," US Census Bureau, Current Population Reports no. P25-1145, February 2020, https://www.census.gov/content/dam/Census/library/publications/2020/demo/p25-1145.pdf, 3.
2. Medina, Sabo, and Vespa, "Living Longer," 3.
3. Eilene Zimmerman, "What 'Retirement' Means Now," *New York Times*, September 12, 2019, https://www.nytimes.com/2019/09/12/business/retirement/what-retirement-means-now.html.
4. "How to Plan and Invest for Retirement Throughout Your Life—Even When It Feels Like You Have Other Financial Priorities," *Real Simple*, April 5, 2021, https://www.realsimple.com/money/money-confidential-podcast/episode-6-claudia-new-rules-retirement.
5. Sarah Laskow, "How Retirement Was Invented," *Atlantic*, October 24, 2014, https://www.theatlantic.com/business/archive/2014/10/how-retirement-was-invented/381802/.
6. "Life Expectancy for Men at the Age of 65 Years in the U.S. from 1960 to 2019," Statista, accessed August 11, 2021, https://www.statista.com/statistics/266657/us-life-expectancy-for-men-aat-the-age-of-65-years-since-1960/.

7. Gratton and Scott, *100-Year Life*, 1; Alessandra Malito, "Good News and Bad News: Kids Born Today Will Probably Live to Be Older than 100—and They'll Need to Pay for It," MarketWatch, June 15, 2019, https://www.marketwatch.com/story/good-news-and-bad-news-kids-born-today-will-probably-live-to-be-older-than-100-and-theyll-need-to-pay-for-it-2019-06-14.
8. "Mandatory Retirement: Is It Legal?," Strategic HR, April 25, 2017, https://strategichrinc.com/mandatory-retirement-guidelines/.
9. "How Much Do You Really Need to Save for Retirement?," Merrill, accessed August 12, 2021, https://www.merrilledge.com/article/how-much-do-you-really-need-to-save-for-retirement; John Waggoner, "How Much Money Do You Need to Retire?," AARP, updated January 6, 2021, https://www.aarp.org/retirement/planning-for-retirement/info-2020/how-much-money-do-you-need-to-retire.html.
10. Peter Coy, "How to Enjoy Retirement Without Going Broke," *New York Times*, August 27, 2021, https://www.nytimes.com/2021/08/27/opinion/how-to-enjoy-retirement-without-going-broke.html.
11. William G. Gale, J. Mark Iwry, and David C. John, eds., *Wealth After Work: Innovative Reforms to Expand Retirement Security* (Washington, DC: Brookings Institution, 2021), 16.
12. James Royal and Brian Baker, "What Is the Average Social Security Check?," Bankrate, April 7, 2022, https://www.bankrate.com/retirement/average-monthly-social-security-check/.
13. "Most Retirees Never Move to New Home, Study Finds," FEDweek, March 19, 2020, https://www.fedweek.com/retirement-financial-planning/most-retirees-never-move-to-new-home-study-finds/.
14. Jane E. Brody, "Keeping Older Drivers Protected on the Road," *New York Times*, October 18, 2021, updated October 21, 2021, https://www.nytimes.com/2021/10/18/well/live/old-drivers.html.
15. Brody, "Keeping Older Drivers Protected."
16. Maggie Germano, "Despite Their Priorities, Nearly Half of Americans over 55 Still Don't Have a Will," *Forbes*, February 15, 2019, https://www.forbes.com/sites/maggiegermano/2019/02/15/despite-their-priorities-nearly-half-of-americans-over-55-still-dont-have-a-will/?sh=2e7683345238.
17. "2019 Profile of Older Americans," Administration for Community Living and Administration on Aging, US Department of Health and Human Services, May 2020, https://acl.gov/sites/default/files/Aging%20and%20Disability%20in%20America/2019ProfileOlderAmericans508.pdf.
18. Lynn Hallarman, "What I've Learned over a Lifetime of Caring for the Dying," *New York Times*, August 11, 2021, https://www.nytimes.com/2021/08/11/opinion/health-care-aides-elderly.html.
19. Lita Epstein, "Medicaid and Nursing Homes: A Quick Guide to the Rules," Investopedia, accessed August 15, 2021, https://www.investopedia.com

/articles/personal-finance/072215/quick-guide-medicaid-and-nursing-home-rules.asp.

20. “What Is Long-Term Care (LTC) and Who Needs It?,” LongTermCare.gov, last modified January 4, 2021, https://acl.gov/ltc.
21. “Formal Cost of Long-Term Care Services,” PwC, accessed July 23, 2021, https://www.pwc.com/us/en/insurance/assets/pwc-insurance-cost-of-long-term-care.pdf.
22. Scott Witt and Jeff Hoyt, “Skilled Nursing Costs,” SeniorLiving.org, updated January 4, 2022, https://www.seniorliving.org/skilled-nursing/cost/.
23. Alexander Sammon, “The Collapse of Long-Term Care Insurance,” American Prospect, October 20, 2020, https://prospect.org/familycare/the-collapse-of-long-term-care-insurance/.
24. Sammon, “Collapse.”
25. Dhruv Khullar, “Who Will Care for the Caregivers?,” *New York Times*, January 19, 2017, https://www.nytimes.com/2017/01/19/upshot/who-will-care-for-the-caregivers.html.
26. “Home Health Aide Salary in United States,” Indeed, accessed August 15, 2021, https://www.indeed.com/career/home-health-aide/salaries.
27. “Nursing Home Aide Salary,” ZipRecruiter, accessed August 19, 2021, https://www.ziprecruiter.com/Salaries/Nursing-Home-Aide-Salary.
28. National Center on Caregiving, “Women and Caregiving: Facts and Figures,” Family Caregiver Alliance, accessed August 19, 2021, https://www.caregiver.org/resource/women-and-caregiving-facts-and-figures/.
29. Carol Bradley Bursack, “Do Parents Really Want to Live with Their Adult Children?,” AgingCare, accessed September 1, 2021, https://www.agingcare.com/articles/parents-living-with-adult-children-152285.htm.
30. Gina Kolata, “More Americans Are Dying at Home Than in Hospitals,” *New York Times*, December 11, 2019, updated December 26, 2019, https://www.nytimes.com/2019/12/11/health/death-hospitals-home.html.
31. “Assisted Suicide in the United States,” Wikipedia, accessed August 14, 2021, https://en.wikipedia.org/wiki/Assisted_suicide_in_the_United_States.
32. Irvin D. Yalom and Marilyn Yalom, *A Matter of Death and Life* (Stanford, CA: Stanford University Press, 2021), 102, 100, 105.
33. Bart Astor, “After Covid-19: What Housing for America’s Oldest Could Be Like,” *Forbes*, July 23, 2020, https://www.forbes.com/sites/nextavenue/2020/07/23/after-covid-19-what-housing-for-americas-oldest-could-be-like/?sh=343e49b71eb5.
34. Suzy Khimm, “The Hidden Covid-19 Health Crisis: Elderly People Are Dying from Isolation,” NBC News, October 27, 2020, updated November 17, 2020, https://www.nbcnews.com/news/us-news/hidden-covid-19-health-crisis-elderly-people-are-dying-isolation-n1244853.
35. Bruce Drake, “The Sandwich Generation: Burdens on Middle-Aged Americans on the Rise,” Pew Research Center, May 15, 2013, https://www

.pewresearch.org/fact-tank/2013/05/15/the-sandwich-generation-burdens-on-middle-aged-americans-on-the-rise/.

36. "The US Population Is Aging," Urban Institute, accessed July 23, 2021, https://www.urban.org/policy-centers/cross-center-initiatives/program-retirement-policy/projects/data-warehouse/what-future-holds/us-population-aging.
37. Barry J. Jacobs, "The Sandwich Generation Feels the Caregiving Crunch," AARP, January 3, 2020, https://www.aarp.org/caregiving/life-balance/info-2020/sandwich-generation-caregivers.html.
38. Esther Koch, "Kiss the Joy as It Flies By," Stanford Business Magazine, November 2006, http://www.encoremgmt.com/images/Kiss_The_Joy_As_It_Flies_By.pdf.
39. Gretchen Livingston, "Adult Caregiving Often Seen as Very Meaningful by Those Who Do It," Pew Research Center, November 8, 2018, https://www.pewresearch.org/fact-tank/2018/11/08/adult-caregiving-often-seen-as-very-meaningful-by-those-who-do-it/.
40. Ezra Klein, "Alison Gopnik Changed How I Think About Love," Vox podcast, June 13, 2019, https://www.vox.com/podcasts/2019/6/13/18677595/alison-gopnik-changed-how-i-think-about-love.

Ten: Be the Change

1. "Civilian Labor Force by Sex," US Department of Labor, Women's Bureau, accessed August 20, 2021, https://www.dol.gov/agencies/wb/data/lfp/civilianlfbysex.
2. "Employment Characteristics of Families—2018," US Department of Labor, Bureau of Labor Statistics, news release no. USDL-19-0666, April 18, 2019, https://www.bls.gov/news.release/archives/famee_04182019.pdf.
3. Debra E. Meyerson, *Tempered Radicals: How People Use Difference to Inspire Change at Work* (Boston, MA: Harvard Business School Press, 2001), xi.
4. Meyerson, *Tempered Radicals*, 17.
5. David Smith, "The Plural of Anecdote Is Data, After All," *Revolutions* (blog), April 6, 2011, https://blog.revolutionanalytics.com/2011/04/the-plural-of-anecdote-is-data-after-all.html.
6. Ian Cook, "Who Is Driving the Great Resignation?," *Harvard Business Review*, September 15, 2021, https://hbr.org/2021/09/who-is-driving-the-great-resignation.
7. Joseph B. Fuller and Manjari Raman, "The Caring Company," Harvard Business School, updated January 17, 2019, https://www.hbs.edu/managing-the-future-of-work/Documents/The_Caring_Company.pdf.
8. Fuller and Raman, "Caring Company," 2.
9. Amy Henderson, "The Secret Society of Parents from Tech's Biggest Companies," *Fast Company*, May 1, 2018, https://www.fastcompany.com/40563270/the-secret-society-of-parents-from-techs-biggest-companies.

10. Francine D. Blau and Lawrence M. Kahn, "Female Labor Supply: Why Is the United States Falling Behind?," *American Economic Review: Papers & Proceedings 2013* 103, no. 3 (May 2013): 251–256, http://dx.doi.org/10.1257/aer.103.3.251.
11. Miranda Bryant, "Paternity Leave: US Is Least Generous in List of World's Richest Countries," *Guardian*, January 29, 2020, https://www.theguardian.com/us-news/2020/jan/29/paternity-leave-us-policy.
12. Lynn Erdman, "Father's Day: A Father's Bond with His Newborn Is Just as Important as a Mother's Bond," HuffPost, June 8, 2017, https://www.huffpost.com/entry/fathers-day-a-fathers-bond-with-his-newborn-is-just_b_5939b1a9e4b094fa859f16c8.
13. Sabrina Tavernise, "The U.S. Birthrate Has Dropped Again. The Pandemic May Be Accelerating the Decline," *New York Times*, May 5, 2021, https://www.nytimes.com/2021/05/05/us/us-birthrate-falls-covid.html.
14. Joe Pinsker, "The 2 Ways to Raise a Country's Birth Rate," *Atlantic*, July 6, 2021, https://www.theatlantic.com/family/archive/2021/07/improve-us-birth-rate-give-parents-money-and-time/619367/.
15. The World Staff, "179 Countries Have Paid Sick Leave. Not the US," The World, March 13, 2020, https://www.pri.org/stories/2020-03-13/179-countries-have-paid-sick-leave-not-us.
16. Emma Jelliffe et al., "Awareness and Use of (Emergency) Sick Leave: US Employees' Unaddressed Sick Leave Needs in a Global Pandemic," *Proceedings of the National Academy of Sciences* 118, no. 29 (July 12, 2021): e2107670118, https://doi.org/10.1073/pnas.2107670118.
17. Joan C. Williams et al., "Who Benefits from Workplace Flexibility?," Slate, March 28, 2018, https://slate.com/human-interest/2018/03/new-study-examines-schedule-instability-in-retail-jobs.html.
18. "Fair Work Schedules," Center for WorkLife Law, University of California Hastings College of the Law, accessed October 11, 2021, https://worklifelaw.org/projects/stable-scheduling-study/.
19. Joan C. Williams et al., "Stable Scheduling Study: Health Outcomes Report," p. 18, accessed October 11, 2021, https://worklifelaw.org/wp-content/uploads/2019/02/Stable-Scheduling-Health-Outcomes-Report.pdf.
20. Claire Cain Miller, "Women Did Everything Right. Then Work Got 'Greedy,'" *New York Times*, April 26, 2019, https://www.nytimes.com/2019/04/26/upshot/women-long-hours-greedy-professions.html.
21. Amanda Zhou, "Washington's New Long-Term-Care Tax Begins in January. Here's What to Know About the Program," *Seattle Times*, October 8, 2021, accessed October 11, 2021, https://www.seattletimes.com/seattle-news/health/washingtons-new-long-term-care-tax-deduction-begins-in-january-heres-what-to-know-about-the-program/.
22. Howard Gleckman, "How Making Public Long-Term Care Insurance (Sort

of) Voluntary Created a Mess in Washington State," *Forbes*, October 6, 2021, https://www.forbes.com/sites/howardgleckman/2021/10/06/how-making-public-long-term-care-insurance-sort-of-voluntary-created-a-mess-in-washington-state/.

23. Terrence E. Deal and Allan A. Kennedy, *Corporate Cultures: The Rites and Rituals of Corporate Life* (Harmondsworth, UK: Penguin Books, 1982; reissue, Cambridge, MA: Perseus Books, 2000).
24. Genevieve Smith and Ishita Rustagi, "Supporting Dual Career Couples: An Equity Fluent Leadership Playbook," Center for Equity, Gender and Leadership at the Haas School of Business, University of California, Berkeley, 2020, https://haas.berkeley.edu/wp-content/uploads/0_EFL-Playbook_Supporting-Dual-Career-Couples_FinalExecSummary.pdf.
25. Many of these questions were inspired by Smith and Rustagi, "Supporting Dual Career Couples."

Conclusion

1. "Huge Study Confirms Purpose and Meaning Add Years to Life," Blue Zones, accessed February 16, 2022, https://www.bluezones.com/2019/05/news-huge-study-confirms-purpose-and-meaning-add-years-to-life/.
2. Kabir Sehgal, *Coined: The Rich Life of Money and How Its History Has Shaped Us* (New York: Grand Central, 2015), 203.

INDEX

21982320630787